What's Bruin?

True Tales and Tall Memories from Bear Country

by

Larry Kaniut

Anchorage, Alaska

Paper Talk
4800 Natrona
Anchorage, AK 99516
Email: kaniut@alaska.net
Web site: www.kaniut.com

Printed in the USA

ISBN 978-1955728249 (paperback)
978-1955728256 (ebook)

Back Cover Photo Background

When I spoke with retired Alaska Department of Fish and Game bear man Lee Miller of Indian, Alaska, he told me, “I’m probably among a select few who have shot a charging polar bear, a charging brown bear, and a charging black bear.”

I told Lee that he was probably the ONLY man to have it happen. Period. Then he explained the picture on this book’s cover.

“We were in our camp on Black Lake on the Alaska Peninsula. We used a three man crew—Lee Glenn, the leader of the project, myself and one other, mostly Chuck Irwin and the chopper pilot. The plane is a PA 18 used for flying crew, hauling extra fuel, and spotting bear. This day was too windy to hunt. We were in camp when across the pumice blow used as an airstrip came a bear into camp. We caught it and processed it, and while waiting it’s recovery from drugs, just were goofing around and put it into the Cub. And I got in with it...just something to do on a day we were stuck in camp. As I remember it was a young 3 to 4-year old. He later rose up and walked off.”

Lee gave me another picture of a bear receiving a blood transfusion on the Alaska Peninsula in 1972 in the Black Lake area and explained:

“I took a blood specimen from a bear in conjunction while on an ongoing study to see if there were any differences in the dispersed brown bear populations brown-grizzly bears...a long, ongoing study at the time. We handled around 500 bears during our tagging operation at different times all through the 1970’s.

“I’m taking blood and I noticed an old bandage on my left

wrist from a bear that bit me when I was taking a tooth from its mouth. He kind of woke up. We wondered at the time if he had AIDS, but flushed it out with Vodka and put a bandage on it. It turned out it was okay."

(Lee told me they considered sending the picture and a write up to the National Enquirer, stating that after a transfusion of human blood, the bear thought it was human, followed them around in a human-like, friendly manner. He joked that the National Enquirer would probably publish it as true.)

DEDICATION

I dedicate this book to my wife, Pamela, whose idea it was.

INTRODUCTION

My wife, Pamela, wanted me to do ***What's Bruin?***, a collection of humorous bear vignettes showcasing normal and humorous aspects of bears. Although this volume pretty much focuses on laughter, there are a few episodes that relate to more violent aspects of bear stories, like the Ron Cole and Alan Lee Precup follow up items.

Table of Contents

Open Doors

From 1967 to 1973 I tried unsuccessfully to encourage publishers to produce an anthology of Alaskan adventures. I assumed an editor could whip up a book and my English department would authorize purchase of a classroom set. Then I could incorporate high adventure for my literature of the North students at Anchorage's A.J. Dimond High School.

There were no high interest books to speak of so I persisted in using my manual typewriter, onion skin and carbon papers to pound out a 14-page outline with some vignettes. I kept a copy for my next rendition, whenever the spirit moved me, which was a few times a year. No cigar.

I received some wonderfully worded rejection letters that included nice letter heads on publisher stationery and my return address all nicely typed. (Going into the late 1990's the rejection standard evolved into a form letter with boxes and check marks)

After our friend Al Johnson was mauled in Denali National Park September 11, 1973, he said he was going to write a bear book. Following several years of failed effort to acquire a publisher for an adventure anthology, I received confirmation from Byron Fish in 1974 that Alaska Northwest Publishing Company thought I could "do a bear book." I immediately contacted Al and told him "you plan a bear book; they want a bear book; when it's done, let me know and I'll buy a copy."

Al informed me he'd changed his mind (he gave me a slip of paper with two men's names on it—Lloyd Pennington and Bill Brody [?], who might have stories). I contacted the publisher suggesting I'd give it a shot but not to hold their breath.

In order to begin my formal research, I visited ***Alaska Magazine's*** local office January 1975. I scanned every bear related piece I found back to 1935 but the person in charge of the magazines so intensely protected the bound volumes that I wondered if I'd have to leave my birth certificate and a sample of my firstborn's blood. By March I had completed that research by copying and pasting anything related into nineteen Manilla folders ranging from false charges to fatalities.

I wearied of bear stories...wanted to see no others forever.

With nary a copy of the manuscript, I mailed a 14 pound box to Jim Rearden of Homer, Alaska, editor for ***Alaska Magazine***. He arrived at our home with the original red-lined manuscript, said it was the best bear research he'd ever seen and wished he were doing the book, pumped me up and left.

The manuscript and I were within a few steps of the fireplace when my wife intervened. I told her I'd assured the contributors their story would be in the book and in their words...not part of it. She asked if it wouldn't be better to have some of their story than none. She had a great point.

The book sat on Rearden's desk for two years while he edited a North American mammal book; ***Alaska Bear Tales*** was published in 1983. Then another publisher wanted a bear book. Next came requests from more publishers for more adventure oriented books. (APPENDIX 2 provides a brief history or our writing)

Pam got her wish and I compiled a ton of "non-violent" material. I wanted to start ***What's Bruin?*** with Stan Price of Southeast Alaska fame.

Stan Price

There are two acceptable spellings of Kootznahoo/ Kootznoowoo. "Kootznahoo generally refers to specific places such as Kootznahoo Inlet; Kootznoowoo is a more regional term. Both are derived from the Tlingit word for 'bear fort.'" ("Admiralty Island Fortress of the Bears," ***Alaska Geographic***, Volume 18, Number 3, Page 9)

6/25/2003 I was unable to validate all names * —persons and places—with Stan because he passed away before we revised the transcription of our interview.

Stan Price is a gnat of a man with a heart as big as Alaska. For many years I read about him. I wrote him a few times requesting his permission to visit him at his Pack Creek home. He invited me but his cancer treatment necessitated our meeting in Juneau. Finally on August 14, 1989, while on a book signing tour for my second book with my son Ben, we had the privilege of meeting Stan at Juneau's Gastineau Hotel.

Stan was a diminutive man with thinning white hair. He wore gray wool pants, a plaid shirt and logger's suspenders. He had a runny nose and the entire time we visited he kept dabbing at his eyes and nose with a handkerchief. Stan was vibrant talking about his "little rascals" and chuckled constantly, recalling his happy memories with his little bear cubs.

It was wonderful listening to him relate his experience with the animals he loves—raising orphaned coastal brown bear cubs and "taming" others. We wished we could have spent days with him as he reminisced about his "tame" bears of Pack Creek.

He has acquired a wealth of knowledge about these huge rain forest dwellers.

The following is a transcription of our interview:

We came from Seattle in February 1922, and went there from town to shut down the camp and drain the boilers when Jay Crocker/Crawford * was loggin'. I was workin' on the salmon streams at the powerhouse for Westinghouse who had a bad generator. In the spring we came back with the natives and lived there about a month.

Peterson was the first man who brought the blue foxes from the Pribilofs out here and started raising foxes on the islands there. His hand got infected and he was going to sell out. I bought half an interest in his outfit there and Jay Crocker/Crawford took charge of it and supplied him with his food for the Columbia River gill netters. I moved in that area there discovered the federalization in a wide area. I lived there in the bay for 25 years by the sawmill.

Then I got tired of workin' there and I came over to Windfall Harbor to work on the mineral deposits with Brandt McGill, Petersburg, and I've been there ever since.

The first event to come was getting the wood supply for the winter. Out where my garden is a big sweep of wind went through and knocked all them big trees down in a bunch. They've been down for several years; it was darn good wood. We cut 'em up and stacked the wood up and had wood for four or five years.

When we got the wood off, we planted a garden around the stumps. One day in the early part of June 1948, we had a fine day to get out of the wind. We went down to work and after we got through, we'd been working with the flowers all afternoon. We heard a lot of racket and when we got ready to go home, there was a, looked like a porcupine, all wet and ragged in the kelp, trying to find something to eat.

I couldn't see it very well but my wife said it looked to her like a porcupine. We knew that there were no porcupine on Admiralty Island. I went out to take a look.

I got out there about fifteen feet away and the little bugger jumped out of the kelp and said, "Wwoooow!" Scared me half to death.

All the reading we'd done about bear stories the general thinking was, beat it; when you come to a little cub, the sow's not far away. You're gonna have a battle on your hands.

It didn't happen.

So we left the little rascal. He'd been eatin' on a seagull. He had it all gone but one part of a wing. He was gnawin' on that. We went home about 1500 feet to the house, had supper and went to bed.

But that little rascal out there by himself got to workin' on our minds. My wife was convinced that he was an orphan and we'd better get some feed down there. She fixed up some oats and put it in the sink and cooled it off.

About dark, why, I put on my clothes and went down to feed the cub. I looked down but I couldn't find the little rascal. We'd piled the brush up so we wouldn't have to be walkin' over it to dry the wood.

I walked over to the brush pile, and he jumped out at me again and said, "Wwooow!" So I walked over to him and dumped the oatmeal onto the grass that had been stomped down.

The little rascal stuck his nose in there and went right over and went to lickin' it. We've had a bear ever since.

We went home. I wasn't sure that there wasn't a big sow in the brush some place that would come out and tear me limb from limb. But it didn't happen. So we went to bed. Without the hearing aid I can't hear anything. She gave me the signal that something was going on outside.

I stuck my hearing aid in my ear, and she said, "We've got company on the porch."

I put on my pants and walked to the door and opened it. There was the darned cub. We raised that one for a while and another one came along about the same place. It was a bigger one. The second one we named Belinda. It had received some milk from the sow for it was so much bigger than the first one that we had, we called Susie.

We had to hold one of 'em there by the nap of the neck while the other one ate.

We raised them till the first of January when we had the preacher out for about a week. He was writin' up his sermon there stayin' in my little cabin. On that day the boat came out to take him to town and both cubs went to hibernation, the first day of January.

We tracked them in the snow to the brush pile. I came back and could see that they'd dug a hole under the brush pile. I didn't think they were in there because I couldn't see anything. The little rascals. One of 'em went in there and hibernated. We didn't know whether Belinda or Susie hibernated. I dug around under about ten inches of snow where body heat come up through the brush.

I reached down and turned the little rascal over. Like a baby it didn't want to get up. It turned over and went back to snoozin'. I played with it there for about four months.

I'd take the deer out for a walk and come to the brush pile and they wouldn't go near it.

In five years we had both cubs back. In six years we had cubs. We had two each. Both of 'em had sows. From there on we had bears all over the place. They stayed with the cubs for three years and on the fourth year, they were born in January or February. They breed the last two weeks in June. It's quite an event.

The first boar that we had there was a huge old boy we called Jake. He was much bigger. Big game guide Carl Lane shot him. Jake had a 9 ½ -foot beautiful hide, they had a terrible time, the new boar came in and tried to start a harem. They fought among themselves and he killed cubs. I suppose they kept them away three years. We never had any cubs born.

Then another boar came in and drove the 6-year or 7-year old boar away and established a good harem there with the 6 or 7 sows. The most we ever had at one time was about 10 sows. We had them for 20 years. One sow must be around 35 years old. We call her Mc Keany. She has two cubs this year. That makes 81 and 82 cubs has been born since we came in October in 1947.

After all that, the attrition and hunters has kept the bunch down to about 28-30. My records showed that last year we had 31 bears. The fish and game and the forest service get to fightin' over who's goin' to administer these bears.

Visitors were getting' pretty heavy. About a thousand people would come and sign our books. So they come in and gave me the privilege that I'd always had there, I could do almost everything I'd always done. But other people had to be guided by the bureaucrats. It didn't work out very well.

These bears have all been born to tame mothers. That helped to tame the cubs. I came back there on the 12th of July in 1989 from Seattle and Portland where I'd been in the hospital four months. The fish just begin to run. I was pretty weak from being in the hospital for so long. I went down to the creek and watched the bears, but there was almost no fish in the river for food.

Bears depend on them long stemmed salt grass for eating. They consume large quantities of it, goes right through 'em... they can't chew it like a cow can. And as soon as they get tired of fish, they go back on the grass and roots. But in Pack Creek the bureaucrats sit there on the fence and all day long makin' racket, makin' a disturbance. The bears didn't like it. They retired to the other side of the river and nobody could get closer than 300 or 500 feet. Most of the bears were out a thousand feet and the tide was comin' in. People spend their money to come but they had no equipment to take pictures of bears 300 feet away with these little dinky cameras.

I came back to see what the bears were doin' and I was pretty much disappointed. All the bears were on the wrong side of the river so people could get pictures walking among 'em.

They were too tame.

On the 14th and 15th I went down about 7 miles to Summit Creek. Some of my friends came up and said there were a lot of bears up there. There were three of our tame sows with 7 cubs. Three of the cubs were almost as big as their mothers. You could hardly tell the difference between them and their mothers.

We come in there in an aluminum boat, we couldn't row it was a swift stream. We couldn't run the outboard because of boulders. There was quite a run of fish, maybe a hundred of 'em. We had to walk in our boots and drag the boat behind us. It's so darned flat you can't get a motor started when the wind's a blowin'. You've got to row out and get in deep water. The first three there was one sow and three cubs and they just got out on the bank and watched us go by and went back into the creek and went fishing. They was tame bears. I seen right away they come from Pack Creek.

We walked a little farther and we had a sow and two cubs.

In the edge of the alders was another sow with two cubs. They was two years old, both of 'em. We walked right in by 'em and they got on the creek and let us pass 'em and get in there. No wild bear would ever do that. That convinced us right away that they were Pack Creek bears. They went out of Pack Creek and had taken refuge up there in this creek where it's about a half a mile to tide, hard to get in there.

We went as far as the alders and we could see in the alders at the edges of the timber there was two more bears, one layin' down in the water. These were wild bears because they went into the woods in a hurry. The tame ones were gettin' along quite well with them, only 500 feet apart.

When I left…last time I went down there another guy was there and the bears were in the same place. There were more fish in there at the last of the season than there was in the first of the season. The bears made the creek their new home.

Pack Creek has only got 4 or 5 bears. When we left there in the fall of 1988 there were 31 bears. When you live in a place like that, you're with the bears when they come out in March. On that mountain where they hibernate, you can see them in the snow playin', slidin' down. They move on down the first of July. The tame bears used our place as their home. Other bears came there and they crowded out the wild bears.

Bears of the same family get along fine together but when a new, wild bear comes in, they begin to have battles. None of 'em actually comes to grips. They make all kinds of false charges, threats and break false runs, but they seem to know that if they go into battle, one of 'em is goin' to get hurt. They fight very rarely.

As soon as the sows come in there, they drive the old ones away. If a boar comes in to catch a cub, he will kill the sows. Several sows protect each other and graze on that 20-30 acres of grass. There's no more salt grass on Pack Creek than any of the other 30 salmon streams around there, but there aren't any bears on those streams. What happened?

Something happened when we went in there and raised these bears and tamed them. They stayed. We're convinced now that a bear moves into a territory for a long period of time. He lives there; he's going to die there—he doesn't go any place else.

You know they've tagged 'em, trapped 'em, turned 'em loose, and they come home again. That's where they was born and raised.

The Pack Creek bears never knew any harm. When the forest service and fish and game came there, they were all carrying guns on their backs. People come there 50, 60 at a time off the cruise ships and walk among the bears, and none of 'em's got a big gun.

Anyway the bears have begun to leave Pack Creek now. They're a thousand feet away and you can't tell which bear is which. They're too far away to tell what their characteristics are.

We had all the bears named. My record book has been kept for around 20 years. Sows and cubs and the years they were born, as they grow up. We had one brown bear come there, she's Susie's fourth, maybe her third. She was born brown and stayed brown. Well actually people see these bears in Pack Creek when they're out of the woods in July. The bears shed their hair, it dies and it turns brown. They call 'em brown bears.

But as soon as the old hair is sluffed off, it sometimes comes in great chunks, and it comes back black. Brownie was born brown and she stays brown. She's had two silvertipped cubs, and the hunters killed both of 'em. There's such a demand, you know. It's such a beautiful hide.

Most of the bears, the sows we have there, had bad hides. I

think that attributes to their long life because the hunters mostly want the bears with the good hides. We named one of them there Bikini because she didn't have much clothes on. Several years back they came out with bathing suits with two pieces they called bikinis. She's still with us. She's got two cubs, 81st and 82nd cubs to be born in Pack Creek.

People come out to see the bears. They leave and there's lots of time with no people around. When the bureaucrats came out there they stay all day and half the night. The bears wouldn't get into the observatory. The bears come and look at the river to see where they can get in to fish. They fish with their cubs where there aren't other bears fishing. They come and look for a place, lay on the ground until they find a spot where the other bears won't be.

A bear is a kind of a coward, a big coward. They are afraid of their own kind more than they are of humans. When humans came over there, the bears didn't pay no attention to 'em. You could walk around with 'em. I would like to show you my films. I've got more than a hundred reels of film, the life history of the Pack Creek bears going back more than 16 years. But now it all ends. I'm going to have to take 'em down this winter.

It's pretty lonesome out there without the bears. We also raised deer there. If I had a place where I could keep a bear, I wouldn't mind havin' one of 'em as a pet. They play rough among themselves. They'll drag each other around by the ear, but you have a little rascal there. They come up and get a hold of your pant's leg at feeding time and growl and make all kinds of fuss. The little rascals got sharp teeth. As the old ones grow up they have blunt teeth like a dog's teeth.

In all these years thousands of visitors have come to see these bears. Not one ever made an attack on a person. A bear will run like the dickens at you and stop about 10 feet away. They call that an attack. That's a rush. It's not an attack.

Wild animals have pretty much the same behavior. Dogs, you got a dog on the other side of the fence from the sidewalk and he'll follow you from one end of the fence to the other, and he'll bark at you like he'll take you apart. You open the gate and the rascal will run under the house. A bear's pretty much the same way. They bluff. Even their own kind. I've seen 'em playin', photographed 'em. On TV you see a bear for three seconds. You can't tell much about a bear's behavior in that time.

I stay with a bear until I get a whole doggone reel of him, the way he does, the way he eats, and his behavior.

The key to staying alive all these years with the Pack Creek bears is the behavior of the people. Bears come and sit on our porch. Cubs are curious like human kids. Turn some little kid lose in this house here and he'll have everything on the floor, by golly, and you have a lot of things you never knew you owned before. A bear is curious in the same darned way. You get him in your place, you hang your wash on the line if they can reach it, the cubs will pull it down. You hang your sleeping bag up there, and they'll do the same thing to it.

Joel and his sidekick went out. They've had tents out there where they stay. A dozen people camp out there. Food in the tent, valuable cameras, clothing. The bears never entered the tent. Not one of 'em. The forest service had crews out there, cooked chicken, none of the bears ever bothered 'em.

Now they put the regulations out there, not supposed to do any feeding, not to bother the bear, put the tents up. I worked a big garden there for years to feed the deer in the winter time. Carrots, celery, strawberry, red raspberries. Lots of 'em. I built a fence around the garden I left a path between the hillside and the fence so that the bear could walk across without climbin' my garden fence.

I was down on my knees there in July and Joel and John they set their tent up there. They had a little dog not much bigger than the bear's head. They saw a bear come down, swingin' his head in Joel's tent. I stood up and watched him.

He went over there and the dog was tied to the tent pole. Joel filled a little pan with little round dog feed pellets. The bear goes over there and eats the doggone pellets and the dog sat there and looked at him, not much bigger than the bear's head. He got all the feed and walked away.

The next day it happened again. The bear had been doing that for several days, I guess. Now he had a habit. The next day I brought my camera down. Joel and John went out on a photographing expedition and left the little dog there tied to the tent pole with a string.

I rushed and got my camera. The bear come up there and begin to eat. The dog stood there four-feet away watchin' the bear eat out of his pan. That's a pretty doggone smart bear. He can say, "Well, I'll eat this little dog and have one meal. But as long as Joel has got money, he'll feed that pup, and I'll have enough to eat every day."

Talk about a bear bein' vicious and wild, that bear could have killed that dog a hundred times.

I'll tell you another little tale. We had visitors come out. I'd go out to the plane to meet 'em. The first plane came there six people in it. They came into the house and they carried a package of beer and set it on the wood pile by the big stove. I didn't think that was the place to store beer. I don't drink it nohow, but I was waitin' for the other plane to come and I picked it up and set it on the porch.

Went down to see the bears. People come to visit the bears there and five of 'em got off. We started up the path. We stopped to talk a little bit and got to the garden gate. Here was a bear there havin' a beer party. It carried that carton of beer cans out there, scratched a can out of the carton and bit a little hole with their sharp teeth and begin a squirtin'. He put his paws over the top of it to quiet it down. Then he begin to lick the can and stirred it up and it squirt again in his face. And here we were, six people without a camera. The bear took out five of these tin cans. Of course, he didn't get much of the beer because it squirted up into the air. He got up and walked right by us and went down to fishin'. That was better than a beer.

Reason for moving to Pack Creek:

They passed a new regulation in Congress allowing bureaucrats to collect money for use of national forests and parks and such as that. They charge people to go into all these parks, Yosemite and Yellowstone. And they came out here. They started out by charging $50 to canoe into Pack Creek and $35 for a kayak. I think they dropped that. Some of the places are still collecting money there. I think they collect money to visit the McNeil River, do they not? Well with a thousand people at $10 a day, they couldn't see that as a gold mine. The forest service and fish and game want money at the same time.

Beginning to work with bears.

We started working with the bears because of the curiosity and behavior of these little rascals. You'll love 'em. They're just like a doggone dog. Man never had any animal that was more faithful than a dog. The bear is nearly the same darned thing. They get attached to you. They follow you around. Even the big brownie, 19-years old, she followed me down to the garden, laid by the gate and followed me back home. People see that down there and say, "Look at that old Alaskan, Larry, he's got these big bears tamed and they mind him."

The mother brings the cubs down to the beach around the 5th to the 10th of July. They're just tiny little things. They've never been in the water before. It's interesting to watch those little rascals get tamed. They don't fish themselves until they're 3-years old. They get in the water. The fish hit their feet and they leave the water for the bank and cry for mom.

They get lonesome for people. Same way of a dog if you treat the dog right, he's going to follow you around. The bears'll do the same darn thing. You can talk to 'em. I believe, take these little rascals, we had a Mrs. Feltenstein from Germany who owned a black bear in Germany. She had to build a cage for it because the people were afraid of the bear. They had an estate and the bear had the run of the estate. Her kids grew up with the black bear but after a while they begin to be afraid of the bear and they made her build a cage. The kids would go into the cage and play with the bear.

They'd maul it and ride it. She took lots of pictures of the boys growin' up with the black bear there.

She came over here and she's responsible for some of these bears' tameness. She was away a year for an operation with cancer. She came back and was such a favorite with the brownies, that when she got off the plane and came to see the bears fishing in the river, she said, "Come on, Donnie."

Believe it or not, brownie come. Astonished all those people standin' around that a brown bear fishing in the river came up to one woman.

I doubt anybody would have the patience. Bears are destructive. Although I've lived there all these forty years, and they've never been in my house except when we leave the door open. They take the peanut butter bottle or sugar bowl out in the yard and lick it till it's all gone. But they never break into the house.

I don't think you could build a structure out of wood that the bear can't get into.

In Windam Bay we had to keep large quantities of food for our workmen. We had hams and bacon hangin' in the house. A bear pulled the damned door down and got into the house. The bear carried them out. It cost me several hundred dollars damage in the fall of the year.

Man obliterates any of these wild animals. They don't increase that fast. If they did, the country would be run over with wild animals.

I've got to go down to Seattle to have a final examination in three, four weeks. I'm gonna go back to Pack Creek. I live there. I like it. I run into all kinds of movie traffic there. I've had some problems here in civilization getting along. I got trapped in the bathroom when the hinges came off, and I was the wrong side. I put my hand on the railing to read what was on it, and the damned fire alarm went off. I never had the bears treat me like that all the years I was out there.

I'll learn to live in civilization after a while. But I've got to edit all my film so I'll have something to do to keep me busy.

I have better shows here than I ever see on that TV they've got on the stand in this room. Every year for the last eight years I've gone into public schools and talked with students about bears and showed my films. I've been on TV ten, fifteen times. I was on PBS on Portrait of America, which should have been Portrait of Alaska, on four or five shows. Last one made came on broadcast from Riverside, California. People came up here on a ferry boat in March. The Forest Service is playing it on boats for entertainment.

Those people asked me if I'd put on my show in Riverside, California.

Stan enjoyed sharing his films with people and telling them about his bears, enjoying the children's facial expressions when they learn of the big bears.

My wife spent the first twelve years documenting the history of the bears, the date we got them. Somebody from the University of Alaska was studying for a biology degree and lifted the book and took it from our house. I would pay $250 to anyone who would bring that guest book back. There were only two people there at the time it was taken. Make a note of it in case you hear about it and can get it back for me.

There's another bear tribe at Jim's Lake where sows raise cubs. They've got to have a boar with one or two sows in order to survive. Four or five sows get together there and raise their cubs. I don't believe there are very few sows that raise their cubs among the boars because they're tormented all the time and don't have any protection.

The Pack Creek old big boar bred these sow bears for many years.

Bears don't care who's filming them. They get that tame. When people came there they'd stay a little while, an hour up to three, sixty at a time among the bears. Man has a kitchen smell. Every man smells different to a bear. The dog has the same quality following an odor to find his way home. Bear comes down there and there's so many kitchen smells, he goes among them sniffs at them, opens his mouth taking in wind that goes through his nose so he can get the smells. He's lookin' for the source.

If you had a candy bar in your pack and took it out, the smell remains in the pack a long time. The bear comes along and gets into it, causing him to rip it open. They say "don't feed the bears," but you bring the feed with you when you come in there—man smell.

People that tent there the bear goes into the tent. The Forest Service has four, five or six people working there. None of the bears bothered any of them.

It's not the same now as it was. It took us so long and so much patience, two people would say the bear came into the house and they kill it, get the whole thing over with. The bears come in and get the feed, we'd leave the door open. They didn't come in through the windows.

Aggression and firearms:

My own observation there for forty years convinced me that the bear is not an aggressive animal. You've got to be the aggressive one, and they'll defend themselves. Several things could have happened to those. You go out into the woods with a gun and you're inviting yourself to a battle. You're depending on aggressiveness to help you and the bear turns up some place, he may be out there a thousand yards away. He's no danger to you whatever. Even close up.

But if you've got a gun along, you're brave, if a bear comes along, you're gonna let him have it with a gun. A bear actually come along, you shoot at him. You don't have to hit him to disturb him, it just goes by, some racket puts him on his guard. He might then attack you, or he might run away.

I've tried several times over the years to convince people you can fire a 12 gauge shotgun over them creatures and they don't even look up. And other times one will be out at the edge of the woods and they hear a sound and it turns around and runs back into the woods. It's not sure that they will do one thing or another, they can do both. The idea is don't encourage them when you make a noise to disturb them to make them think they're in danger.

You may shoot your darned gun in the ground or you may shoot at him and wound him. If you wound a bear, you can't get away from him. They're still, even if broken down in the back, they'll drag their front quarters. If they're not broken down, you can't get away from 'em. You can't climb a tree to get away from 'em. So you've got a battle on your hands and you're gonna lose. They can chew you up.

I first saw a bear kill a deer and kill cubs. They bite the head off first. You read all these stories about a man gets his scalp all tore up by a bear when a bear battle comes on. That's the way they kill their food.

So I read the other day some guy come out of the woods with his head all scratched up and he didn't say whether he had a gun or not. I don't believe a bear will attack a person unprovoked unless he is disturbed in some way…if he has a gun, why he disturbs the bear by firing the darn thing at close range. And if he had meat on him, the bear may attack to get the meat.

At Eliza Harbor we had a bear attack a man and kill him and the bear got away. He took the deer away from the man before he killed him. If you've got a bear that wants that meat, you can't take it away from him. You might kill him, but the chances are you wouldn't. They die slowly. It takes five, ten minutes for a bear to die with a bullet hole in him.

Started taming cubs and keeping a journal shortly after the Japanese bombed Pearl Harbor. I suspect that this will be the last…the year after next year they'll be bred again. They'll be out and the wild bears, you can see 'em now, it will be the last of the bears at Pack Creek.

What will become of Pack Creek place:

They gave me a lifetime lease several years ago. I've got two home sites there, about 6 acres. There's no interest out there for me without the bears.

When you first arrived at Pack Creek, Windfall Harbor, what was the main attraction?

When the bears had value for their hides. All the big game guides wanted to hunt close to town because they could get there quicker. They pretty much killed all the bears off the northern part of the island. They started out there $50 a day for hunting. Now it's around $5,000 for a bear.

They killed the bears off there. We hardly ever see one down there. I've been in there prospecting and we had tents up, and the bears never bothered us at no time. We stayed from the time the snow was gone at 1,500 feet until October when you had to leave due to deep snow.

All summer long we had the tents there for the workmen, for the cook shack and the bears never bothered us.

I hope someday somebody will start and have the patience to establish another area for tame bear and let the people be the managers. They know more about the bears than the G-- ----d bureaucrats. They send these kids in there and they've never seen a bear except on a piece of paper or photograph. You've got to have some animal husbandry degree to manage and live with animals. They don't have that.

People come to Alaska by the hundreds of thousands to see the wildlife and all they see is the junk shops and the beer halls—they've got them at home. It cost $125 now to go to Pack Creek to see the bears. It used to cost only $12. The government makes airplanes take out a $125,000 liability on these seats, and we've got to pay that. I'll take my chances with any of these bush pilots. They know how to fly planes and bureaucrats don't.

Why do you say there won't be any bears there in three more years?

Let me begin at the beginning. The natives lived in that area before I came in 1932, Johnny Wise and Jerry Watson and their families, about fifteen of 'em. And they had no other way to make a living except the land. And the bears was their chief target. They get twenty-five, thirty dollars in gold for the hide. And believe it or not...they killed bears with a .22 long rifle. They would die in a half hour to an hour. That's not unusual. They killed whales out there with a .30-06. They shoot the whale there, skin 'em out.

Looks like the fish and game and forest service people are cowards to come with guns.

Forest Service says it's a regulation that they're required to carry a gun, but I guess it's to protect a game warden from another human not a bear.

Pigs

Pigs take residence in Fortress of Bears

TRIAL: Controversial plan tested by the case of the wandering pig.

By MIKE CHAMBERS, *The Associated Press*, September 8, 2003

JUNEAU -- Hunting guide Les Kinnear's plan to turn a disused Sitka pulp mill into a zoo for problem brown bears has plenty of detractors.

And that makes the case of the wandering pig that much more intriguing.

Recently, a single pig was found outside a waist-high plywood pen and wandering around inside one of two 192-foot-diameter concrete tanks where Kinnear hopes one day to house large bruins.

Kinnear formed a nonprofit group called Kootznahoo-Fortress of the Bears in January with the idea of converting the two large clarifier tanks -- with walls a minimum of 12 feet high-- into a zoo for brown bears that have shown a penchant for digging into garbage.

But first, Kinnear must prove he is capable of handling animals in order to get the necessary state and federal permits. So he's keeping pigs in plywood pens inside the tanks as part of a demonstration project that will be monitored by the state.

The proposed bear display has drawn the threat of litigation from an environmental group and has generated numerous letters to the local paper from people who fear it will turn into a carnival for tourists.

And it raises questions in the recent case of the liberated pig. Sitka police have no leads, but some people think it's more than a joke carried out by bored youths.

"They feel pretty confident that somebody had to assist the pig out of the enclosure," Sitka Police Chief Bob Gorder said.

Kenyon Fields, executive director of the Sitka Conservation Society, suspects it could be the work of someone opposed to the project.

"It's likely not just a teenage prank and more likely represents the disagreement with the project that's been echoing around town," Fields said. But the chief is not willing to go that far yet and hasn't ruled out the possibility that the pig simply squeezed out of the poorly constructed plywood pen.

To get his permits for the Fortress of the Bears, Kinnear must devise a plan to ensure animal welfare and safety and prepare for the possibility that a bear would escape.

"We've taken additional measures to provide security," Kinnear said, dismissing the seriousness of the recent pig escape.

He contends that criticism of the project has come from a "very small, very vocal" segment of the town.

The Sitka Assembly has provided $25,000 for the project that Kinnear must match with $75,000. It could cost as much as $250,000 to get the project started, Kinnear said.

The borough also agreed to a 10-year lease for the 2.5-acre site with two five-year options. Eventually, the facility would pay $36,000 a year in rent, said Sitka Administrator Hugh Bevan.

Kinnear anticipates having between six and eight juvenile brown bears housed in the two large tanks, connecting the enclosures with a 6-inch-diameter pipe left over from the Alaska Pulp Mill. Water would run through the pipe, and the bears would have foliage in their tanks. There would be viewing platforms for the public.

"We anticipate once we are open to the public, we will generate enough revenue to make this self-sustaining," Kinnear said.

The Center for Biological Diversity, a Sitka environmental group, has vowed to fight the project.

The facility would be next to a noisy glass crusher that is on site and the holding tanks are too small to accommodate the number of bears Kinnear plans to house, said the center's Corrie Bosman.

Also, a fertile female bear inside the tanks would attract wild bears to the grounds, Bosman said.

Diana Weinhardt, curator of large mammals at the Houston Zoo and a member of the American Zoo and Aquarium Association's Bear Taxon Advisory Group, visited the site at the request of the state. Weinhardt told the Daily News that the project is feasible but needs public support.

Also, the Angoon Native Corp. has told Kinnear's group to drop the name Kootznahoo -- an English derivation of the Tlingit phrase "Fortress of the Bears" -- from its project. Kinnear said he would.

Kinnear is still clearing debris and making modifications to the site of the proposed bear pens. Once that is complete, the pigs will be allowed to roam free inside the concrete enclosures and the one-year demonstration project will begin.

"Not only do we see how they handle the animals, we look at various educational programs," said Ryan Scott, permit biologist for the state Department of Fish and Game.

Cruise ships bring about 700,000 visitors to Southeast Alaska annually, more than the population of the entire state. "We anticipate this may be a feature of their itineraries," Kinnear said.

[Author: You can Google Sitka Bears, find "sanctuary," and view some of the sanctuary's bears.]

Robin Candrow

I heard about Robin's story and contacted him. He responded with the following email.

Email received 1/1/2004

Dear Mr. Kaniut,

Here is my story, as promised. I hope it's what you are looking for, and if not, I hope you can at least enjoy it. You asked me what I did here in Whitehorse, well, at the moment I am an unemployed Class 1 driver, but just recently got out of employment as a mover for a local moving company here. It seems as if I may be leaving the north soon to go work for a trucking company in Labrador, but rest assured, I'll be back. The north is my home, and could never stay away.

hope you enjoy, Robin Candow

My story begins in the summer of 1998. It was an exciting summer for me, as I had just finished school, was turning 19, and planned on doing a little exploring of the Yukon. That was also the summer of the great Fox Lake forest fire. Some friends and I drove through some real bad smoke filled spots on our way up to the Dawson City Music Festival. On the drive back from Dawson that weekend, I showed my friends, where just a few weeks earlier, I had my very first encounter with a huge grizzly bear. At least, I thought it was huge.

It was getting around the end of June, and I had decided to take a trip up to Dawson City, just for kicks. Not having any money for gas, I figured I would just hitchhike. So I packed my tent, clothes, a couple cooking pans, some food, and an old hunting knife I found to attach to my belt. In a way, I'm really glad I hitchhiked. I wasn't getting rides all the time, and those that did pick me up, were only willing to go a short distance before dropping me off again. Normally, this would just irritate me, but every time I got dropped off somewhere, I would walk along the road until somebody picked me up, and would get a really good view of the Yukon's great outdoors. It was really exhilarating; as I've driven this road many times, and never felt the freedom I felt that day.

Well, I finally made it to Dawson City in the early evening, just in time to find an old friend and set up camp in "Tent City". You had to catch a ferry across the river to get to Tent City, and then back again to get back into Dawson. So I did, then my friend and I went to a local diner for some grub and hot coffee.

My whole weekend in Dawson City was quite memorable, as I was able to see all the great historic sites of the old north and see how much life has changed from the gold rush. I even met some really nice people while I was there, including a small group of people staying in Tent City that I would talk to long into the nights.

Then on Sunday morning, I packed up my tent and clothes, and threw my cooking pans and left over food back into my bag. It was time to head back to Whitehorse. I grabbed my old hunting knife and went to strap it onto my belt, but the sheath snapped right at the belt attachment. I tried to rig it up so it would just hang, but every time I walked it banged against my leg and started to hurt, so I just took it off and put it into my backpack.

Sunday was worse for rides. Out of the entire 533km between Whitehorse and Dawson, I truly believe I walked 200km of it. There was next to no one on the road that day, and I was starting to debate whether I should keep going, turn back, or find a place to set my tent back up and camp the night.

I had passed the Dempster Highway cut-off, where someone had dropped me off, and walked down the road for a little over an hour without seeing a single car traveling in either direction. Boredom began to really sink in, and I was trying to find things to keep myself busy. I started picking up small rocks and began tossing them into the trees that lined the side of the road. After a while, the trees seemed to be going away from the road, as a small ditch began to form. So I threw the rocks harder.

Every once in a while, I would hear a noise in the trees like a squirrel, and would aim my rocks in that direction, knowing I would never hit anything, or so I thought. I threw a nice rounded rock as hard as I could towards the sound of a snapping twig. I heard a thump, a grunt, and then the bushes began to move.

I knew immediately I was in trouble, and whatever was down there was big. I hadn't seen a vehicle in about an hour and a half, maybe more, I was in the middle of nowhere, and all I had to protect myself was an old hunting knife that I...MY KNIFE! I tapped my hip, and remembered I had put it into my bag. Just as I started to take my bag off my back, I looked down into the ditch to see this huge Grizzly staring me right in the eyes.

My mind raced faster than it ever had. Don't move! Play dead! Run! Don't look It in the eyes! Help! Dear God, please help! I was frozen with fear. Sweat poured down into my eyes, but I didn't dare even blink.

I tried to think if I should go for my knife, and risk this bear coming right at me, or to just stay still, and hope he goes away. As it turned out, this bear had no intentions on just going away. He began to saunter slowly towards me, and I could feel my heart stop, or so it seemed. I started to slowly back up, now more scared then I thought possible. I didn't know what to do,

I mean, I've never taken courses for this kind of stuff. I wished someone could have yelled out what I needed to do, cause my brain had just shut down.

The bear was about 50 feet away, but continued to walk slowly towards me. Suddenly, I saw a slight flash out of the corner of my eyes. I looked up the road to see, to my amazement, the first vehicle I'd seen in almost 2 hours. A blue pick-up truck came around the bend up the road and was heading right in my direction. My heart began to beat again.

As the truck came closer, the bear stopped and looked at it. Then, I did the one thing that could have gone either way from saving my life, to ending it. I threw my backpack back around my shoulders, and ran to the middle of the road and began waving my arms as hard as I could. I wanted more then anything for that truck to stop, but as it got closer, the driver turned and went around me.

I just about started to cry.

The bear, now triggered by my sudden movements, came towards me again, only this time, faster then before. At that exact time, I cursed to myself as I turned and ran towards the departing truck, which slammed on its brakes once the driver saw me turn and run in his rear view mirror, as at that time, the driver finally saw the bear.

Now I've heard stories that bears can outrun any human, but this day I won the race. I probably broke a speed record that day as I ran for the opening door of that beautiful rusted blue truck. Within what seemed like an eternity, but must have been a split second, I reached the door, threw my bag around my shoulder and into the truck, and jumped in myself, yelling for the driver to go. He had his foot burying the pedal the second I had hopped in the truck.

Suddenly, just as the truck began to move, we felt a huge

jolt. I looked back to see that the bear had hit the side of the truck, before deciding to stop its chase. I couldn't thank the man driving that truck enough.

A little while up the road, we stopped at a rest area for a quick pit stop. I was surprised I held it in as long as I had, and didn't leave any for the bear to sniff in my tracks. Once I had jumped out, I looked to the rear of the truck to see where the bear had hit. It was quite obvious as there was now a nice sized dent about the size and shape of a football in the side of the truck.

The man gave me a ride to Pelly Crossing where I had to walk again, this time though, I stopped within sight of town, and had my knife tucked into my pants.

I'll never forget that day as long as I live, and haven't hitchhiked any great distance since then. Every once in a while I get the opportunity to take a drive up back up to Dawson for a quick visit or for work, and every time I do, I shiver at the spot where I was sure I was a grizzly's lunch.

Tim Bowman

I played volleyball with Tim and he consented to provide this story after he'd told me about it.

Just Park the Bear in the Garage, Honey

By Tim Bowman, Anchorage, Alaska

I returned home from a 5-day kayaking trip in Prince William Sound on July 22, 2001, about 8 PM. My girlfriend Veronica and I each grabbed an armful of gear and headed for the garage. I unlocked the garage door and opened it only about 8 inches when it hit something behind it and jammed. I stuck my head in and saw that my garage was trashed. There was stuff everywhere; tools, camping gear, hardware, a bike, lumber, pieces of drywall, all strewn about. I thought I'd been robbed. I closed the door and told Veronica I had to check the main house.

I walked up on the deck, entered through the back door, and walked through the house to find everything intact; just the way I left it 5 days ago. I thought that was strange. Why would someone rob, or vandalize, my garage but not the rest of the house. So I took another look in the garage, and something didn't make sense. It just didn't look like the work of a vandal or a thief. Then I saw one, then two piles of bear crap, and it was starting to make sense. But how did the bear get in there; the garage window wasn't broken and the doors were shut.

I walked around the perimeter of the garage and still could find no sign of entry. I figured that my renter, who rents the apartment above the garage, must be the key to the mystery, although she was gone. In retrospect, I guess I also had a mostly subconscious notion that maybe the bear was still inside. So I took one more long look in the garage, noting that the fully inflated Zodiac I had inside the garage was intact. I also noted the black bear crouched behind the boat in the corner peering back over his shoulder at me!

It wasn't a very large bear, but I noticed he had ear tags and I thought I saw a collar as well. I quickly shut the door. OK, what now? I figured that Fish and Game might have an interest in capturing the bear, after all, Rick Sinnot, the area biologist, had been up to my house before to dart a bear and replace its radio collar.

I called Rick's cell phone but couldn't get through, so then called the cops and told them that I had a bear locked inside my garage and that I could just open the door and let it out, but I thought Fish and Game might be interested in getting their hands on it since it was tagged and couldn't be easier to dart where it was. The dispatcher said she'd try reaching someone at ADF&G and to hold on. She came back a minute later and said a trooper advised that we just let it out.

OK, no problem, except that the bear was facing the overhead door with his nose just about against it, and I was afraid that if I hit the door opener, the bear would freak out and damage the Zodiac.

Veronica and I talked it over and decided there weren't many other options. Veronica had left her Subaru parked in front of the garage door, so we thought we may as well milk the opportunity and get some good photos of a bear, so Veronica took a camera and sat in her car.

I opened up the small garage door a few inches, reached around and pushed the door opener, and watched. The door opened only about 18 inches and jammed on something that the bear had tossed in its path. To my relief, the bear didn't freak out and just slipped under the door, cautiously creeping out only inches from Veronica in her car. The bear made for the woods and bolted.

We then pushed open the door and took stock of the damage. It stunk to high heaven. We found 7 piles of bear crap with nothing really discernible in it except a few sunflower seeds.

The window was smeared with his paw prints, but he apparently didn't have the sense to bust through it. He did, however, rip off the molding and hardware and tried to claw his way out through the frame. He also tried to tear his way out through a wall, and got through the drywall and urethane insulation but was stopped by the outer plywood sheathing. The insulation blanket on the back of the rising door was ripped to shreds. That was the worst of it, the rest was just a colossal mess. But the mystery remained -- how did the bear get in there? About that time, Kristin, my renter, and her sister drove up. She knew something was wrong because she could see the grage door partway open and all the shredded insulation hanging down. And the looks on our faces probably revealed something was amiss.

"What happened?", she asked.

"Take a look inside," I said.

"Ohhh, there's been a bear in here, huh? How'd he get in?"

"I was hoping you might have some insight into that," I said.

"No, we've been gone since Friday morning and it was fine then." Kristin explained that they did have the small door open for a little while Friday morning while they were loading the car for their weekend trip, and after talking about it for awhile, we came to the only possible explanation, that the bear entered the garage during that time, probably attracted to a stinky bag of trash, and Kristin, on her last trip out, walked right through the garage (with bear in it) and locked the bear inside. Where it stayed for the next 3 days!

Curiously, the bear apparently ate and drank nothing during the 3 days, despite the fact that he'd dragged out and spilled 2 full bags of dog food and a partial bag of sunflower seeds, and never touched them, the bag of trash, or a couple cases of beer, either. I figured I was pretty lucky, as it could have been a lot worse. As it was, I declined to claim it on insurance and pay the deductible.

Ben Ballinger

I met Mr. Ballinger in Kodiak where I was seeking bear stories for ***More Alaska Bear Tales***. He kindly chatted with me and I've not used his information until now. Because my hearing is not the greatest and I was not able to finalize my interview with Mr. Ballinger, I probably have mis-heard and mis-spelled some of the persons mentioned in his interview.

When I first started working with bears here, I was assisting, ah...first of all, the way I got into this wildlife work, I'd been studying wildlife through correspondence courses through (Yousaucie?), it's a military thing. I was in the Navy, a deep sea diver for twenty years.

When I got stationed in Kodiak, they needed a game warden, this was during Territorial Days. The game warden stationed here was a US Deputy Marshall, a US deputy game warden and an agent for the Alaska Department of Fisheries, which was the forerunner of Fish and Game. I had all of these authorities. I wasn't limited to the base. I worked directly for the command and I wore civilian clothes. Every morning I could come and go out of the gates, carry firearms, I had cards from everybody—all authorities. I just reported every morning to the fish and wildlife service, "what you got to do?"

I was on patrol on the road system. They didn't have a protection officer here; I was it. That's what started it in Kodiak in 1956. From 1956-58 I had this position.

I made my own cases, took them to the local magistrate, set them up, carried them through the court system, the whole works.

I really was, the purpose of the job was to keep the military service? But, you never knew with someone in civilian clothes out there whether they were military or civilian so you weren't restricted to military. The enforcement thing worked into both civilian and military

The marshal quit, so for a while I was the only marshal on the island. They got to running me all over the damned island and one thing and another. Finally the command finally got on the marshal's office in Anchorage and told them to "get a marshal over here the purpose of this job is wildlife enforcement, we want to cover him on this job and keep him safe."

I worked with Will Troyer, he was the Refuge Manager and he hadn't been there very long when I got here. So, Atkinson said, "Hey, how about we go up and make up some composition counts?" We started this project. Nobody'd done that in Kodiak. Most of the deer at that time were restricted to the north end of the island. You get down to Uganik Bay and you run out of deer, they were all down on this end of the island.

This road system out here, we had deer in huge numbers. We could probably have had three, four months of doe season with no problem. But the U.S. Fish and Wild Service didn't want that. They had this thing imprinted about bucks only. They never had a doe season until after Statehood.

The same time I met the ranchers. They were concerned about the bears. I went up and witnessed some of these kills, bear signs all over, fresh hemorrhage. You know it had to be bear that killed them, it wasn't just an old hide that was winter killed cattle.

The refuge manager was more interested in managing bears and requested me to intercept the ranchers for him so he could manage bears. He wanted to get to Karluk Lake and start a tagging program. They trapped the first bears with culvert traps.

I worked with the ranchers, sympathized with them for two years. I lived part of my life in Colorado on a cattle ranch, I could see where a lot of bears were killing quite a few cows. They were very efficient.

The Navy built a culvert for them. Built it in sections so we could pack it up to where we could use it. I arranged it for them. We could fly it down there in pieces so it could be handled. Two men could carry a piece and assemble it on site.

We used bacon rinds and halibut heads and bait in the back of the trap. Bears would go in and pull on it and the door would shut. They put canvas over the top of the trap and they had these little squirt guns filled with ether. They squirted it in until the bear went down. We'd drag them out and process them.

Of course the bear would have saliva flying out of its mouth. We were afraid they were going to drown. We nearly drowned a couple of them. It wasn't very effective.

I think we processed three or four bears the first year.

That was before the muscle relaxant was used. Before the sophisticated drugs and later dart guns. The first ones were air guns with the little O rings always leaking on them. You never knew if you had a load in the damn thing or not, whether it was going to carry twenty feet or fifty feet. Compared to the capture guns of today with the .22 blank loads in them, three loads, heavy, medium, light.

Then we started trapping with these wolf traps, we cut the jaws off, put tape on the jaws to soften them more. We set them on the bear trails along the rivers when they were feeding in the summer. We had a drag on them. This was pretty effective, the only thing is when you have an adult in there and even some of the smaller bears that were big enough to be dangerous, they'd go back in the thick alders.

When you went in there after them, you didn't know if it was on that end of the chain or this end. The alders were all moving and you couldn't see which end of the chain the bear was on. The minute they smelled you, the alders were thrashing.

We found out if you put one of those CO2 bottles in there and shoot the bear at close range...at first we were using these aluminum poles with a syringe. You had to get close enough to reach them. We were bending needles and wasting drugs, it was slow. Then we found out if you put one CO2 load, you could get up 5-feet from him and administer the drug that way. It made it a lot easier.

You wouldn't dare use one of these capture guns even with .22 loads, a bear hemorrhages about three-inches. I broke a deer's leg one day. I tried for the shoulder and missed. Hit it in the leg and broke it.

Once we got the muscle relaxant drugs things went a little smoother with one exception. And that was judging the weight of the bear. You look at one bear and think it would go about 400 pounds. But you get him down and he's got thick fur and it was maybe an emaciated bear and he'd die on you.

We got to where we could look at a bear and guess its weight at 400 pounds and load the drug for 300 pounds, go light on them. That would at least slow him down and not kill him. We'd follow them until they got woozy. Then we'd give them another small dose to put them down.

Once over on McNeil me and Eide (Sterling) misjudged a bear and had to put five darts in it. I said, "Hey, let's not put any more in it." Finally it went down.

We didn't kill a bear that year of 50 that we anesthetized. We made sightings of these bears later. We had one bear stay down nine hours and we were afraid the tide was going to get him. He was down on the mud flats, and we got a couple of photographers to help us drag him onto a grassy knoll.

She had two cubs, and we were able to get in front of her on a crossing.

We had good luck with the Karluk Lake culverts. The lake is twelve miles long, thirteen feeder streams with red salmon. There are bears all along the lake in the summer. There are trails all along the edge of the lake and up the streams. It was pretty easy to trap bears. We'd have a dozen traps set. Take the boat in the morning and start making our rounds.

Some days we'd have, after a night's setting, we might have three or four bears to work on. That would take most of the day to tattoo and collar them and everything. Of course we were making some of our own radios and stuff. The radios have changed drastically since those days, much better and better signals too. The double antennas on them now enable better receiving.

Over the years, this bear-cattle thing in Kodiak. That started in 1964, the spring following the earthquake. All the roads were inundated. They were building new roads and it was really hard to get out to the ranches. I approached the Navy out here and got them to let us use a helicopter to go to and from the ranches.

They were real cooperative and dropped us off in the morning and picked us up in the evening. The biologist where was Sterling Eide. It was his first permanent job with the Fish and Game. He went to Juneau to discuss this with the director and the commissioner. They said, "Set it up into a study and then we'll look at it. We're going to kill some bears and we're going to be under the gun so document and watch what you're doing."

He was in a great habit of keeping records and being very careful, not keeping anything from the public. Put everything up front. Collect all specimens, all hides, all bears that we killed; we had to make a hell of an effort to get those.

The money that we were spending...when I'd get in an airplane in the morning and go out here and look for bears, the money that I was using was management money that was coming out of the state coffers. It wasn't that PR money. Once we had a bear killed and was down, and we had to collect the specimen, we could go off that management money cause then we were looking at research—we were collecting reproductive tracts, blood samples, all these different tissues, master muscles, all this information was going into our research program in Anchorage.

We had to be very careful about flight time, money. We had to keep these budgets separated very carefully. If there was any question, we put it into management. It was hunters' money to represent excise tax to kill bears. It was kind of crazy.

Eide was a young biologist just out of school. Oh, he'd worked temporary for the state for a couple of years, him and Ron Sommerville. It was kind of against his grain. Here's the first job he gets and it's kind of a predator control issue, disenfranchised him. But he did a hell of a job on it. He was a sharp kid. I was real pleased with the way he conducted the project.

The paper he wrote on it I think was...he presented that at the fish and game commissioners' annual meeting when we were the host back in '66 or '67. This program lasted four years. In '68 when Loren Croxton was the director, we got so much bad publicity on it. Jim Rearden wrote that article for ***Outdoor Life*** and he got some public attention on it. They finally stopped us.

I knew it was in the making. In fact I called Juneau once in a while cause I knew him pretty well, and I said, "What's the story are we going still kill bears over here or what?"

He said, "Any day now it's going to stop. But right now it's still go."

The day they called me and said, "That's it. No more," I took the Super Cub and flew around to all the ranchers and told them, "Hey, they just cut this program off."

They took it well. They said, "We kind of figured one of these days they'd stop it—especially after that article." That was the last year, 1968, after it went about four years.

The night Eide left and there was a guy came here by the name of Jack Alexander. He didn't want a thing to do with it. So they said, "Let Ballinger run that thing." After Eide left that bear-cattle program was kind of on my hook there about eighteen months.

Alexander was the area management biologist.

Jack didn't like the ranchers and he let them know it. I kind of give him credit for standing his ground and saying he was for the bears and not the cattle ranchers. I used to get in trouble at home with my wife and my mother who said, "The bears were here first." There's logic to what they're saying.

It is marginal cattle country, let's face it. I've never seen a cattle rancher here really make any money from ranching. What they did is they came in, they settled, they got a herd started. Where they'd make the money was where they sold it to the next guy who got it, not from actually producing meat for the market. They're not really productive.

Tagging program started in the summer of '57 on Kodiak.

Bears that ate cows...

We estimated the number of bears within the five leases were somewhere around 50 bears. We did this by walking the streams and measuring and counting tracks and differentiating their sizes. In one section you'd find a 6-inch track for a hundred yards, that's one bear. Then we'd find a sow with two cubs of the year with 3-inch tracks, there's three bears. Then we'd find a 7-and-a-half-inch track.

We did this with all these streams on the road system. They'd send us a couple of temporaries from Anchorage to assist us. They're a tough species to work on. We go by trend counts. We consistently fly stream counts, alpine counts, check salmon and bears feeding on sedges. We count year after year and look for trends, reproduction for instance, cubs per 100 sows, cubs per sow.

A high percent of the 50 bears were males. The habitat hasn't changed much with the cattle feeding there. Territory unoccupied by bears or nowhere near the saturation level, boars were the first ones to move in there. Very few sows and cubs were there. Something like 83% of the bears we killed on the cattle ranges were males. Many of them were huge bears, just huge. Several big record book skulls.

Even when we were working with them the ranchers killed a few bears that they never reported. They just shot them and the bears ran off into the brush. We'd find a carcass of a bear. We couldn't always find ...people along the road system, new people especially, shot bears and the bear died 500 yards away.

Number of bears Hirst and Zentner worked together, ranches abutted one another from Sultery Cove to Pasagshak. They were such good hunters and trackers that they wouldn't give up. It wouldn't be unusual for one to help the other to track down a bear.

The ranches were around 3,000 some of them. The grazing area including mountain tops and so on, they ran the lease by drainage from the mountain top down. Only the lower elevation was good for cattle of course. It wasn't uncommon to see them up quite high in the summer time, in the sub-alpine areas.

The ranchers didn't have any control, they didn't have any fences.

We made an agreement with them, "How about we put a fence there to check these bears, to find out where they're coming from, which direction, and how they react to fences?" The state spent thousands of dollars on all fencing stuff. We were going to test them, put up a 4-inch pig fence wire, 4 strand barb wire, electric fence and so on. We had all these different type fences that we were going to test.

We were going to run them from Middle Bay over here up over the top down into Saltery Cove. The state felt that most of the bears were coming from the Hidden Basin working this way onto the cattle ranches. We were also going to start a tagging program in Terror Bay and Hidden Basin to see if the bears showed up here. But we didn't have the money and the personnel. We did a little tagging in Terror Bay and we got a few bears tagged, and most of those were harvested within a year or so, and we didn't learn much on them. We needed more money for that.

All of a sudden the ranchers said, "We don't want any fences up there."

One rancher on this side said, "You're going to feed all those bears right into my cattle. They'll hit that fence on the other side and follow it right into my cattle."

They wouldn't allow us to put the fence in. At the same time they were starting that moose project at Kenai and they needed to fence it. So I put it all on a couple of big trucks and got in on the ferry and sent it up there so it didn't go to waste.

We were going to get some help and put this up for bids so we wouldn't be strapped with doing that ourselves. But they never did allow us to build the fence.

We found that bears often hit a fence and turned away.

Some found a spot where they could cross.

The cattle grazed throughout their range, wherever it was accessible for them to go they went. The ranchers didn't fence the ranches that well. They didn't really know where their stock was half the time.

In a lot of areas they were easy prey for bears because they grazed into their bear area. When we found a bear-killed cow, we filled out a form and tried to collect data—how far was it from the nearest cover for bears, condition of the animal, where the hemorrhage was. Quite frequently they'd get them in the neck and come down on them and open up the back and find two or three vertebrate broken in the neck. Sometimes there wouldn't be a piece of bone over quarter of an inch big. There'd be two or three vertebrates busted right over the top of the neck. The mouth did the damage. They'd bite them just forward of the shoulders right on the neck.

Whenever a bear had been around the cattle, the cattle were real spooky. Their tails would go up and they'd high-tail it. You could figure there had been a bear around.

You never knew if the bear would come back to a cow it had killed or not. There was enough range and cattle that he might be over the next range or half a mile away feeding on a different cow. He never did come back to this one. We put traps on them, a number 6, great big bear trap.

When we did that, we built corrals around them and put up a sign so that if somebody investigated and got in that trap, they could get out of it. We were a little spooky about those traps. We put great big chain around a log so the bear would have to drag it.

We were successful in trapping a few bears but it wasn't that productive. If that had been a black bear, we'd have had a lot of bears. But those brown bears are either more reluctant to go into a baited trap like that or their noses are much keener or something. We used gloves and boiled the traps to get off all the scent, very careful about handling them.

We had a professional who'd worked in Washington trapping black bears for the forest service down there. He assisted us with that, guy by the name of Jones, Doug Jones, out of Palmer. We'd get him in the summer time down there. He was good. He said, "These brown bears just don't come into the traps like black bears." He got 91 black bears one year in Washington, and he knew what he was doing.

I never had to shoot a bear when we worked with them. I had one time where I was just about to pull off on one, but all of a sudden it stopped and ***woofed*** at me. It looked at me, sidetracked, went around. I don't know what changed its mind. They're so damned unpredictable.

Maybe a healthier bear population now than we had in the 1960s, some huge boars still.

Harvest date before statehood isn't very reliable.

Jack Alexander

I met Jack some time ago. His son was on the wrestling team I coached at A.J. Dimond High School. Jack received his Bachelor of Science degree from Brigham Young University and joined Alaska Department of Fish and Game in 1966 as a Kodiak area biologist. He trapped many bears on Admiralty and Kodiak islands. Jack commented…

Most of the cattle people down there were probably just getting by. They had supplemental incomes in town. Cattle ranching was always a difficult proposition down there. It was there, we saw it and everybody knew it, a lot of animals were lost the same winter forces that all wildlife is subject to. All winter is icy conditions, poor nutritional value of the feed that they were subsisting on. Is it really true that the bears were taking additional cattle or were the bears taking cattle that had already died or were near death. It was quite often the case.

Put yourself in the ranchers' point of view. There wasn't anything you could do about the winter. You couldn't go to the legislature and the governor but you could do something about the bears. Whether they were taking healthy cattle, you've got frustration and something to do.

Tim Burton and his brother came up here and bought the ranch from Beaty (Joe). So Beaty, they took turns working in town and were probably the most aggressive, knowledgeable cattle ranchers Kodiak had seen at that time, and probably still are. I know they're still working at it, how well they're doing I don't know.

You look around and generally find a viable industry has

some growth in it, capital improvements and buildings, roads, equipment. I doubt in thirty years there's much in the way of new buildings, construction. Burtons have gone into beefalo. They actually have hunts out there. Hunters come out and shoot one if they want to.

As for the rest of the ranchers, I couldn't attest to their financial conditions, but I have my doubts and reservations that there are many who have made much money. Like a lot of things around here, people develop and sell and that's when they make their money whenever they turn over something, sell the company.

It's tough to survive, the market, quality of what they're producing, state has built a slaughter house out there back in the 70s specifically for processing beef. I think it shut down in a couple of years then reopened. I think it's a fairgrounds building now. In spite of the state's best efforts it still didn't work.

Garbage Bears

Biologist kills bear on Kenai

EUTHANIZED: Grizzly with taste for garbage and hurt by buckshot runs out of chances.

By Craig Medred, ***Anchorage Daily News***, August 4, 2001

A grizzly bear died in a ditch near Cooper Landing on Thursday -- euthanized by a state biologist who discovered the bear's shoulder riddled with buckshot earlier that day.

The bear's two young cubs were captured and sent to a wild portion of the Kenai National Wildlife Refuge.

Alaska Department of Fish and Game biologist Ted Spraker, who administered the lethal drugs, said people, circumstances and bad luck finally caught up to the young sow and her brood.

Three years ago, when Spraker captured the bear that biologists labeled C-5, she was a youngster developing a taste for garbage in Seward. He darted her, crated her up and hauled her 70 to 80 miles out of town.

Then he fitted her with a radio collar and set her free. With the isolated Kenai Peninsula brown bear population struggling at about 250 animals, the last thing biologists want to do is lose a potentially productive sow.

Back in 1999, C-5 looked like she might have a chance.

"That fall," Spraker said, "she went back to Dave's Creek," in the mountains above Sunrise.

The biologist assumed the bear found a supply of spawned-out red salmon. He hoped she'd lose her memory of eating the discards of food, fish waste and dog food found on the edge of civilization.

She hadn't.

Last summer, signals from the grizzly's collar started being heard in Avalanche Acres, a subdivision near Tern Lake, at the intersection of the Seward and Sterling highways. Homeowners complained about a bear on their decks.

"She ... got into trouble a few times over there," Spraker said.

Last fall, researchers working in the Kenai Mountains above Tern Lake darted her, weighed her and released her.

As winter settled over the Kenai and the grizzlies headed for their dens, biologists could only hope for the best. They didn't know C-5 was pregnant and would give birth to a couple cubs over the winter.

And Spraker was optimistic when the bear stayed out of sight through early summer.

That didn't last.

"About three weeks ago," the biologist said, she showed up back at Avalanche Acres. She was into everything, up on decks, looking in windows, pushing on doors."

The danger couldn't be ignored. An adult grizzly can easily kill a child with a casual swipe of its paw.

So Spraker caught her again -- this time hauling C-5 and her cubs as far as it was possible to drive out onto the Mystery Creek access road that cuts into the heart of the Kenai refuge.

They didn't stay long.

"In about three days, she was up at the Princess Lodge (in Cooper Landing)," Spraker said. "She was into the dumpster, leaning on the kitchen doors."

Cubs in tow, she worked her way along Cooper Landing's Bean Creek Road, stealing dog food, getting into garbage and showing an ever-diminishing fear of humans.

The three bears literally went door-to-door, paws against windows and sometimes nosing into vacant cabins.

"She pushed on the door pretty forcefully," homeowner Richard Dunn said. "My wife was sitting there having a cup of coffee. She thought it was an earthquake at first."

When Dunn's wife, Barbara, saw the bear, she screamed and ran out the back door to the neighbor's house, he said. Her scream sent the sow ambling away.

Longtime Bean Creek resident and retired bear biologist Will Troyer, who keeps his garbage and dog food indoors, heard the sow's snorts, too.

By last week, the family of bears was a regular at the dump near Sunrise, a roadside stop along Kenai Lake just east of Cooper Landing. She'd lost almost all fear of humans, Spraker said.

"She'd be feeding 10 feet from my truck," he said.

"Six days ago, she got into some guy's camper," Spraker said.

The man told Spraker he fired a warning shot at the bears in bad light.

"He thought he shot over her," Spraker said, "but he hit her in the shoulder."

On Thursday, Spraker tranquilized the bear again, thinking he'd relocate her once more. Then he discovered the damage from the gunshot wound.

"It was a bad state of affairs," he said. "She was in really bad shape."

Given her past behavior and the handicap of her wounds, Spraker decided her survival was linked to foraging around humans. Grizzlies habituated to human food can be aggressive, and someone could be hurt.

Better, the biologist decided, to put C-5 down before that happened.

So on Thursday, with C-5 already sedated, Spraker trickled more drugs into her veins. She died of an overdose.

When her carcass was skinned (the hide will be sold by the state at auction), the biologist found six buckshot pellets in her chest.

"One shoulder was all bloodshot," he said. "She was in pretty rough shape."

The 45- to 50-pound cubs were aggressive and hard to catch, but with the help of others Spraker corralled them and took them to a wild area of the refuge with plenty of green grass, water and climbable trees.

There was no other option, Spraker said. Zoos already have more grizzly bears than they want, and if one of these cubs survives it will help the Kenai bear population.

"There's no place to put them," Spraker said. "At least this way they've got a fighting chance."

Cubs have been known to make it on their own.

"These were big, strong, strapping cubs," he said. "They have a 50-50 chance."

Spraker knows, however, that 50-50 may be optimistic. Making it through the year will be tough.

"The real problem is they have a tough time denning," Spraker admitted.

That is something their mother would have taught them.

Now, the odds are that if another bear doesn't kill the cubs by fall, winter will claim them.

Dump Breeds Problem Bears

COOPER LANDING: Unfenced transfer site lures bears out of wild.

By Jon Little, *Anchorage Daily News*, August 4, 2001

Soldotna -- Cooper Landing's garbage transfer site along the busy Sterling Highway is doubling as an unofficial bear viewing area.

People actually bait the big metal bins with dog food and have even tucked fish carcasses into dumpster handles, apparently hoping for a cute photo, said Mayme Ohnemus, head of the Sexy Senior Dumpster Cleaners, a group that contracts with the Kenai Peninsula Borough to maintain three waste sites in Cooper Landing, Moose Pass and Hope.

Ted Spraker, a state wildlife biologist who trapped one boar and euthanized a sow there this week, said he's tired of it. "This needs to be addressed," he said Friday after disposing of the sow's body.

The site is unfenced and open 24 hours a day. It is just too much of a magnet for bears, opportunistic feeders that will return again and again once they've found something to eat, Spraker said.

Ohnemus said she has one idea. She said she admires transfer sites in Willow and Houston, which are fenced and appear to have electric gates.

She is scheduled to meet Kenai Peninsula Borough solid waste officials and Spraker at the Cooper Landing waste site

Tuesday to talk about the problem.

Cooper Landing's transfer site is one of 12 borough-operated garbage drop-off points on the Kenai Peninsula. Some are more developed than others, with fences and buildings. Garbage from the sites gets trucked to the borough's two main landfills, in Soldotna and Homer.

Bear problems crop up at some of these sites from time to time, but nothing on the scale of Cooper Landing, said Holly Hastings, the borough's solid waste contract administrator.

The Sexy Senior Dumpster Cleaners spruce up the transfer sites once a week, raising money for their senior center. Ohnemus said it took a crew of 14 people 45 minutes last Monday to pick up trash strewn about the woods by bears. In the winter, a smaller crew will be done in 10 minutes.

Spraker said he watched the sow gobble down plastic and paper bags last week. It was 10 feet away from his vehicle and paid him no mind. Residents have said they had to lean hard on their car horns to get the bear to budge.

If a bear's around, six to eight cars will line up there, waiting for a safe moment to get out and dump trash, many of them seizing the opportunity to shoot a photograph, Spraker said.

It was one of the reasons he decided to kill the sow, he said. Even with an injured left leg, the bear was faster than a human. She could have wheeled and smacked someone.

"It's the old story that a fed bear is a dead bear," Spraker said. "If you let 'em get into something, they're going to get killed."

Bear Opens Garage Door

Bear Opens Garage Door, Saunters into Family's Kitchen.

By KORRY KEEKER, *Juneau Empire*, August 9th, 2005

JUNEAU, Alaska (AP) - Geri Anderson was sitting in the computer room in the back of her Sunset Street home when she heard a noise in her kitchen just after 9:30 p.m. Sunday.

She went to the kitchen to investigate and found a black bear, eating garbage and licking the plates from her family's rib dinner, a few hours before. The bear turned around and snorted at her.

"All the bones were in the kitchen garbage, and he had it spread out all over the floor," Geri said. "He had a pretty good mess going by that time." "I turned around and I didn't make a sound or anything," she said.

The bear entered the house through the Andersons' connecting garage, Geri said.

"The switch on the garage door was turned off so there was no power in the door," she said. "He was able to lift the garage door up and come in, and the garage door went down behind him."

Geri came out, but didn't see the bear, which was already in the garage. She went back, heard another noise and came out again.

She found the bear this time – about two feet away, she said.

As Geri walked quickly back to the bedroom, the bear followed her eight feet down the hallway.

"I felt him," Geri said. "I just turned around and started walking away really fast, and I got down the hallway, opened the door and closed it and said, 'Bob, there's a bear in the house.' I just fell apart, I was so scared."

Bob, her husband, jumped out of bed and went to the door. He opened it and saw the bear staring back at him.

"I've been in Alaska a long time," said Bob, a 46-year resident. "I've seen a lot of bears, and I lived in Yakutat for 18 years and I've hunted and been in different situations. My wife, she's never had that."

"I closed the door, and I put my weight against it, and I could feel the door being pushed," he said. "It was a big black bear. When he turned, his rump went up against the door."

The bear knocked off a small decorative shelf at the end of the hall, just outside the door.

"I think he saw himself in the mirror and took a swat at himself," Bob said.

"But he wasn't aggressive. He had a lot of guts to walk into a house through the garage door."

Geri called 911 and said she got through to the police at 9:51 p.m.

"They said, 'Where's the bear?'" Geri said. "We said, 'He's right outside the door.'"

Three officers arrived in the Andersons' front lawn just before 10 p.m. and continued to speak to Geri on the phone. That's when, according to the police report, the bear stood up on its hind legs, put both front paws on the glass, broke through the window and escaped into the woods.

"I was talking to them on the phone in the bathroom and Bob was still holding the door," Geri said. "They said, 'The bear leapt through your living room window.'"

The bear crashed through the glass, ripping down the blinds, clawing the radiator and almost shattering a framed, glass decoration of a raven that hangs in front of the window.

The Andersons' landlord estimated the damage at $5,000 and will pick up the bill, Bob said.

The Andersons have lived at their Sunset Street home for 10 years. They've seen bears sniffing around their house and garage before, and once took a picture of a baby bear crawling on their deck.

"That was frightening, but not like this," Geri said. ***Juneau Empire*** reporter Tony Carroll contributed to this report.

Garbage-grubbing Bruin Sparks Afognak Fire

Garbage-grubbing Bruin Sparks Afognak Fire

Logging Crew Extinguishes Blaze Before It Spreads

By Lucas Wall, *Anchorage Daily News*, May 31, 2001

It's a rare camper who hasn't heard Smokey Bear's message: "Only you can prevent forest fires!" Some of his species on Afognak Island apparently aren't so concerned.

Bears are blamed for a four-acre fire Monday night at a Danger Bay logging camp. An Afognak Native Association fire truck and a crew from the logging camp extinguished the fire, which caused little damage in the logged-over area but has provided some chuckles for forestry workers who usually must cope with human-caused blazes.

"They were burning some of the trash and evidently some bears came along and decided to dig around in it," said Andy Williams of the Alaska Interagency Fire Information Center. The bears tossed some of the burning debris onto the ground and sparked the fire.

"I've heard of fires being caused by animals nibbling on power lines and things like that," Williams said. "It's the first time I've heard of a fire being caused by a bear. It is definitely unusual."

Ric Plate, fire management officer for the Alaska Division of Forestry, said he suspects some leftover food was among the trash being burned in a barrel.

"There must have been something in there that had

attracted the bear," he said. "It's a new one for me."

Forestry division staffers took the news that the popular fire prevention mascot was implicated in an outdoors arson in stride.

"It's a little bit of humor to our normal business here," Plate said. "Oh well, those things happen I guess."

Allen Hasselborg

Ralph Young tells of Allen Hasselborg making noises like a brown bear. Young once encountered a wounded and moaning brown bear, avoided it and then ran into Hasselborg. After assuring Allen that Ralph was unmistaken in his assessment of the origin of the sound, Hasselborg told him, "'Well, that wasn't no wounded bear you heard back there...that was me.'"

"I could scarcely believe what I heard. The growling and moaning couldn't have been more realistic had it been made by a bear. It was the first time I had heard Allen Hasselborg talk like a grizzly bear. Later I would hear him talk to the bear and the bears talk to him." (Pg. 116, ***My Lost Wilderness***)

John M. Holzworth wrote ***The Wild Grizzlies of Alaska*** which he dedicated to Allen E. Hasselborg. "It was the Fall of 1927 that I made my initial acquaintance with Admiralty Island and Mr. Allen Hasselborg. Admiralty Island is unsurpassed as a field museum for the study of the Grizzly and Big Brown Bears of Alaska, and there are few men living who have more first-hand information about them than Mr. Hasselborg, who has lived alone on the island for the better part of twenty years." (Page 4)

Bear Trails or People Trails

Bears vs. People

Who gets the Rabbit Creek greenbelt?

By ROSEMARY SHINOHARA, *Anchorage Daily News*, June 2, 2003

Some South Anchorage residents are trying to carry out a long-held dream of carving out trails through the public greenbelt stretching from the mountains toward the sea along Rabbit Creek.

The idea has been in city plans for more than 15 years, notes Rabbit Creek Community Council president Dianne Holmes.

But State Fish and Game area biologist Rick Sinnott says the trails, if they attract many people, will disturb one of the city's busiest bear habitats and will increase the chance of dangerous conflict between people and bears.

"I wouldn't want to be hiking along there when the salmon are running," Sinnott said.

He is urging that the builders move one piece of the proposed trail "well away from the creek" and that they leave the trail muddy to discourage use. Runners and bicyclists would be particularly likely to startle a brown bear, Sinnott said, so the trail should be designed for walking only.

Since the Rabbit Creek trail system was conceived, development has squeezed out much open space in Anchorage. In the remaining public wild land, residents and officials must weigh competing values: How hospitable should Anchorage remain to its bears, moose and other wildlife while also accommodating people's use of parks and greenbelts?

The Rabbit Creek trail proposal is pending before the city. The Parks and Recreation Commission, which advises the Parks Division, will likely make a recommendation in July, a city official said.

Holmes and Nancy Pease, leading the trail builders, say they are taking into account the fact that bears use the Rabbit Creek valley and are planning only a packed-dirt trail with boardwalk or gravel in wet areas that would be used mostly by local residents. Leaving a trail muddy isn't sound design, Holmes said. "You never would do that."

"I feel that the city parkland there has been unfairly targeted by strong language from Mr. Sinnott as a sanctuary-type habitat when it wasn't intended for that," Pease said. "Our little trail is about the lightest use of the land we could make."

The Rabbit Creek Community Council and the Anchorage Trails and Greenways Coalition, with help from the city Parks Division, last summer built a narrow three-quarter-mile dirt trail in the east end of the Old Rabbit Creek Park, on the upper Hillside south of De Armoun Road.

They won grants from public and private sources to help pay for it; volunteers did the work.

The trail switches back and forth through tall spruce and alder up and down a hill, to a bridge crossing Rabbit Creek. Near the top, a volunteer set up two pieces of burl at a rest spot. "We call it table and chairs," Holmes said.

"The design of the trail dictates who uses it," said trail supporter Susanne Comellas. "If you have roots and shrubs in a narrow area (as this trail does), it's not going to bring bicycles."

The creek gushes and gurgles below for most of the way

but is not visible until the end of the path.

A segment of trail the community council and other volunteers want to build next would begin at the bridge and follow an existing foot trail through a flat, grassy area. They've also proposed a loop in Griffin Park, off Cannon Road and DeArmoun, and a couple of segments to connect the main trail with neighborhoods to the north and south.

Sinnott said there's little hard information on bear use of the Rabbit Creek valley, but based on what's known and on his own experience, the valley is one of the top five spots used by black and brown bears in the Anchorage Bowl.

Black bears will probably adapt even if more people trek through, Sinnott said. "They're forest animals. They'll move into the brush or climb a tree," he said.

But brown bears, which could be feeding at any time when the salmon are running, don't climb trees. They either run away or attack, he said.

While the trail planners say the paths are just for the immediate neighborhoods, he notes, long-range plans would connect long stretches through the greenbelt and some streets.

Al Meiners, a retired Chugach State Park superintendent who helped plan the trail the council built last year, seconded the notion that brown bears can be dangerous near salmon streams. He recalled three incidents in the 1990s when people were injured by brown bears on the Albert Loop trail near the park visitor center in Eagle River.

In each case, the bears were drawn by fish, he said, so the park closed the trail when the fish were in.

But most of the existing Rabbit Creek trail is rough enough that people will have to walk it and the trail is high enough above the creek, Meiners said. As for the segments yet to be built, bears are “a concern, but I don’t know that it’s much greater than many other places people hike in the Anchorage area.”

“You’ve got to remember, moose are more likely to hurt you than bears,” Meiners said.

“And more people are killed by dogs across the country than bears.”

Daily News reporter Rosemary Shinohara can be reached at rshinohara@adn.

People Say the Darndest Things

I've been accused of many things by people who have read or heard about our books...even been told I needed to see a shrink. Hmmmm. The following vignettes capture some of those events.

STUDENT: "What do you do with all your money?"

In the mid-1980s a student asked me a question as I sat before my tenth grade English class. I laughed so hard I nearly fell off my little stool. When I stopped laughing, I asked Kim to explain her question.

She said, "Well, you told us you had a Leer jet agency with offices all over the world."

I agreed, "Yes, I said that."

"And you said that you made 1.5 million dollars last summer on your lawn mower business."

I concurred again, "Yes, I told you that."

"And you're rich and famous," she concluded.

I fought the impulse to ask this tenth grade brunette if she were wearing a blonde wig. Then, without insulting her by asking if her hair was dyed, I said, "Yes, I told you all those things. I assumed you students knew that I was only joking about owning a leer jet agency and a lawn mower business."

Bears Nearly Evicted

AP, ***Anchorage Daily News***, B-1, January 9, 1993

Concerned for his six children's safety, Bob LeBlanc called the Alaska State Troopers. He forbade his children from playing in the yard after his wife Harriet saw "steam" arising from the ground two weeks previous.

Bob had seen fourteen bears in his yard.

By the time a front-end loader had arrived in his yard 100 miles north of Juneau, Alaska, the bears had left. LeBlanc said, "They booked."

Bear Visits Inn

BEAR PAYS INN LATE-NIGHT VISIT STARTLED:

Guests heard breaking glass, saw bruin in lounge.

By Marmian Grimes, ***Fairbanks Daily News-Miner,*** September 23, 2002

Fairbanks -- Barbara Claspill advertises "a view of the wilderness" to potential guests at her Stampede Road bed-and-breakfast.

The wilderness opened the door and walked inside early last Saturday.

A ringing telephone at 2:30 a.m. jarred Claspill awake in her upstairs bedroom of the Denali Touch of Wilderness Inn.

"The guest in Room 3 called me and said, 'You have a bear in the house,' " she said. "It was right outside her window." That would be a window into the lounge area, Claspill explained, not outside.

Guests in two of the downstairs rooms had been awakened by the sounds of thumps and glass breaking outside their bedroom doors.

The guest told Claspill that the bear finally settled down but was right outside her door. "She looked out her window. She said, 'I think I made eye contact.' I think it scared the bear." Claspill quickly dressed and started down the stairs.

"Then I realize what I am doing," she said. "I don't even have a gun with me."

Her husband, Dan, had the gun. Ordinarily that would not have been a problem, she said, except he was sleeping in a trailer about 200 yards from the house because he hadn't been sleeping well with all the hustle and bustle of the bed-and-breakfast.

"I call my neighbor next door and I wake them up and say: 'I have a bear in the house. Could you come over? I can't get a hold of Dan,' " Claspill said.

Claspill said she thinks the bear got in by pushing against an unlocked lever handle on her door.

Neighbor Michael Owen arrived and spent a tense few minutes, going from room to room in the darkened house looking for the bear.

"(I) had flashlights on and just basically started going through the house trying to clear the thing," he said.

Meanwhile, Claspill's husband woke up out in the trailer to see armed people with flashlights moving around in his house. He grabbed his gun and flashlight and headed to the house.

"He yells in there ... 'come out and show yourself because I have a gun,' " Claspill said.

Owen yelled back: "It's Mike and Pat (from) next door. Don't shoot. There is a bear in the house."

"I said that very forcefully and clearly," he said.

Sometime before all of the commotion, the bear had apparently left through the same door it came in.

No one saw it clearly enough to say whether it was a grizzly or black bear or how old it appeared to be. But state Department of Fish and Game spokeswoman Cathie Harms said it sounds like something a young bear would do.

"Most of the time when a bear goes into structures or goes

close to people, it is a young hooligan that has been kicked out by mom," she said. "They are highly curious animals."

While she can laugh about it now, Claspill said it was scary at the time. "I was afraid that maybe it would panic and not be able to get out."

Despite the drama, the bear caused relatively little damage, Claspill said, and nobody was injured.

"It knocked over our monitor, our printer, all of the plants," she said. "I have got a claw mark on my rug in there." Perhaps the worst damage was the slobber.

"I had this bear goopy stuff all over everything," she said.

Charlie Brown

Alaska Sportsman, August 1966, John Walatka

Three one-year-old brown bears made their way one windy day to Kutik Lodge on the Alaska Peninsula—a family of two sows and a boar. They made themselves at home, becoming both pets and nuisances. Within a year the boar came to camp munching handouts from the kitchen. He was named Charlie Brown, sleeping by Charlie Blue's tent, often placing his paws on the tent porch. He followed Blue to the kitchen at 5:00 AM.

Every day Charlie Brown sauntered to the lake for a bath, usually twice. The bear usually came when his name was called. It was common to see him tossing sticks and rocks into the air and catching him in his mouth. Also, he followed guests or preceded them to the fishing holes.

Charlie particularly enjoyed mechanical things, often standing near someone who worked on mechanical items—especially when John started a tractor, which was noisy enough so that Charlie wandered away.

Within four years Charlie had become a 9-foot, 800 to 900 pound and beautiful animal.

He did not show up in 1965 and folks thought a local guide harvested Charlie.

Cruising Bear

Curious bear on cruise, *Anchorage Daily News*, B-1, Cathy St. John, July 19, 1995

Just west of Ketchikan at Thorne Bay, the just departed skipper and guests on the boardwalk was surprised to learn of a bear aboard his boat. The small, 4-foot tall bear seemed right at home. People chased it from the boat and it found room atop an approaching boat. The captain remained inside until he was a hundred yards from the shoreline. The cub jumped overboard and swam to shore.

Sea Going Bear

Seagoing bear gets ear oared, *Anchorage Daily News*, July 19, 1994, B-1

Surprise! Surprise!

Anchored in Kalinin ay the Silver Fox, skipper Mike Maher of Juneau, felt the 30,000 pound boat shift somewhat in the water. He looked overboard and came face-to-face with an adult brown bear. Maher jumped back but the bear swam to the other side of the boat and tried to board.

Maher grabbed a wooden oar and slammed it against the bear's left ear. With that how-do-you-do, the bear swam away from the Silver Fox and onto the beach.

Spirit Bear

White black bear wins protection

'SPIRIT BEAR': Rare bruin wins reprieve as hunting season nears.

By Larry Campbell, *The Associated Press*, August 24, 2002

A rare white-colored black bear got a reprieve from hunters' gunsights Friday morning.

In a teleconference meeting, the Alaska Board of Game ordered an emergency closure on hunting of all "white phase" black bears in the Juneau area. Effectively, that covers only one known white phase bear, the one spotted and photographed last week by local photographer Pat Costello.

Costello petitioned the board Thursday asking that the bear he's dubbed "Spirit bear" be exempt when hunting season opens Sept. 1.

"I'm thrilled with what the board did," Costello said Friday afternoon. "They realized there's an extreme interest in this bear."

Costello had the backing of hundreds of e-mail messages received this week after he posted a picture of the bear on his Web site, www.juneauphotos.com. People all over the world don't want to see the bear harmed, he said.

"People recognize this is a unique animal. It's important to them, whether they ever get to see it or not," he said. "They don't want to see it just made into another rug."

Game Board executive director Diana Cote said board members agreed, and the Alaska Department of Fish and Game told the policy-making panel it also supported the hunting ban. State game officials say they also have been flooded with phone calls and e-mail messages this week urging them to spare the bear.

The bear is creamy white, almost like a polar bear, but with a distinctive raccoon mask around the eyes. Most likely it is a variation of what biologists call a glacier bear -- genetically a black bear, but with a light fur coat that can run from cinnamon to golden-retriever blond to blue-white.

While glacier bears are somewhat scarce, a bear this white is rare even among glacier bears. Biologists in Southeast Alaska said they have not seen another like it.

"Actually, there are a lot of different color morphs with black bear," said Neil Barten, Douglas area biologist with the Alaska Department of Fish and Game. "But not quite this white. This is definitely unusual."

The hunting ban will last at least until the Game Board's regular meeting Nov. 1, when they will ask for public testimony and decide whether to extend the ban through the rest of the hunting season, which ends June 30.

State biologists in the area have known of the bear's existence for a few years. But knowledge of it became public after Costello took its picture.

The bear had emerged from some woods near town while Costello was waiting to take pictures of other black bears. The state capital city has a continuing problem with bears coming into town and raiding trash cans and bins.

He found himself standing in awe at the first sighting and hadn't snapped a shot before the bear disappeared back into the trees.

The white bear showed again about 45 minutes later, Costello said: "And I took 22 shots in about 60 seconds. Then it went back again into the woods. It was exciting. I was visibly shaking."

Taking any black bear out of season in Alaska is a Class A misdemeanor, punishable by up to one year in jail, a maximum $5,000 fine and a $600 restitution fee for the value of the bear to the state. Conviction would also result in forfeiture of the weapon used to kill the animal.

Cool Juneau Photos an ongoing photo-essay from Juneau, Alaska

08/23/2002 - Great News! I've just come from the emergency meeting of the Alaska Board of Game. 6 members of the Board participated via teleconference to consider my petition to protect this white-colored black bear. They voted unanimously to close the season on the taking of white bears in Unit 1C (Juneau area). This action is effective immediately and will be in effect for 120 days. The Board of Game will consider whether to enact permanent regulations to protect this bear at their regularly scheduled meeting here in Juneau in November.

Public input played a huge part in this victory and I thank-you all very much for your support. Your e-mails, phone calls, and other shows of support for this bear reached all the right people and it was obvious that this extreme interest by the public is the reason.

My request was approved. Thanks again for taking the time to get involved. You all made a huge contribution.

The photo and story of the Spirit Bear have reached all corners of the US now, on television stations and in newspapers and websites across the country. I heard there was even a mention in ***USA Today***, ***CNN.com***, etc. Simply amazing! In response I received nearly 1,000 e-mails from people from around the US. Thank-you all for letting me know where the story has appeared and for offering support. You're the greatest. Please accept my apologies if I don't personally respond to all these e-mails, as I'm a bit overwhelmed with it all.

So what's in store for the Spirit Bear? Well, hopefully permanent protection for this bear will be granted in November. And hopefully he won't become the target of poachers, those folks without scruples and little regard for the law.

Me? I've been privileged to have my moment with the Spirit Bear and I probably won't look for him again anytime soon. I'm sure I did the right thing by publicizing this animal and seeking protection but all this attention certainly has its downsides. It would be nice to believe that he could continue to live a life free from intervention but that might not be possible now. Let's just hope for the best for him...and don't bother asking where he's at, because I'm not telling!

Cheers! Pat Costello

Collision with a Grizzly

Collision with a Grizzly, By Robert R. Nelson

I was a school administrator for the Lower Kuskokwim School District in western Alaska when the incident occurred. On May 23, 1994, I finalized my work in Kipnuk, closed up the school, and left for Thorne Bay in southeast Alaska, where I was building a home during the summer months. As usual, I planned to stock up on food and construction supplies before driving to Thorne Bay.

When I left Kipnuk, I flew first to Bethel and then on to Anchorage. From there I went to Kenai to pick up my truck, a heavy duty Ford diesel. My friends in Kenai were storing it for me during the school year. In addition to a lot of food supplies, I picked up two 6 KW generators and extra batteries, electrical conduit, a fifty-five gallon drum of diesel fuel, copper napthaline, creosote, and a large amount of electrical wires and components. Both the cab and the bed of the truck were filled to capacity.

I left Anchorage on May 25 and drove through Beaver Creek at the Canadian border at 6:00 p.m., continuing down toward Haines Junction. I arrived in Haines at 10:00 p.m. and drove to the U. S. border. I drove through Dezadesh at about 2:00 a.m. on May 26th which happens to be my birthday. I was planning to stop at the U.S. border to sleep because customs didn't open until 8:00 in the morning.

At 2:30 a.m. I passed Mile Marker 19 and then I came over a rise in the road. The terrain consisted of rolling hills with no trees on both sides of the road. It looked barren, and there were snow banks on either side of the road. This was a straight stretch. I'd set to cruise control at 55 mph and 1900 RPM's. It was dark outside and there was no moon. Visibility in the barrow pits was zero. From the left side of the road, out of the barrow pit, a dark shape came up onto the road and ran across the right side.

I immediately recognized it as a bear. There was a guard rail on the right side, so, after checking to see that there were no oncoming vehicles, I steered the truck into the opposite lane to avoid the bear. I was traveling along in the opposite lane, not touching the brakes because I believed the bear was going over the guard rail. Unfortunately, he didn't.

As I was pulling past him, he bounced off the guard rail like it was a trampoline and flew across the highway, hitting the right side of the truck at the front tire. The front of the truck rared up and ran over the bear. It dragged the bear down the road for 300 feet while the back end came around. Now the truck was going down the road backwards.

It went through the right hand guard rail backwards and rolled over in the barrow pit 1 ½ times. It landed upside down in the barrow pit. The bear was back on the road 20 – 30 feet from where the truck had left the road.

The truck was laying on the driver's side. As it rolled, I saw a big splinter of gravel, lights and glass. When the truck stopped, the engine was racing. I reached up above me to turn it off. The steering wheel was above my head and I was pushed down into the seat. The front windshield as about eight inches high. The driver's window was about eleven inches high because the top of the cab was squashed down. I was jammed under the steering wheel.

The next thing I remember was hearing a steady "ding, ding, ding" warning me that my lights were still on. I straightened out the bent light knob and pushed it in. I tried to wiggle out of the driver's door and couldn't.

Finally, standing on the driver's door, I broke out the window on the passenger door and crawled out. I was still wearing one boot laced up, but the other was gone. The amazing part is that both boots had been laced up to the top when the accident occurred.

I had a case of rum, a gallon of dill pickles, 3 large bags of pistachios and a variety of other food items. Rum, pickles, and pistachios were everywhere.

I took stock of everything and started to pull out anything I could to keep myself warm because it was about 32 degrees outside. I pulled out floor mats, a jacket, rain gear. As I was hunting for things, I found my other boot, still laced up.

The truck canopy was gone. The generators were on their skids and had rolled down the barrow pit, one about 5 feet from the truck and the other about 150 feet. One of the batteries had come out of the back of the truck and was about 300 feet down the road. It was less than half of its original size. A person could follow the black streak down the road where the truck had skidded and there was fur on the road for about 300 feet where the bear had been drug underneath the vehicle.

It was cold out, the wind was blowing 10-15 knots. Water from melting snow was running into a creek alongside the road.

I went up on the road and tried to push off any debris so that it wouldn't be a hazard to other drivers. The sky was turning gray as it was starting to get daylight. There was a black lump visible where the guard rail had been torn up. The canopy and a bike I'd been carrying lay on the road. I looked back up the road to where the truck had gone through the railing. About 50 to 100 feet back was a big black shape. I was beginning to feel shocky from my injuries.

I pulled out everything I could from the truck, including a

duffel bag and I made a bed. I laid down and fell asleep for about 20-30 minutes. When I came to, the sky was still very gray. I could hear growling and moaning just above me on the road. I could also hear the unmistakable sound of teeth popping together. I opened one eye, and about 12 to 15 feet above me was a large, black head—the grizzly's head and shoulders swayed back and forth. The bear was snapping his jaws every 10 seconds or so. I thought to myself, "I didn't go through Viet Nam and several other nearly fatal experiences to lose it here."

He stood there for what seemed like an eternity, rocking back and forth, snapping his jaws, and looking down at me. In reality it was probably only about a minute. Then he turned, looked up the road, put his head down, and disappeared behind the canopy.

I wasted no time in scrambling to my feet and getting to the opposite side of the truck. I looked up over the truck. He was still in the same place with his head down.

I started up the creek moving as fast as I could parallel to the road. When I got 200 feet up the creek, it disappeared into a snow bank. I crossed the snow, making a crunching sound. I knew the bear could hear me and expected to the worst, but nothing happened.

I thought I was far enough away, I went up onto the road. I was limping and I had lots of cuts all over me. The entire time I was walking, I kept looking back, waiting for the bear. I couldn't see much yet because it still wasn't daylight.

When I was about half a mile from the crash site, two ptarmigan flew up right at my feet. This was the closest I've ever come to soiling my britches. The bear was still not coming.

I walked back into Canada about 6 miles, to mile marker 22 where I remembered seeing a truck parked off the road. I hammered on the truck door, and the trucker came out of his berth. He seemed pretty hesitant when I told him my story. Then he looked at me again and agreed to take me to Canadian Customs.

When the trucker and I passed the crash site, the bear was still alive. He was lying in the road. He got up and started to run, but lost his hind quarters and he left the right side of the road. He control-tumbled down the barrow pit, regained his hindquarters and went through the creek. Then he lost his hindquarters again. He started up a rock knoll and using his front legs, pulled himself to the top and stopped.

When the trucker stopped where he could see my truck and the bear, I got out and looked for my wallet in the wreckage. I could only find a briefcase. I was looking for something so that I could identify myself. We drove down the road 8 to 10 miles to Canadian Customs. It was 5:30 a.m. so no one was there yet. We went to the residences and knocked on the doors, but no one answered. The trucker couldn't go through customs without clearance. He could take me no further.

The U.S. Customs was a few blocks farther down the road, and I knew two of the customs officers, the Truebloods. I got out of the truck and walked toward U.S. Customs. As I was walking along, guess what darted across the road in front me? You guessed it, a bear. Only this one was a black bear.

I went past the customs station to the Truebloods' house. They let me in and I laid down on their floor. They called Canadian Customs and Jim Stanton who was my maintenance man when I was a principal at Klukwan. He lived at Mile 22 just off Mosquito Lake Road. Jim came to get me immediately; it only took him about 30 minutes to get there.

He and I drove to Canadian Customs. When we arrived, the woman in charge of customs was leaving with two other agents to find the bear. Jim and I followed them. We were about

5-6 yards behind them when they arrived at the crash site.

The bear was coming up from the knoll toward them. All three got out of the vehicle with rifles and shot at him. On the ninth shot he was wobbling. On the tenth shot, he finally fell dead. The agent's discovered that the bear had been speared by the truck springs which is what had drug him down the road.

I arranged to get the truck and my other things later. Jim drove me to Haines Junction where I flew to Bartlett Memorial Hospital in Juneau. I had a lacerated kidney and a broken rib. They treated me and then reluctantly released me.

I went immediately to the Alaska Marine Highway office to let them know that I was not going to be on the ferry with my truck. I told the agent that I had been in an accident with my truck. She acted as though she didn't believe me and demanded to see my tickets before she would consider giving me a refund. She watched me open my briefcase to look for the tickets. It was filled with gravel and pistachios. The corners of it were destroyed. She didn't argue anymore; she just refunded my money. I checked in at the super 8 Motel and slept for 8 hours straight.

Woman, Bear, and Broom

Seldovia woman fends off bear inside her home with a broom by Aaron Bolton, *Anchorage Daily News*, October 17, 2018

Karen Mahan worked at her computer just before 2 a.m. and heard a noise coming from her living room and kitchen. Thinking it was her two youngest sons, she checked. However a black bear had broken and entered through her front door and stared at her from her entryway.

As the critter watched her, she fetched her pistol from her bedroom not realizing her ammo was old. She said, "I'm walking out my bedroom door in a hurry, he's already in the living room standing between my couch and my rifle cabinet. He starts peeling is lips back and growling at me. I pull my gun to shoot on him and it dry fires."

When her pistol failed to fire a second time, she grabbed a metal broom, hitting the bear and pushing it toward the entryway. The 200-plus sized bruin growled, spit, clicked its teeth so she shoved him out a two story window. He bounced off her son's truck, denting the door, made all sorts of noises and split.

Seems a bear or two has been scavenging garbage in the Seldovia area. That bear probably wishes he'd not entered Mahan's home…or that a mini-tramp had reduced his bruises.

Golf Course Bear

Golfers let bear play through, *Anchorage Daily News*, B-1, June 21, 1998, by Isaiah Wilner

A young, 150 pound black bear was caught on the greens in Anchorage. Area biologist Rick Sinnott said, "We have scores of black bear in town. This one had a good head start on us, and once they get back in the woods you're not going to find them. They know you're there."

And so the animal tried to find a way to escape the golf course near the ninth hole.

Golfer Nancy Avery said, "He was running back and forth trying to figure out how to get out of the course. Poor guy."

And he did finally escape, going over the fence.

Bikers and Bear

Biking family outruns grizzly down Hillside trail, *Anchorage Daily News*, May 14, 1996

The Pautzke family, celebrating Mother's Day, rode their bicycles before being interrupted by a brown/grizzly bear. Their 14-year-old son Brian stated, "I saw the bear," and he turned around and peddled downhill. Brian's father Clarence heard him yell at the dog. Clarence said, "It wasn't in any sort of real pursuit, but it was loping along."

Alaska Department of Fish and Game stated that they "have had numerous report of brown bears on the Anchorage Hillside in recent days." And the paper reported "Hikers and mountain bikers can expect to meet bears at almost any time and almost anywhere in Alaska in the summer."

Sightings

SIGHTINGS: Biologist darts bruin that had eluded him for weeks. By Jeff St. John, *Anchorage Daily News*, June 22, 2001

Rick Sinnott's fourth black bear of the season lay in the bed of his pickup, eyes closed and nose twitching, with plastic yellow tag number 25 pinned to its right ear.

He looked like he might be dreaming.

This urban black bear had left a trail of sightings and reports across South Anchorage -- from Oceanview to Kincaid Park -- and on Thursday afternoon had been happily munching from a pail of sunflower seeds in Jeff Lowenfels' backyard. Then Sinnott, the state Fish and Game Department biologist, showed up, waited for the bear to bare its behind, and shot it with a tranquilizer dart.

Soon he would be driving the 2 1/2-year-old, 140-pound bear to a sparsely-inhabited area of the Kenai Peninsula, where he hoped it would stay out of trouble.

"He's not a garbage bear," Sinnott said, "though he does like his birdseed. We'll give him a chance, see what happens."

Sinnott's job is to track down, tranquilize and relocate black bears that wander into Anchorage neighborhoods before they become a nuisance, or a menace, to people.

About 250 black bears inhabit the city and the nearby mountains. This time of year they show up all over town. Fish and Game has been getting up to 20 calls a day from people spotting them, from Turnagain and Bayshore to Hillside and points beyond.

Kincaid Park staffer Kyle Van Solten said he has received reports of a young black bear nosing at garbage cans near the 8.5-mile point of the Tony Knowles Coastal Trail and another near the upper tunnel area at Kincaid, though none had threatened park visitors.

Centennial Park in Muldoon, closer to the Chugach Mountains, has seen a rash of black bear incursions. City park ranger Tiffany Opp said that for the past few days, two boars have been tramping through campsites and trying to chew open the lids of camp trash bins. Earlier this month a sow and her two cubs came through the park. One of the cubs came back a few days later, ate all the food left out at one campsite and was starting on another when Sinnott showed up with his tranquilizer gun.

Sinnott had caught and relocated three black bears before Thursday: one in West Bayshore, one on the Hillside and the cub in Centennial Park.

But Thursday's bear had eluded him for weeks. He'd tracked it from Klatt to Oceanview to Bayside to Kincaid Park, following a trail of more than 40 calls. Thursday morning a Bayside homeowner called in, but by the time Sinnott reached the house 10 minutes later, the bear had disappeared.

He wanted to catch this one before it learned to love garbage.

"If a bear has shown it's hooked on garbage -- because garbage is such good food -- we just kill them," he said. "We're not going to move our problems into someone else's backyard."

Sinnott shot 14 black bears last year but hasn't had to kill any this year. It's early yet. Most bears get addicted to garbage later in the year, he said.

Luckily for number 25, most eyewitness accounts had him bypassing the garbage and heading straight for the birdseed.

That's where Lowenfels, Anchorage Daily News gardening columnist, found him on Thursday. He had just gotten home when he discovered sunflower seeds scattered around the birdseed pail. He heard a noise, looked up, and "there was the bear, up in the tree."

He called Sinnott, who walked around the house, spotted the bear and darted him.

"He very carefully and gently tranquilized it, with expert marksmanship right in the back thigh, and waited for the little fellow," Lowenfels said.

"Thanks to Rick, not one petunia was scratched," he said.

Lowenfels said he's learned his lesson. From now on, he's leaving his seed pail in the garage.

Zoo Bears Go Fishing

Zoo bears go fishing for trout.

A GOOD SHOW: Oreo takes the lead after keepers stock pool.

By Zaz Hollander, ***Anchorage Daily News***, July 7, 2002

The 50 rainbow trout darting through the bear pool were supposed to outrun Ahpun and Oreo.

The two furry Alaska Zoo celebrities -- Ahpun the polar bear and Oreo the grizzly -- had made short work of the last fish placed in their exhibit: The five silver salmon got eaten in 45 minutes in 1999. This time, zoo managers hoped, the speedy rainbows would be too quick for the bears and the whole thing would provide a good show.

They were about half right.

By day's end, zookeepers counted at least 25 surviving trout swimming in a school in the deep part of the tank.

The zoo stocked the pool with trout Friday afternoon and shut the bears in their dens. By 10:30 a.m. Saturday, about 200 people eager for action had packed the viewing areas in front of the exhibit. A few were betting on the trout. Most thought the bears had a sure thing.

"It's going to be ugly," said Kim Welborn, a zoo regular from Anchorage who witnessed the salmon carnage in 1999.

Just after 11 a.m., the bears came out. Ahpun hung back. Oreo headed for the water right away, stuck her head in and

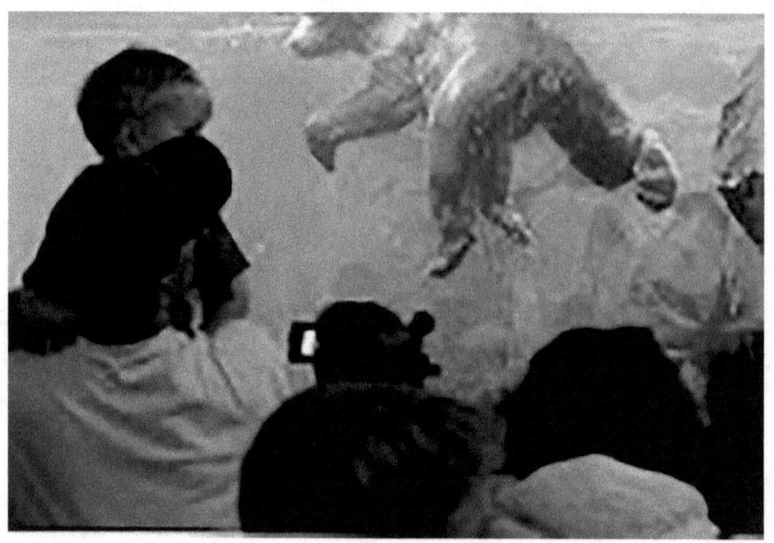

To the delight of the crowd gathered, Oreo the Alaska Zoo grizzly bear, above, searches for rainbow trout Saturday in the bear pond of the special enclosure she shares with Ahpun the polar bear. The zoo got a permit from the Alaska Department of Fish and Game to stock the pond with 50 rainbow trout, small and fast enough to test the bears' hunting skills and possibly elude them and live in the pond. (Photo by Evan R. Steinhauser / ***Anchorage Daily News***)

came out with a dead trout. She clenched it by the tail, like a silver cigar.

Oreo nibbled at it, showed it off to the crowd, then dropped it on the rocks around the pool before gulping it down. Soon she was back in the water for another dead fish. Then she trapped a few slow-moving trout in drains at the sides of the tank.

Ahpun got one fish, a live one.

Then Oreo put her foot down, chasing Ahpun away from the water.

The two bears, both females just over 4 years old, grew up together at the zoo. The unlikely bonding of a polar bear and griz is a hit with visitors, and the exhibit is the zoo's centerpiece.

On Saturday, however, the bears weren't sharing. Oreo ruled, catching most of the fish and showing little sympathy for Ahpun's hunger.

Around 1 in the afternoon, Oreo lumbered off and left the pool. All eyes turned to Ahpun. With the brown bear out of sight, the polar bear could finally show her stuff.

Ahpun put her wedge-shaped white head down on her huge white paws and closed her beady black eyes for a nap.

That's when the heckling started.

"Come on, Ah-PRUNE," yelled one young spectator.

"Ahpun's a wuss," said another.

Keepers say Oreo usually dominates Ahpun at feeding time. And it's possible that the polar bear was just pretending to sleep so Oreo would drop her guard, said Tex Edwards, zoo spokesman.

"Ahpun is very much the thinker," Edwards said.

By the end of the afternoon, Ahpun had managed a few mouthfuls of trout when Oreo's attention wandered.

The zoo plans to keep the trout in the tank as long as they survive, he said.

Polar Bear Gathering Closes Trail

Polar bear gathering leads to trail closure

CONCERNS: Barrow village corporation fears tour vehicles could send bruins into town.

The Associated Press, September 17, 2002

Barrow -- The local village corporation in Barrow has closed the trail to Point Barrow at the end of the road north of the old Naval Arctic Research Laboratory.

That's because the trail leads to a record number of 60 polar bears that continue to take residence around Barrow. The bears are camped out about two miles past the start of the trail.

Craig George of the North Slope Borough Department of Wildlife Management, said the trail was closed to prevent off-road vehicles from carrying tourists out to see the bears.

In past years, the bears have congregated out toward the Point, feeding at whale bone piles, but would rarely venture closer to Barrow, on the coast of the Arctic Ocean. But this year, there were more sightings and encounters in and around town, he said. No residents have been injured.

"The thinking was that all the tourists going by this year might be disrupting the bears and sending some of them back into town," George said.

He said since the trail was closed there have been fewer bears in town.

"We had been getting four to six calls a day about polar bears," he said Saturday, "but since the trail was closed off, the

About 60 polar bears have been seen feeding on the pile of whale bones a few miles outside of Barrow in the past month. The village has closed the trail to the bone pile to prevent off-road vehicles from carrying tourists out to see the bears. It is thought that tourists are disrupting the bears and sending some of them back into town. (Photo by Craig George / The Associated Press)

number of calls is way down."

George said during the last big polar bear gathering around Barrow in 1992 there were about 30 to 40 bears sighted. To his knowledge, 60 bears is a record number.

On Saturday, about 40 residents attended a presentation on how to better live with polar bears. The seminar was held at the Ukpeagvik Inupiat Corp. Science Center at the old Naval Arctic Research Laboratory.

George told the standing-room only crowd that polar bears feed primarily on seals, but they have been known to attack beluga whales and walruses as well. And they can also be scavengers and eat carrion, he said.

"If there is a superabundant food source around, normally solitary bears will congregate," he said.

George warned the public to be careful but keep the bear situation in perspective. "They can be dangerous," he said, "but statistically not as dangerous as four-wheelers or snowmachines."

"Look around when you step out," George said. "Don't assume that you are safe because you are in town. And you always want to see the bear before it sees you."

Hungry Polar Bear Samples New Kind of Sub Sandwhich

TASTY? Bruin chews on the rudder of the U.S. submarine Connecticut.

By DOUG O'HARRA, *Anchorage Daily News*, May 30, 2003

A polar bear gnawed on the rudder of a U.S. submarine and then attacked it after the sub surfaced in the ice pack during maneuvers between the North Pole and Alaska this spring, the U.S. Navy reported last week.

The submarine Connecticut, a new Seawolf-class sub, had partly surfaced with its sail and rudder sticking through the ice on April 27.

"When an officer looked around outside via the periscope, he noted that his sub was being stalked by a hostile polar bear," the Navy reported on its news Web site.

In a series of pictures captured on the periscope's camera, the bear apparently chewed on the rudder, then batted it around. The Navy reported the damage was minor. "It wasn't designed as a polar bear snack, but that's how life is sometimes," the story said.

Polar bears are federally protected marine mammals, but biologists with the U.S. Fish and Wildlife Service in Anchorage hadn't heard about this encounter, said spokeswoman Catherine Pearson. "It would be very unusual for polar bears to be north of the 80th parallel, as there are very few places with open water."

Strategy Page July 11, 2003

Bear Attacks Sub

During the ICEX 2003 naval exercises near the North Pole, the American submarine Connecticut (SSN 22) poked its sail and rudder through the ice. The sub surfaced in an area of polar ice between Alaska and the North Pole Subs in the arctic have long ago learned to look out for polar bears, especially if some of the crew are allowed out on the ice. In this case, a large (700-800) pound polar bear was seen approaching the sub. For about 40 minutes, the bear loitered around the subs rear rudder. It took a bite out of the rudder and, finding it inedible, stayed around the area of broken ice around the rudder for a while, apparently thinking a seal (the bears favorite food) might use it as an air hole. The bear finally left when he heard the noise of an approaching helicopter. When an officer first looked around outside via the periscope, he noted that his sub was being stalked by a hostile polar bear. The periscope cam was turned on, and these photos of a polar bear chewing on the subs rear rudder resulted. The damage was said to be minor. The SSN 22 is a Seawolf class boat, one of the navy's newest submarines. It wasn't designed as a polar bear snack, but that's how life is sometimes.

There are over 20,000 polar bears living in Arctic waters (although some live in Hudson's bay and down the Pacific coast of Alaska.) The bears normally live on pack ice or ice flows and prey on seals. Some come ashore during July and August, when offshore ice melts. There they live off their fat, or dead sea life that washes ashore. Some have been seen as far north as the North Pole, but there's little food for them up there.

American submarines have been operating under the Arctic ice for over half a century. In August, 1958, the American nuclear submarine USS Nautilus, passed under the ice at the North Pole for the first time. In the Summer of 1962, two U.S.

nuclear subs surfaced at the north pole. All of this arctic activity was to prove that nuclear subs could operate up there, and that ballistic missile subs could launch their missiles there as well. American, and Russian, subs have been operating up there ever since. They have also used their sonar to measure the ice thickness and report that the ice has lost 40 percent of its thickness in the last 20 years. This has caused problems for the polar bears, who feed on seals that surface near offshore ice flows or through breathing holes in pack ice. Some bears are forced to come ashore earlier because of the longer warm season. This is caused by a combination of global warming and the normal fluctuation of Arctic ice thickness.

Submariners have seen polar bears in the past, but this is one of the few times that the bear saw the sub first, and apparently mistook it for the world's largest chunk of bear food.

Grizzly-Polar Hybrid

HYBRID Strange bear was grizzly-polar hybrid, tests show

Martel wasn't very happy, having spent $50,000 on his trip. He was also worried he wouldn't be able to take the hide back home with him to Idaho.

ENR will return the hide to Martell, who is already back in the territory – on a grizzly hunt.

Wed, 10 May 2006, ***CBC News***

The DNA of a bear shot in the Northwest Territories in April shows it was a hybrid of polar bear and grizzly — perhaps the first ever seen in the wild.

From APRIL 26, 2006: **Hunter shoots grolar bear – or was it a pizzly?**

Scientists with the territory's Department of Environment and Natural Resources compared the animal's genetic makeup with samples taken from polar bears in the area and with DNA previously collected from grizzly bears along the coast to the south.

They concluded that the bear shot by Jim Martell was indeed a rare hybrid of the two types of bear. Officials say it could be the first recorded polar-grizzly bear hybrid found in the wild.

Martell, a sport hunter from the United States, was on a guided hunt when he shot the bear on April 16 near Nelson Head on southern Banks Island.

American hunter Jim Martell will be allowed to keep the pelt of the hybrid bear he shot on April 16. (Courtesy of Jim Martell)

Since it looked like a polar bear but had strange colouration, the hide was turned over to the Environment and Natural Resources department for testing.

It was considered nearly impossible for the two species to mate, since polar bears mate on the ice, while grizzlies mate on land.

'Some of the elders here in town say in the past there's been grizzly sightings but usually they fight.'-Hunting guide Roger Kuptana

"It's a total surprise," said Roger Kuptana, Martell's guide.

He said the relationship between polar and grizzly bears is usually more adversarial.

"Some of the elders here in town say in the past there's been grizzly sightings but usually they fight."

Additional analyses are underway to determine whether the mother was a grizzly bear or a polar bear and to determine the age of the bear.

Martell had a tag that allowed him to hunt polar bears, but conservation officers were threatening to charge him with shooting grizzly. It could have landed him 12 months in jail.

Wayward Bear

Wayward bear scampers through city.

Animal jousts with its reflection, gives runner, walker a start By Peter Porco, *Anchorage Daily News*, August 8, 2001

A young bear wandered through the heart of Anchorage on Sunday, popping up on streets and greenbelts and scaring the devil out of several people. But the bear seemed just as frightened, according to those who encountered it.

The bear apparently tried to pick a fight with its own reflection in the windows of a Spenard house. It bolted away from a runner after what seemed like a charge, then warily crossed Lake Otis Parkway as cars stopped short for it.

The bear hasn't been heard from since Sunday, when its appearance prompted more than a dozen calls to Anchorage police, said Rick Sinnott, a biologist with the Alaska Department of Fish and Game.

From what witnesses told him, Sinnott said Tuesday, it was hard to know for sure if the bear was a grizzly or a black, or even if only one bear was involved. One of the encounters, however, was almost certainly with a grizzly, he said.

That incident involved Todd LaPorte, a financial adviser who lives in a basement apartment in a house near Westchester Lagoon.

About 10:35 a.m. Sunday, LaPorte was sitting in a living room chair inches from one of three picture windows. The windows look out from below an overhang to the backyard lawn and a thick stand of trees.

LaPorte was talking on the phone when he heard a loud crash over his right shoulder.

"Out of nowhere something comes into the side of the building, hits part of the window frame and the concrete foundation and rolls upward against the window," LaPorte recalled Tuesday. "If it crashed through the glass it would have come right into my lap."

Only when the bruin stood back and swiped at the window, and LaPorte saw the foot pad and claws against the glass, did he realize what it was.

"I was six inches from the window, looking at it in shock. It took that entire time for me to realize it was a bear."

He yelled into the phone, "I'm being attacked by a bear!" he said. He jumped up, tumbled over another chair and fell on the floor.

"I look up and the bear is charging again." The bear smashed again into the heavy frame and the concrete wall beneath the windows, and deflected upward. It tried to bite the glass, slobbering over it, he said.

On Tuesday, the glass still showed signs of the bear's encounter with itself -- paw prints, the tracks of its tongue and lips and dried slaver.

LaPorte got up and ran to the closet at the far end of the room where he keeps his gun. He tore the sliding door off its runners, cursing himself because the gun case was locked. He ripped it open.

The bear, meanwhile, dropped to all fours, paused, "and then just bolted" through the trees, LaPorte said.

"I remember thinking, 'It's going to run into a chain-link fence. It will feel trapped and then come up again and be really pissed.' "

Twenty minutes went by, and no bear. LaPorte walked outside, and found the 5-foot fence down.

"He tore it like tissue paper," said LaPorte. The metal posts were bent and the cross bar bellied out.

Sinnott guessed the bear had come loping down the street into the yard, turned the corner around a large bush and ran toward the windows at an angle, seeing only the reflection of the trees. After hitting the window, it may have thought it was in a fight with another bear.

It likely was the same bear that surprised Sven Ole Jordan and Mike Mark Anthony, who each saw it Sunday afternoon along the Chester Creek greenbelt.

Jordan said he was running west at mid-afternoon when he heard a crashing in the trees to his left. He thought it was a moose and stopped, thinking he'd have to dodge the animal.

About 20 yards behind him on the trail, however, the bear came out of the woods, sliding on to the bike path "like a dog on a linoleum floor," Jordan said.

The bear faced away from him, then turned, saw Jordan and "comes full tilt at me," he said. "I was slightly scared, then full-blown terror."

He yelled for help. The bear ran up to him and skidded again, stopping at his feet. It then backed up. Jordan also backed up and got behind a tree. They looked at each other, "doing the peek-a-boo thing," he said.

"For some strange reason, it turned, took off and ran back into the woods just as fast full-tilt as it came at me," said Jordan. "It never growled, never took a swipe. It could easily have killed me."

Anthony was unavailable Tuesday, but his fiancee, Monika

Hensel, said he was walking one of their dogs on Lake Otis Parkway near the greenbelt when he heard a car brake to a quick stop. He looked to the right, and a brown bear was trotting across the street toward him and the dog, Hensel said.

"Mike was very surprised," she said. "The dog stopped. And the bear stopped three feet away from my dog."

The dog, a 5-year-old female German shepherd named Paisley, has been trained not to bark at moose, Hensel said. Paisley turned her back to the bear and looked at Anthony.

"The bear tried then to get a little closer, and my fiance was concerned and started yelling," she said. The bear turned and took off at a trot back into the trees, said Hensel.

Black Bear Tracks Pizza

Black Bear Tracks Pizza Scent, Destroys Car in Juneau.

A black bear has destroyed a Juneau Pizza employee's car looking for food in a residential neighborhood, raising concerns from wildlife experts that the animal will have future encounters with people.

By *Associated Press*, Aug. 8, 2020

Juneau, Alaska (AP)—A black bear has destroyed a Juneau Pizza employee's car looking for food in a residential neighborhood, raising concerns from wildlife experts that the animal will have future encounters with people.

"I think it was the delicious smell of the pizza that drove the bear to the point where he could not resist the urge to go into the car," said Andrew Fairchild, who owns the car. "It's pretty totaled on the inside. The seat belt was ripped completely out. The panel where the stereo is off."

Fairchild was woken up Friday around 3 a.m. by noise from the neighbors in the Mendenhall Valley area north of the Juneau International Airport, the Juneau Empire reported.

Fairchild said there was no pizza in the car, but the bear likely smelled the scent from his job.

"No playing favorites," Juneau Pizza said on Facebook. "If the bear wants a pizza, he has to call it in just like everyone else."

The bear destroyed the inside of the vehicle before returning into the woods.

"Luckily we have local insurance and they completely understand what's going," Fairchild said, adding that the car is already in the shop getting repaired.

"If we were able to catch up with the bear, then we'd probably have to capture them. I don't know if we'll necessarily set up a trap and wait for someone to report it somewhere we can find it," Alaska Department of Fish and Game biologist Roy Churchwell said, adding that it is likely to be euthanized.

'Residents are encouraged to keep food out of their cars and keep their doors locked to avoid similar situations," Churchwell said. Things like birdseed, dog food and other strong odor foods could tempt bears and other animals.

Black Bear Charges Motorcycle

Eagle River black bear charges, rams moving motorcycle.

Bent and broken, bike doesn't go down, but 5-foot bruin goes down for the count

By TATABOLINE BRANT, ***Anchorage Daily News***, August 4, 2004

A woman and a young boy enjoying a low-key motorcycle ride in the sun Monday nearly toppled over on Eagle River Road after a large black bear chased the machine and rammed it with its head.

"The bear acted like a dog," said Dena Boughton, who was driving the Harley-Davidson at the time and was home Tuesday with a sprained ankle and a broken bike.

Cameron Ryckman, 9, the youngster riding with Boughton, said the episode was "probably the scariest thing that ever happened to me."

The collision with the animal "was the first time that I ever actually touched a bear," he said.

Monday evening was perfect for riding, Boughton said. The road was dry and the air was warm.

Boughton, who said she has about 30 years of experience on a bike and also teaches motorcycle safety classes, decided to swing by the Ryckmans', longtime friends, and take Cameron on his first-ever motorcycle ride.

Boughton drove Cameron around Eagle River for about 15 minutes to see if he felt comfortable. He did, and so they decided to cruise out Eagle River Road to the Eagle River Nature Center, she said.

Once there, they stopped and stretched their legs and then turned around to go home.

About two miles down the road, Boughton spotted a bear standing in the other lane. She slowed to figure out what to do. Boughton said she thought the bear was a cub and that other bears could be nearby, and the best thing to do was motor by.

But as they neared the bear, the animal started after their bike. "That's the most bizarre thing that's ever happened to me," Boughton said. "I was surprised at how fast that bear could run."

The bruin rammed Boughton's left foot and Cameron's shin with its head. It broke the gear shifter on the Harley and bent a foot peg before falling into the street. Boughton said when she looked back, the bear was still.

Cameron remained calm the entire time, Boughton said. "Had he freaked out and wiggled, we might have gone down," she said. As it was, the bear had made them swerve sharply.

"At first I thought we were going to fall over, because it was a pretty big bear," Cameron said. "We're lucky we didn't crash, because then we would have been stranded."

Boughton kept going. She said she thought it was too dangerous to stop, especially with the broken shifter and her injured foot.

The pair cruised into Eagle River. Boughton dropped Cameron off near the Eagle River Wal-Mart near his house because she didn't think she could make the final mile to Cameron's home with her gear shift broken, the pain in her ankle and the youngster on board.

Boughton parked out front of Cameron's house and started yelling and honking for help. There wasn't any blood on her bike, but there was bear hair stuck in the front forks.

Cameron's parents rushed outside.

"My first thought was, 'Where's Cam?' " said the boy's dad, Dave Ryckman.

About that time, Cameron came walking down the street. Cameron's mom took Boughton to get medical help -- she initially thought her foot was broken -- and Cameron and his dad went to look for the bear.

Police were at the scene when they arrived, and Cameron and his dad set about explaining what happened. Cameron said he thinks another vehicle hit the bear, because there was a lot more blood on the road than he remembered and the animal was in a different spot.

Ryckman said the bear was lying on the side of the road and looked to be about 5 feet tall.

"I kinda felt bad for it," Cameron said of the animal, which was dead when he arrived. "But then I thought it wasn't exactly all our fault. I think it had the ability to sit there and not chase us."

Cameron said he probably would ride a motorcycle again but not right away. "I feel really shocked," he said.

Boughton said she will never forget what an emergency room computer monitor alerting medical personnel she was on the way said: Ankle Pain -- bear versus motorcycle.

"I thought that was pretty cute," she said.

Battered Biker Bear Tale

HELMET SAVES LIFE: Pelvis broken, new motorcycle destroyed.

By ZAZ HOLLANDER, *Anchorage Daily News*, August 10th, 2005

WASILLA -- The bear was at a dead run downhill toward the Old Glenn Highway when Garrett Edgmon came around a bend on his new Kawasaki motorcycle.

Edgmon barely caught a glimpse of the reddish-brown fur coming headlong at him out of the corner of his eye as he drove south at about 45 or 50 mph.

Then the bruin's ribs slammed into his front wheel, sending the bike hurtling across the pavement.

"Bears ain't exactly soft," Edgmon said by phone from Anchorage on Tuesday afternoon. "Trust me, they're not. It hit me pretty hard."

The commercial fisherman from Dillingham ended up with a broken pelvis, numerous bumps and bruises -- and a heck of a story to tell.

As man and bear locked eyes, Edgmon didn't think he would see his 41st birthday next month. Then he was thrown onto the bear's head and neck. The two skidded together for a little ways on the highway, about two miles from where the Old Glenn leaves the northbound Glenn Highway.

Edgmon felt his head bounce. He heard his helmet shatter.

Meanwhile, Palmer resident Scott Hanson came up in his red pickup and pulled over. Hanson later told Alaska state troopers the bear did a flip and then disappeared under a guardrail. Edgmon only remembers getting up, shocked and in a great deal of pain, and trying to drag off the road the 750-pound 1200cc Kawasaki Voyager he bought last month.

Hanson called 911.

Edgmon was treated at Valley Hospital. The full-face helmet he wore saved his life, he said. “If I didn’t have a helmet on, I would have been dead.”

Edgmon is staying in the city with his wife as she undergoes cancer treatment. He said his bike was insured. But he doesn’t plan to get on another motorcycle any time soon.

Doctors told him he’ll need a walker to get around for the next two months, effectively through the fall fishing season.

State biologist Gino Del Frate said he knew of no plans to track down the bear, described by Hanson as a young brown.

Trooper Mitch Lewis said he scanned the slopes above the highway with a scope on Monday but saw nothing. It’s unlikely the bear wandered off and died, Lewis said.

But Edgmon figures the critter must be badly hurt.

“If not, he is one miracle bear,” he said.

Sow Attacks Car

Anchorage Daily News, July 5, 2002

Alaska Digest

DILLINGHAM, *The Associated Press*

Protective brown bear sow attacks car, leaves driver shaking.

While many residents in this corner of the Bristol Bay region have encountered brown bears, not many have had an experience like Ross Armstrong's.

Driving home to Dillingham from Aleknagik on June 23, Armstrong and a passenger came upon a sight seen by many people who travel the winding, gravel road: two bear cubs, on their right. Armstrong stopped to watch the young bears go about their business.

Armstrong's mother, Pinky, who owns the car, said her son's eye then caught something moving from his left. By the time he turned, a sow's mouth was already on the car.

"Right here you can see where the top and the bottom teeth hit," Pinky Armstrong told the Bristol Bay Times.

The highly protective mother attacked the windshield on the driver's side. The bear cracked Armstrong's windshield in baseball-sized spider-web shapes in two spots about 14 inches apart.

"That kid isn't afraid of anything, and he was shaking like this when he got home," Pinky Armstrong said of her son, holding up a trembling hand.Ross departed for a commercial salmon fishing opening in the Nushagak District after the incident. Pinky is wondering what to do about the cracked windshield.

"Boy, what do I tell the insurance about this?" she said.

Lars Monsen

As I sat signing books in the summer of 1997 at Barnes & Noble in Anchorage, a stalwart, blonde Viking stood rigidly nearby off to the right of a line of people. I saw him out of the corner of my right eye. Unable to give him my attention while addressing those in line, I completed our visiting-signing then turned to him.

I asked, "May I help you?"

He stepped somewhat rigidly forward, bent at the waist and asked in his Norwegian voice, "Do you accept gifts?"

Taken aback by his question in light of previous signings, my response was, "Well, it would be a first. People don't usually give me gifts at signings."

He then handed me a rolled up 8x10-inch glossy picture of him shouldering a shotgun and a brown bear closing on his dog Toini. I was impressed and told him it was a nice picture. He said he didn't have to shoot the bear. Then he handed me a book, a very nice coffee table book of pictures and text. I jokingly said, "Oh, thanks. You give me a beautiful book of pictures and text which I can't read because they're in Norwegian!" Part of his inscription to me reads: "Anchorage July 31st, '97...Your book ***Alaska Bear Tales*** scared the s—t out of my girlfriend, I loved it. Thanks for the inspiration, and do continue writing books. If you ever come to Norway, and need help in any way, contact me!

Best wishes from Lars Monsen."

We laughed and talked. His desire was to get his books

translated into English. Over the intervening years we kept in touch and became friends.

Lars is an incredible individual who loves the outdoors. You will discover a great deal about him as you read his summarization of his Alaska bear experience from having travelled solo or with a partner over vast areas of the state.

He provides great advice on how to co-exist with our ursine neighbors. I find it incredible that in all his miles and months in Alaska's wilderness that he has NEVER fired AT a bear.

Enjoy reading about a modern day Viking!

Letter from Lars:

Trout Lake, some 120 air kilometers E-SE of Inuvik, Northwest Territories, Canada, July 28th 2000

Dear Larry!

How are you? I hope all of you are doing fine. You're probably busy writing, and fall is a good time to do so, don't you agree? At the time being I am spending some 20 days by this 60 kilometer shoreline lake in the midst of nowhere, or actually, where the small Kugaluk River starts its way northwards. My days are highly leisurely, I have one base camp (tarp) and canoe around for trips up to 10 days or just stay here, mostly fishing, writing and exercising the dogs. No bears (!), or moose or caribou, but one wolf very close (it was curious, ran away, young one) and another one distant. Fishing for lake trout is excellent, I catch some 10 kgs every day (rod), enough to feed myself and the dogs.

Anyway, I have written 20 pages for you, all bear stuff from my expeditions. I hope you like it. Feel free to use it in your coming book "What's Bruin?", but don't feel obliged to use it. I do have slides if you need that, and also, if you have questions, I'll be glad to answer them.

I'll mail this letter in the beginning of Sept., and I'll probably be in civilization for a couple of weeks, camp around Inuvik, to do some work for my sponsor. I have one hour's access to the Internet and email every day, at the library. We can communicate then, if you have received the letter. I'll get in touch with you, and we'll figure it out!

I don't know where I am going to spend Sept-Oct-Nov, it may be here, or maybe up in the Yukon Mountains. I'll probably be back in civilization in Nov/Dec., when I start up again from Tsiigehtchic (Arctic Red River) with dogsled and all. We can communicate more then, and as I go between Fort Good Hope, Norman Wells, Fort Franklin, etc.

Take care, Larry, and keep on with the good work!

All the best from Lars

P.S. Translation of my '95 Alaska book is very present in my mind.

(Lars was in the midst of his cross-country voyage, which took three winters. He'd hole up in the summers and await more snow. At one point he was forced to shoot a polar bear—through the cabin door which it tried to enter. That's the only bear he had to kill.)

BACKGROUND

Born in Oslo, Norway, 1963

Became a teacher (elementary school) in 1988, but quit after two years to do what I love the most and know the most—spend time in the wild woods and mountains.

Today I have spent 2700 nights plus in the open, average is 200 nights a year. More than half is above the Arctic Circle in winter time (Nov-April).

My father taught me to love and respect nature, he let me spend the first night alone in the woods as a 9-year-old, I "slept" under the open sky. Had a terrible night, seeing the axe killer as ever. Wanted more and was allowed to.

Spent every night possible out in the woods during my school years, one year 51 weekends in a row, normally around 40. Lived for weeks and twice months in the woods while attending high school and teachers training college.

All 26 in a row summers (8 weeks) spent in the mountainous terrain south of Bodo (above the Arctic Circle) where my mother was born. The cabin they lived in is my base today, no road leads there, either boat across the fiord or 2.5 hours walk over the wild mountains. Ptarmigan, brook trout, sea trout, (silver) salmon (up to 30 pounds normal), reindeer, wolverine, lynx, rabbits, foxes and lots of eagles in the nature up there. The weather in these coastal mountains can be as fierce as anywhere, and taught me always to be cautious and prepared.

Didn't have much money, learned to use whatever available. Got my first real hiking boots as a 23-year-old, but still used cheap cotton clothes for a few years. After the first long expedition, 365 days and 2542-plus kilometers hike along the Norwegian borderline to Soviet, Finland and Sweden (1989-90), people got to know me because I started writing articles often. This was in 1989. Since then I have more or less been sponsored on all gear, and today I can choose what to wear, what brand to use. This "business angle" can be the other side of the coin, outdoor life is big money today, so I always try to focus on what's really important: the basic skills of surviving all conditions.

I've always wanted to explore new things, and if people say something isn't possible, I get especially interested. Everything is possible with proper preparation respect.

I've been weather bound in snow storms and fog at least 200 nights, up to 9 days (the wind blew me off my feet).

I've survived solely on dog food for a week four times, both in summer while hiking 10 hours a day with a 70 pound pack in the bush (north Finland) and while lying still in a tent in 40 below in December. The latter was perhaps hardest, nothing happened, left with my longing thought for food. You can live on dog food, but with constant headache and a slow stomach maybe a month.

I've lived four winter months in the mountains, half above tree line without a tent, but with a tarp 2x3 meters and a good shovel. Dug a lot of snow caves.

I know physical pain. With experience and will power you can learn to walk two more hours after the "knives start hunting you" (feels like walking on knives) in the end of a day's hike. Pure muscle power is important to a degree, but what really decides survival or not is your mind, your attitude, your ability to always look for possibilities, keep up the good spirit.

To become fearless (not respectless!) you must learn to sense your own fear, your own limits. I deliberately hiked through the woods when 13-14-years-old in totally black October nights to feel what that was like. I crossed rivers in the dark (not swimming much!), felt the bottom with my feet, got soaking wet, dried off by the fire.

In spring time I often don't bring a sleeping bag, only a thick wool sweater, matches and fishing gear, plus salt, bread and coffee. You learn to appreciate the small things.

Skill hour 1 is orienteering. Hour 2 is making a fire under all conditions (one match only, no artificial help). I've lived for months in the mountains above tree line without a stove.

After the 1995 crossing of Alaska (see www.larsmonsen.net for more details on expeditions) I fell in love with one animal in particular: the brown bear. It has it all. Strength, beauty, total control of the environment (boss!), it demands respect, it rules and there's a lot of mystery. So I decided to get more experience, and do it all the way, really thorough. Why not cross all the three areas with the highest brown bear (grizzly, same animal to me because they wander from the inland to the coast and back again) density in the world: canoe through Katmai, walk across Kodiak and Admiralty! Get right in there, into the beast's living room, on its premises as a humble guest passing through. (I had never been to any of the places before, but I hadn't been to Alaska or Canada before '95). Would it be possible to live with a tent, sleeping bag and fishing rod in the thickest of bear country without any dramatic episodes? Without having to shoot at a bear? How close would I come? What could happen in the alders in the middle of July on Kodiak, was obvious, but can one crawl through there on one's knees in the bear trails, and get away with it? Would the bears come to my tent at night? Were there differences in their behavior in Katmai, Kodiak and Admiralty?

General: Katmai bears were habituated and were not afraid or shy of humans, the Kodiaks and Admiralty brownies were, probably because they are being hunted and/or aren't used to humans around. I have no reason to say one was more aggressive—they would try to avoid us. Always exceptions though!

All these questions burned inside me. I had to find out. The fact that no one had heard about anyone crossing either Kodiak or Admiralty on foot made the project even more exciting. With proper preparation and lots of respect it would be possible! If you are a macho guy out there, you won't last long. I knew from the start that everything I did had to be done out of respect for the bears during the daily hikes and in camp.

PREPARATIONS

On the 3000 kilometer and 10 month hike in November 1994 to September 1995 from False Pass (Cold Bay) to Kaktovik (Arctic Ocean, some 120 kilometers west of Canadian border) my girlfriend Marit, our husky female Toini and I encountered 46 bears. Before the trip we read as much as possible about bears and talked to "experts." One person in Norway was a former Alaska Trooper, born in Alaska. His obvious negative attitude towards the project (too hard in the bush, too many bears) helped me a lot. I like that.

The idea of crossing Canada and Alaska was not born yet at this stage.

One of the books I read thoroughly was Alaska Bear Tales. My girlfriend wouldn't touch it, she was already struck by serious fear of the bears (it disappeared slowly when she saw them running away, and that our field behaviour actually worked), and she later joined me the last half of the Admiralty hike ('98). I loved the book. Here were all the mistakes we should not make!

We decided to be extremely cautious. After collecting as much information as possible, I wrote down a set of 10 bear safety rules, that would be our guiding stars in Alaska's bear country. These rules are:

1) Always know which direction the wind is blowing. (If a bear smells you, you're fine, that's good. If you walk against the wind, be extra careful. The wind also carries the scent of fish, meat, camp food, etc. Temptations bring bears.)

2) Avoid places where bears spend much time. To minimize the number of bear encounters—one should act like one wants

to avoid all bears at all times!—stay away from places where salmon are plentiful in summer (pass it, but don't camp there), where the grass is green in spring, where the berries are ripe in thousands in fall.

3) Make a lot of noise while hiking. Point is to let the bears know you are there. The sooner a bear knows you're human, the better (a few exceptions). Talk or sing loudly, blow a whistle, step on and break twigs, clap your hands.

4) Avoid all smells that can attract bears. The smell is the bear's best weapon, it's just incredible. Don't wipe off fish blood on your pants (and sleep with the pants in the tent!). Pack mostly freeze-dried, almost non-smelling food like oatmeal, rice, mashed potatoes, soups—chocolate is okay. Spit out the tooth paste on the fire or in running water, not on the ground in camp (I pick up even small grains of rice).

5) Do not store, prepare or eat food in your tent. The bear will smell it and come to investigate. As you know, once the bear is inside, you're in trouble. The food should be stored in air- and waterproof (also makes them smell proof) bags or containers, preferably 100 meters away from the tent.

6) Organize camp with bears in mind. Don't put up your tent in the middle of the bear trail or close to a river or lake edge. Go at least 50, preferably 100 meters, into nowhere land where bears are less likely to come wandering. You can eat and make a fire on the beach or river edge, but spoil as little food as possible on the ground, burn all fish bones. Clean all fish and game away from camp (straight away, where you get it). Fire and eating place should be 100 meters from tent, or more. Store food in trees, at least 5 meters above ground, 100 meters away from tent, preferably also 100 meters from eating place. If you're on a spit with wind blowing food smell out across the lake, that's perfect, but keep an eye against the wind.

7) Always be prepared to defend yourself. Carry a gun powerful enough. I prefer shotgun because of tremendous power at close range and possibility to hunt small game. Bear country is ptarmigan, grouse, duck and rabbit country as well. If I go 10 meters to urinate, the shotgun is with me. If I go 11 meters to get wood, the shotgun is with me. You should feel naked and be alarmed if your weapon is not a part of your body in bear country. Choose a weapon you know. A .45 revolver is powerful, but difficult to handle for beginners. You want to kill with the first shot—a wounded bear is deadly dangerous—and keep on shooting till the bear doesn't move. A shotgun is best for beginners, easy to operate and easier to hit what you aim at. Bring 10-15 extra slugs and practise somewhere safe. Sleep with a shotgun in the tent, no slug in the chamber though!

8) Always look out for flocks of eagles, ravens and crows. This may mean there is a dead moose or caribou lying in the bush, most likely with a bear close by. It will kill to defend its food.

9) Always look for signs of bear. Footprints, claw marks, scats, rotten trees turned upside down, roots tore up, bear fur on bushes, half eaten salmon and nesting places are the most common. The more signs, the more bears around, and the fresher sign, the closer the bear!

10) Expect the unexpected. Bears are smart and unpredictable. Always be on guard, don't rule out anything. The bear you saw running away scared as hell is not likely to return, but it may. A bear wandering up river steadily may suddenly turn around. A bear may not be frightened by a shot in the air, and you never know, maybe the taste of pepper spray is like candy. My attitude is that I won't be surprised if a 10-foot and 1800-pound grizzly comes walking into my camp, drowns its cigarette in my soup and asks if it can borrow my fishing rod.

There are many more things to be said about each rule. I'll try to take them into the rest of what I write.

BEARS ON THE ACROSS ALASKA EXPEDITION 1995

(Lars and Marit spent 9 months traversing Alaska from False Pass to Kaktovik which he turned into TIL FOTS GJENNOM ALASKA, the book he gave me in 1997)

We saw 46 bears, about half grizzlies, half blacks. We were close to several hundred more, but scared them away with our scent and noise. This number is very low for such a long trip in Alaska and shows how important smell and noise are, and also organizing camp right.

Scats and footprints are the two by far most common signs of bears.

The area where there were most bears around us was Alaska Interior south of Ruby and Yukon River, towards Tahotna, the signs were absolutely all over, mostly black bears. We saw only a very few, however because of bear safety rules and thick brush (we passed Alaska Peninsula January, February and March).

We used trip wire almost all the time. It was activated 4 times—one by Marit, one by Toini and two by me! Still, very nice psychologically easier to fall asleep (see also Kodiak comment).

One snowy day in the end of January I decided to get above the alders to avoid the tiresome tussocks and deep, meandering creeks in the lowland (This was close to the Aghleen Pinnacles northeast of Cold Bay. I walked this leg to Nelson Lagoon alone). To my delight, walking was considerably easier higher up, especially where the wind had blown the snow solid.

As Toini and I entered a little gully, I noticed some fresh prints in the snow and bent down. Bear! I could see every claw clear as my own fingers. They were only minutes old, the wind was blowing snow and in 20 minutes they would be wiped out.

That's when I saw that the prints led straight towards the mountain wall only 10 yards away, disappearing over a man-tall snow-knoll and into the mountain! I was right by its den, and it had just been out for a little winter walk...I drew my shotgun, walked away and turned around at least a hundred times the next four hours, until I set camp.

The temperature was mild, around minus 2-3 degrees C. A few days later it rained. Marit and I walked into a big brownie in February in 70 centimeter deep snow. It chose to disappear when I fired a shot in the air at 200 yards. This was east of Nelson Lagoon and not many meters above but close to mountains at sea level, maybe 50 meters.

I saw fresh bear signs 4-5 more times in January-February which were never really cold as to degrees minus.

Conclusion: the bears are occasionally out of their dens in mild winters.

I've had the pleasure of watching wild, non-habituated bears on occasion, blacks and browns.

East of Hughes, in Interior mid July, I lay on a high ridge by my small coffee pot fire, overlooking a steep valley. Suddenly I see bushes moving down there. A mother black bear with one cub. I watch them for a whole hour as they work their way up, eating, playing and resting. The cub is full of energy, slaps its mother with the paws, "Come on, fight me!" So the mother and the cub both go up on their behind legs and hit each other's chests with the paws. The mother very gently so the cub won't fall too hard or get hurt. The cub goes down over and over, up again, "this is fun!" Other times it went alone into the alders. I could see them swaying as it played berserk in there. Cub was two years, pretty grown up.

The day before I watched a mother with two tiny ones, also blacks. I was on that same ridge, looking the other way, against the wind. They were one mile away, so I used my 210 millimeter lens on the camera. After about 20 minutes one of the tiny ones (born this year) suddenly rose to its back feet, smelling the air. Two seconds later the mother did the same, facing me.

Then they ran as fast as they could. Somehow they must have scented me! Incredible at that distance.

A few days south of Hughes I saw a grizzly coming my way, not aware of us. It suddenly lay down in some bushes, atop this open ridge-like plateau. It totally vanished. Marit and I lay there a few minutes, and then out of the bush explodes the bear, runs away from us in sheer panic. It smelled us, some 400 meters away. Not many humans in these parts.

Often they get scared, but don't run very far only to the nearest cover. While walking along one of the highest ridges, somewhere north of Ruby, we startled a grizzly eating berries just 20 meters away, even though we had just clapped our hands regularly. It stood up exactly one second, and down into the nearest alders it went full speed. There it stopped, about 50-60 meters from us. We sat down and talked about the great moment—seeing wild animals, and bears in particular is our reward for working hard—while I kept an eye on the bushes. After a little while I saw a big brown head pop up in there, but just for a second. It was checking us out. "Are they still in my dinner dish?" We left, crossed the valley, put up camp and watched the bear eating berries peacefully at a distance of at least two miles. It was there for several hours. Note that we were walking against the wind and it hadn't smelled us.

One black boar spotted us at 50 meters, looked at us for 10-12 seconds—which is pretty long—as we stood motionless, but talked to it, and it wandered down from the open berry country to the nearest thick group of spruce, some 100 meters away. As we walked by, a black head with two stiff ears was all we saw, it hid the rest of its body in the trees. We later spotted it back with the berries. This was also in Interior, where hardly anyone goes.

A few times we never saw the bear, but I just knew it was there, maybe just 10-30 meters away, lying still in the bushes, watching us. When you spend most of your time out in the wild, you develop a sense of danger, an alarm. These times were all in thick underbrush, my heart started pounding, there were fresh tracks—and I could feel a pair of eyes at me. I walked with the shotgun in my hands, not hastily, but slowly, talked a little even though I knew it wasn't necessary, "Just passing through, bear, take it easy!" Also if you sense that you might have a situation ahead that in worst case might involve shooting, you don't want to breathe heavily, another reason to calm down. If you manage to stay calm, you don't really have to be a master shot at that close range. Anyway, we always came through safe and sound.

For the most part the bears ran away as soon as they understood we were humans. There was one exception, that shows the rule expect the unexpected. It was a beautiful day high up in the Brooks Range with red, orange and yellow all over the fall coloured landscape. We were above tree line with wild mountains to the north and a long valley to the southeast (there's a fall picture of these bears in my bear book, I think).

All of a sudden I spot a single grizzly eating berries, 150 meters ahead. The wind is not good, it can't smell us. We stop, yell loudly and expect that the bear will get scared and run away. That's when we see the two small ones. They come running to mom, who simply sits down on her rump with one cub under each arm! I go a little closer, fire a bird shell in the air, but no—"This is where I sit, and I don't intend to move out of your way!" Normally a mother with cubs would head straight for safety. Not this one. We had to walk in a wide arch around them and they continued their meal.

On the whole trip we had only one dramatic bear encounter, actually on the day before we reached Kaktovik. I was in front, and I made two major mistakes. Firstly, I let the approaching grizzly come too close, 50 meters, before I raised my body from the pack and yelled. I thought it would smell us, the wind was in our back. And secondly, I did not keep our husky Toini to the leash! She thought the bear was a caribou, ran towards, came close enough to see that this caribou had an ugly face, turned around—out to the left, not back to us luckily! Marit fired 4 revolver shots from a 45 magnum into the air, and I yelled as loud as I could, but the bear still went after Toini. When it was 1.5 meter behind her, I was 1/10 of a second away from letting the slug go the 14-15 meters to the bear (which would be a big minus, having to shoot a bear because of our stupid behaviour). But in the absolutely last moment the bear got the scent of man and turned around as stabbed in its nose with a knife. I then saw how fast a bear really can run.

You have to have a certain amount of luck, too, or at least one or two guardian angels with you. They were with us that day.

EXPEDITIONS IN BEAR COUNTRY KATMAI

Twenty months later I returned to Alaska, ready for Katmai National Park. My brother Jan joined me and this trip was 90% in a canoe. We had two portages, one tough one that took 4 days through the alders.

First we spent 10 days along the north side of Iliamna Lake, though. One night we returned from our grayling fishing trip—which was good—and spotted a big 250 kilogram brown bear only 10 meters from my tent, possibly without knowing it was close to our-clean-camp. It was feeding on something on the ground. We were maybe 150 meters away, the wind was "blowing" very little from the bear towards us or sideways. We spoke a few words in immediate joy—this was Jan's first bear ever—almost whispering. It heard us! And off it was, scared as hell.

A few days later we had our campfire on the beach under a steep rock wall (picture of the tent on top and canoe on beach in bear book). As the darkness fell and we got ready to leave for our sleeping bags, we heard the loon screaming out on the quiet lake. When we reached our tents (one each for privacy), we heard heavy steps in the gravel, an obviously big animal was coming directly towards the remains of our campfire. Then we saw it, only some 20 meters away from the fire, a grizzly! It was coming at a steady pace, probably not expecting to see any humans.

That's when I chambered my shotgun. That sudden, metallic sound made it spin around in a split second, and escape back into the darkness. This was one of the very rare occasions when a bear has come directly into camp. If it smelled the fried fish, it must have smelled us too. Maybe the temptation got too big. Or maybe it hadn't smelled anything at all. Anyway, cook the food that means less smell and tempting odors.

Now to Katmai. We landed in the far NE corner at Mirror Lake. Saw no bears up there in the mountains, this was around June 10th-12th 1997.

They started showing up when we got to Battle Lake, close to the origins of McNeill Lake and River. They passed us at 200-300 meters, going towards the pass where McNeill Lake is.

One smelled at our 30 minutes old footprints, followed them for 10 meters, and left them. We yelled at another one, it looked at us as if it said, "What's your problem, why all the fuss?" These bears seemed used to humans.

We portaged back and forth from Battle to Kulik Lake, two times, 13 kilometers one way, mostly thick alders. Nine kilometers took one day, the first one. Jan told me he was not envious of the trip in '95 (which forced us into a lot of alders).

One bear came directly "at us" by American Creek. A 5-6 year old maybe (picture of him as opening picture on chapter in the bear book). Long legs, but he would be pretty big in fall. Anyway, I was fishing and threw the remains in the bushes behind me, not into deep water as I usually do in bear country. Three minutes after he was there, only 30 yards away, and advancing. Jan and I were between his food and him, and he gave us a lecture in bear body language: very slow walk, head mostly down, only looking at us occasionally, his broad side to us, stopped once and licked his paw for some reason. When he was 20 meters away, we were in our canoe and took off. He crossed the river immediately and got into the bushes to get his food. What a proof of its excellent sense of smell—and also how little afraid habituated bears are of humans.

As we got closer to Brooks Falls, we saw a lot of bears. We kept out of their way, let them know we were there, in short followed the bear safety rules. None bothered us, except one youngster at Savonovski River: he came running towards our campfire obviously curious. We stood our ground, side by side, yelled at him, but he kept coming—until I shot in the air. That bang scares them off! He left, although reluctantly.

From the trip to Katmai with John Trampus 1999:

This was later in the year, in August. The bear had left Brooks Falls and we encountered quite a few along the Savonovski River.

We watched them fish the silty water systematically until it got dark (they continued doing the same fishing, we heard them). One bear would walk slowly (wow, they were big boars!) up along one branch, maybe 200 meters. Then he slid into the water, let himself float with the current, and dove! We often saw just the top of the big hump on its back, the head was under. And the water was very silty, maybe with 15-20 centimeters visibility.

He got onto the shore again, walked the exact same distance, let himself into the current and fished the same stretch. This happened up to three times before he tried out another stretch.

We saw two big boars doing this simultaneously, and they respected each other's territory. And they did catch salmon. Then they would sit down ashore and eat it, before diving in again.

Now—the excitement had just started for John and me! As I was filming—yes, I have this on film—my Alaskan friend (actually from Wisconsin, been teaching in Wainwright, Stony River, Red Devil, Juneau and Anchorage for 15 years) tapped my shoulder, "Turn around, look up there!"

There stood a giant boar, the biggest sucker I have ever seen! Forty meters away. His big, fat belly almost touched the ground, and when he started walking, he had those extremely heavy, broad steps, slowly moving. His head was huge.

By now it was getting dark, almost too dark to see. Neither John nor I could tell if he was aware of us, but I think so. He didn't care anyway because he was the KATMAI BOSS.

We were by our fire and eating place on the south side of a small island in Savonowski, maybe 100x50 meters. Half of it was covered with tall bushes (3-4 meters), and our tarp and fireplace was on the south side, our tents on the north of this small "woods."

What do we do?

The beast had simply laid down in a pool, only its enormous head visible—sideways from our point of view and still 40 meters away. As we discussed our options in low, tense voices the Boss rose from the water and disappeared behind the woods to the north side.

John and I packed everything air tight, also the freeze dried non-smelling food, and put it into the bushes, with moth balls on top (no trees big enough for hanging). Then we headed for our tents in almost total darkness. The distance was maybe 60 meters between the fireplace and the tents.

John was by his tent (which was right by mine, on the edge of the bushes) and I was halfway between the fire and the tents when I noticed a big, black log that came down in the middle of the river, some 30-40 meters away. It was so dark I had to look above it to examine it the best way.

The thing was going up and down in the fast current, just like a log would do, but I kept my eyes on it.

That's when the log suddenly rose to the shore and came straight towards me—it was the big boss himself! I shouted, "Hey, bear! Go away. Go away!"

He was then 25 meters away and came right towards me still!

Now I shot one shot in the air 15 meters away, reloaded and yelled, "I DON'T WANT TO HURT YOU!" while pointing my shotgun at him.

He changed his course some 45 degrees. By now John was there, too, also with his shotgun (not using it), and we both kept yelling loudly. The boss slowly moved away.

This incident turned out okay because we, or I in this case, always have my shotgun ready. That big bang did it. Not our yelling, not the sight of us, not our scent, but that big bang. And all firearms are forbidden in the Katmai. I know that. That's a good rule for tourists at Brooks Camp that don't know a shotgun from a rifle, but for outdoors people like John and I—I think it should be allowed to carry firearms. Proper education maybe a hunter's license, could allow one to carry a gun for self defense.

By the way, that big boss had its fishing route right around that very island we had chosen as our camp! It was fishing all night, we could hear it splashing in the water. Do you believe me if I say we slept good for 5-6 hours? We actually did. We figured it had lost its interest in us and "if we don't bother him, he won't bother us." I did, however, John too, sleep with a loaded shotgun right by my side. And I am a light sleeper under conditions like that. A thrilling experience, indeed!

KODIAK 1997

One of the most exciting, tense and physically tough expeditions I have ever been on was the 1997 Kodiak trip. I wanted to walk on foot across the whole island right through the densest brown bear territory in the world, living in a tent, having a new campsite every day.

I came in the middle of July when the bush was as thick as it gets. The small air company owner who flew me out was born on Kodiak and he was most reluctant to fly me out, in fact, he was very negative. In his mind, and others it clearly seemed, this was a stupid thing to do. "You'll have to crawl on all fours in the bear trails through the brush, and in there you're in for a nasty surprise. The alders are too thick, come back in November." And "do it without any drop outs of food?" and "you say you have only been to Alaska once before?" (I didn't tell him what I did in 1995)

Anyway I started from the southern tip of the island. My pack was 28 kilos, everything I needed for 21 days, easily a month if necessary. To put it very short, this turned out to be 99% hard, extremely hard physical work, up and down alder-covered mountainsides, crossing rivers and more alders (and grass, up to 3 meters tall, though most was 1.5-2 meters), to the point that I got "black eyes." That happened to me when I really have to give it all physically and mentally (at least 50% is mentally!): I become so focused on making it that nothing else matters, and to get there I can be ruthless, both to myself and the ones I'm with. That's why I'm alone on this one.

That resulted in no rest for 14 days. On day number 14 I walked into Kodiak downtown. Cramps in both legs and mentally tired—I almost didn't move for a month, no physical activity.

To the bears: I saw 24 and was close to at least a hundred more. The first day I saw within a four hour walk six, because the terrain was open. On day 3 the alders started.

One close one:

I'm trying to follow a bear trail through grass and alders 3 meters tall, but it's hard, you have to "feel" it with your feet. It's more efficient to look ahead and think like a bear—where is the best route? Anyway, I'm clapping my hands and yelling every 5-10 meters. This goes on for three hours, and I still do it. Discipline!

After one such yell, a big brownie explodes up from the grass 10 meters ahead of me and runs through the bush like a bulldozer, passing me 5 meters to the right! It was sleeping and if I had not made noise, I would have stepped on it. That would have been unpleasant: It could have made mashed potatoes out of me in seconds, attacking in fear and self defense. Some of these Kodiaks know they can be hunted by man.

One time I saw a fox coming full speed, obviously scared. I grabbed my shotgun. Then I saw a bear as it crossed my footprints 100 meters away: it stopped, got up on two legs, turned around and quickly disappeared.

In Uyak Bay I spotted two bears fishing salmon at 200 meters distance. I yelled loudly and clapped my hands. They looked at each other for a couple of seconds, as if to say "look over there, a big, fat steak is yelling for us to come and get it!" Then they exploded full speed right towards me. I felt like someone hit me with a sledgehammer and had two reactions: 1) stay still, if you start going away, you're history; 2) I have four slugs in my shotgun, breathe calmly, let them come close enough, and give them two each." If I have to!

I also put a bird shell in the chamber. When they were 60 meters away, I shot in the air. The first and not the bigger one ("smaller" doesn't fit!) continued, but the bigger one in the back halted. After 20 more meters the one in front realized its pal had stopped, and so did he. He turned around as if to say, "Aren't we gonna take him after all?"

They started moving sideways. I started moving backwards, slowly, very slowly, talking firmly to them: "Okay, I take a hint. I'll move back!" I had to turn around to see where I put my feet on the round, slippery stones, which was very disturbing. They did not follow me. In short, I spent two days trying to get unnoticed by these two fearless ones, and finally made it by climbing way up in the alder-covered mountainside.

Another bear got scared off into the bushes in a similar situation, but returned and came my way shortly after even though it must have smelled me. You never know their next move!

One time I crossed a big, grass covered—really thick, 2.5 meter tall—meadow, and I could hear one bear walking only 5-6 meters to the left, parallel to me, and 10 minutes after, one to the right! Talk about high pulse for half an hour—I couldn't see anything! I was yelling though.

There are several reasons that I didn't have more trouble, but mainly because I followed the bear safety rules specific for Kodiak, though:

1. Never camped close to a creek or river with fish in it. Ninety percent of my camps were just above "tree line" (alders only), where I had access to firewood (no stove in summer ever) and the bears were much less plentiful. Sometimes I didn't reach above the alders until midnight, but I pushed on to get a safest possible campsite (plus it doesn't get real dark in Alaska's summers).

2. I experimented with not using the trip wire, (where better than Kodiak?) and to my knowledge I only had two bears close to my tent, and they were both scared off by my scent (I heard them spin around). I made it a routine to walk in a wide circle some 30-40 meters from the tent through the bush if necessary must to put my human scent there, as a "fence' around my tent. I urinated on the tallest bushes and on rocks and in bear trails. I also put moth balls by each stake around the whole tent, they stink!

The result: the bears stayed away. This works!

ADMIRALTY ISLAND 1998

What a wilderness adventure this was! The rainforest down in the southeast is really something, with those huge spruce trees, the often thick areas of berry bushes and devil's club and the smell of fresh plants and sear at the same time.

I started out with my skilled outdoors friend John Trampush, who actually has a cabin on the Taku River, closer to Juneau, so he was already familiar with the rainforest.

Our packs weighed 70 pounds and we had everything we needed for 23 days, easily 5 weeks with good fishing or bird hunting (lots of deer on Admiralty, too, in an emergency).

After only one hour's walk from the starting point at the southernmost tip of the island, I decided to cut across a spit, through the woods. We climbed some 20-25 steep meters, then followed a bear trail through "not too thick bushes." The bear trails are absolutely all over, it's hard not to follow one!

All of a sudden I hear a twig breaking, so I stop. Turn around and look at John, but the sound didn't come from him. My eyes look ahead again, and suddenly I spot a huge, dark brown hump, and then the big head—only six meters away! It's a very big bear, in fact the biggest one we ever saw on Admiralty—and it's on the same bear trail as us, only coming the opposite way, right towards us!

It's amazing how quickly a human mind and body can react sometimes—we can be fast too. I notice that the bear's head is only centimeters from the ground, and it probably hasn't spotted us yet, and therefore I decide to make a short, hasty retreat. I'm some 10 meters ahead of John, who's maybe 2 meters lower and further down behind me.

Maybe it takes me 2-3 seconds to get back to John.

"Bear! Right ahead of us!" I explain as I draw my shotgun and stand ready with it, pointing, if the bear saw my quick retreat and that incited an attack. At the same time both of us yell as loud as we can, clap our hands and blow our whistles. It's 100% certain that it heard us.

I think it's reaction was simply to lie down at the very spot it was. We stood there for a couple of long minutes, listened carefully when we were not making noise and heard nothing. The bear may also have turned around and disappeared very quietly. I know how silent those big animals can be.

John and I decided it was nicer along the beach! We kept on making a lot of noise. To my recollection it seems that we were not making noise before we walked into the bear. This was because we had just started, and the unconscious ways of civilisation still were with us, our habits.

We woke up and got determined to alert our senses to those of an animal—always be on guard.

On the third day we had climbed way up to the highest ridges on Admiralty's southern part through some pretty heavy terrain—dead trees and bushes everywhere, tall grass. I recall we encountered lots of really fresh bear signs, one or more bears had been feeding on green grass in southern slope, a little opening in the woods (the tree line goes all the way up, even though the landscape is much more open most places)—a typical place where bears would be. This was still relatively early in summer, in late June, and the salmon runs hadn't really started yet, which probably meant there would be bears higher up. We knew that but hoped to take advantage of more open terrain—which we did. Anyway, those bears feeding on grass got scared by our noisemaking. They never showed themselves. A proof noise works. And no dramatic encounter—that's how we like it.

Later I woke up one bright, sunny day (near down there), grabbed my shotgun automatically—it's part of my body in bear country—and headed bare-footed for a small source of cold water that came up of the ground, behind and down from a narrow line of spruce trees.

As I came around the edge of those trees, I saw the back of a medium grizzly, 25 meters away! It was moving away from me, and had not sensed me. Since it could decide to go through the small spruce forest and come right towards the camp where John was sitting relaxed with his morning coffee and diary writing, I decided to sprint back to him. I deliberately made no noise in this case, because I did not know if she—I think it was a she—had cubs close by, and if they do, they are very likely to come right at you when the distance is a 100 meters or less! (sometimes distance doesn't matter). Now it was only 25 meters, way inside her space limit.

Bear! I noticed John when I came running, even though that wasn't necessary. He understood as he saw me coming, and we both went up on a little knoll, yelling and clapping our hands. We never saw her again.

I have never been on an expedition in bear country with a more skillful noisemaker than John. He is a big, strong guy (approximately 190 cm, 100 kilograms) with strong lungs, and with discipline, so he was always making a lot of noise as we were hiking. I almost found it disturbing, that's how good he was!

There is no doubt in my mind we scared off a lot of bears because of this, and probably at some distance, too. We gave the bears both time and room, and didn't "step on them."

The undergrowth was many times so thick we spent one hour covering one mile. The slower you move, the harder it is physically, that's a good rule in bush Alaska! Sometimes our noses hit warm, freshly produced bear scats as we had to crawl on all fours! That feeling is something else.

John returned to the other world called civilisation when we reached Angoon, and my girlfriend Marit joined me the last 11 days (it took 22 to complete the trip).

Marit and I saw "her" first bear the first day. A big one on the beach 400 meters away. We hollered and it disappeared (and we crossed its path).

We worked our way through some really thick brush crossing the island from Angoon towards Pack Creek. Here we didn't see one single bear, but lots of bear signs. We scared them off.

As we reached the bays around Pack Creek, they showed however. First we woke one that was sleeping right by a stream on the edge of thick, 2 meter tall berry bushes at 10 meters distance! And we did make noise many times. It ran away, scared.

Seconds after we spooked another one, it also ran away, but not very hastily (50-60 yards away, I'm sorry I mix yards, meters, but it's inevitable when you read American books). And then, 15 minutes after that, one big one came out of the woods, straight in our direction. It didn't care about our noise, so we packed up and left. One hour later a bear spotted us on the narrow beach from 200 meters, and went up into the woods.

As we stopped by a small nameless creek south of Pack Creek, we had our closest and by far most exciting encounter.

I was throwing my spoon (fishing lure) into a school of salmon, trying to get dinner. Marit was sitting at her pack some 30 meters upstream, and it was still 100 meters up to the edge of the forest. We had a good view of the scenery around us.

Suddenly I hear Marit yell, "Bear, bear! Coming right at us!" I quickly turn around and, yes, no doubt, a bear is coming full speed, right towards us, and some 60-70 meters away when I first see it.

Marit and I have discussed what to do in situations like this. Her "part" Is—willingly—to be the one with the camera(!), while I'm supposed to do any shooting with a gun if necessary. So, even though the bear is coming right at her, in the middle of the 10 meter broad, shallow creek, and she's convinced she is the bear's target, she grabs her camera, and takes photographs! Sharp photos, too (they're in the bear book).

I run towards her and the bear, loading my shotgun, aiming at the attacker. But somehow, when the bruin is 30 meters away (and I'm still going to give it 23 more), I see a movement in the corner of my left eyesight. A big salmon! Swimming downstream with half its back in open air.

The bear is not after Marit or me, it's simply chasing that salmon!

Stay still, Marit!" I say, even though that isn't necessary to inform her. She's now thinking, "Why the ... doesn't he fire?"

And then she sees the bear run past her at 8-9 meters, reaches the salmon, water splashing and it stops in the middle of the shallow creek. With the 8-pound salmon wriggling desperately in the bear's mouth, the successful fisherman turns its head and looks us straight in the eye, "Are you going to try to take my dinner?"

No way! And, like a big, happy dog, it enters the opposite creek bed and goes back into the woods with its well deserved catch. Talk about rear (rare?) experience.

FINAL COMMENTS

Most bears, blacks or browns, will avoid humans if they have the time and room to do so. Our main task as guests in their dining room is to give them this time and room.

One very good sentence: avoid to; threaten or tempt bears, and you're a long way to successful trip in bear country.

I always carry pepper spray, simply because it's one more possible way of getting away unhurt (relatively!). I have never used it though, because I always have chosen the shotgun and fired warning shots. If I were ever to use it, I think that would be after the bear has knocked me over and I can't reach my shotgun. To carry a pepper spray as your main defense in regards of weapons, I would not recommend that! It's not enough, or, it may turn out difficult to use. The wind might take most away, the spray only lasts some 10 seconds (!) and the bear might return after a while. Don't use it if the bear is more than 5 meters away, preferably only 2!

I carry the stupid bells that tell every true Alaskan I'm a tourist. That's because those bells are one more way of letting bears know humans are around. They hardly weigh anything. I don't think they are very efficient unless it's almost no wind and very quiet.

Sometimes, maybe 1 in 50, it's not a good idea to make noise. If you're too close to a bear and it sees you, it might trigger a charge. If it hasn't spotted you, consider retreating silently.

Do not fire at a bear at longer range than 7-8 meters. This is how close I'd let a charging bear come after my warning shot(s). If it still comes full speed after the warning shots, I think its intention is to kill you, it's not just bluffing. Fire over and over until it doesn't move any more, and be very cautious when approaching it. I have never fired at a bear.

I consider all bears equally potentially dangerous, blacks and browns, coastal and interior, and take the same precautions in black bear country as in brown bear country.

That's it, Larry.

Author Tracks Bear

May 13, 12ish o'clock (2005)—on the trail of *Ursus americanus.*

I was working at the computer when the phone rang, Brad Risch excitedly explained that "a black bear waist high to me just crossed Huffman in front of the house."

Waist high to 6' 3" Brad would be a pretty big black.

I asked him how long ago and he replied, "20 seconds." He was returning Pam's call, and I told him I'd take her the phone in the garden area and come down with my camera to see if I could get a pix of Ursus americanus.

I stuck my serrated hunting knife in my right pocket, hung my Olympus from my neck and drove Pam's white Suburban to Brad's, pulled into the drive and he said he'd go with me to cruise a couple of cul-de-sacs in the Van Derhouwen neighborhood north of the 6 to 8-acre woodlot into which the black bear had melted (in the Lower 48 people would refer to it as a woodlot, but here it's called a patch of woods).

The sun shone brightly on a 60-degree day as we drove into 4 culdesacs, turned at the end of each, saw a boy around 8-years-old roller blading in the street (it appeared his pop was an APD officer/car in driveway and garage open), noticed a couple of yards without fences where a bear would have no trouble passing through, turned around and took Brad home.

He said he'd finish re-working his flower bed, and I told him I was going into the woods. With a twinkle in his eye and a smile on his face he said, "If you don't come back, I'll come looking for you."

I showed him my Jerry Anderson knife and said, "If you find me and see this on the ground, it means I couldn't get it out of the sheath. You can take it out and save me."

I entered the birch thicket about 15 yards east of the sidewalk on Lake Otis and paralleled that street north. Within a hundred feet I opened the buttons on my polar fleece shirt to access the camera and pulled it out. I held it in my right hand (strap around my neck) with the lens half way out.

Within 50 yards I encountered thicker trees in the form of black spruce. It wasn't jungle-like but definitely a spruce thicket where dwarf trees 4-6-inches in diameter and 15-20 feet tall grew 2 to 6 feet apart. It was darker in the spruce where damp moss covered the ground, softened the sound and proved quieter "tracking" turf. Hearing steady traffic on both Lake Otis and Huffman Road, I continued slowly north through the shadowed spruce thicket.

About halfway to the subdivision, sneaking along and looking everywhere among the black shadows for any sign of the bear, a dump truck on Lake Otis (to my left) banged its bed and gave me a quick start. I kept walking and thinking about my assessment of those who get into bear trouble...*most are doing something goofy. And what am I doing? Walking into and through the woods where a black bear preceded me by half an hour or so. How many photographers have gotten closer for a picture before getting mauled!? I repeat, what am I doing?*

Of course, I entered the woods with a couple of assumptions: 1) The bear's on the move and passing through. It will be long gone. 2) The bear's not interested in people or it could have all the customers it wants on the bike trail. 3) Its hearing is so acute that there's no way I'll be quiet enough to "sneak" up on it.

Slowly, silently I slipped along toward fenced back yards of the subdivision.

Then I emerged from the trees onto a power-line type area bordered by numerous wooden fences. I turned east and followed the fence line at my left past a couple of houses to the end of the fence, where it made a 90-degree turn to the north. A few feet ahead on the ground lay a weathered, white moose foreleg bone and two scapula.

I crossed the open back yard to the next yard about thirty yards and turned south, working around water filled pockets in the dried brown grass. About 70-feet from the fence I came to a tree house, one story about 5 feet off ground, a second about 12 feet up, a yellow nylon ¾ inch rope hanging to within a couple of feet of the ground and a ladder leaning against the second story. A broken white plastic chair resembled a moose rib cage and signaled bear food, giving me a quick adrenaline rush.

I walked under the bottom story bent over and turned at a 45-degree angle left, sneaking along and looking ahead and to both sides. *Lots of black shadows clinging to the spruce. Remind me again how most people get into bear trouble!*

I picked my way along moose trails, walking over brittle brown leaves, sticking to the mossy areas and moving silently, paralleling my original approach about 30 yards. I encountered occasional patches of unmelted snow.

Eighty feet beyond the tree house I encountered a foot-diameter birch with 2x6 steps a foot long nailed to the trunk every 18-inches or so. I prayed that the Lord would show me the bear and let me get a picture of it…thinking *how can a person with knowledge of the bear's hearing expect the Lord to answer that prayer!?*

I stopped about 80 feet past the "laddered" birch and looked back toward the north. At the edge of a spruce patch about 3-feet off the ground was a round, black bear's head with a black round right ear. The bear was facing me at about 75 feet, its black blending perfectly into the black shadows of the spruce thicket. *Hmmm. So, let's get the camera, hope he stays there, or moves more into the open, and take a pix.*

I zoomed in on his head and couldn't find him in the viewer. Looked up and back down to the view finder hurriedly, hoping he wouldn't decide to leave before I took a pix...and wondering if he'd want to investigate me! My mind was starting to race because I thought he'd vanish instantly and before I could focus and click.

I finally found him in the view finder and took the picture. Then I looked at him again, hoping he'd move forward into a more open area away from the spruce. And that quickly the head ghosted back like a vanishing black shadow and was gone. Less than thirty seconds had elapsed from my sighting till his disappearance among the shadows.

Should I follow him for a closer picture? Since he knows I'm here, will he allow me closer? Will I be able to see him in the thick stuff? Maybe wisdom is the better part of valor...I mean stupidity! I replaced the camera in my shirt and turned to leave, looking back every so often and wondering if I were being followed.

The bear kindly allowed my stupidity to reign and probably went off into the thick stuff wondering about two-leggeds!

Troy Hurtubise

"Showdown," ***We Alaskan***s, F-6, October 5, 1997, by Stephen Smith

Self-defense takes many steps where bears are involved. Troy Hurtubise has toyed with different ideas and come to the conclusion that he would be safer around bears with armor. In 1997, he was a 33-year-old Canadian living with his wife and 4-year-old son. Having spent $100,000 creating and refining his bear proof suit of armor, which he called Ursus Mark VI, he determined that nothing was going to happen to him should he encounter a bear.

Composed of fireproof rubber, chain mail, inflatable cushioning and a motorcycle helmet that fit inside a titanium-alloy unit. He self-tested it and has endured 12-guage shotgun blasts from twenty feet, purposefully falling from a one hundred fifty foot cliff, beatings from friends armed with baseball bats and a splitting ax. His 147-pounds of titanium, rubber, plastic and chain mail stands just over 7-feet tall.

He has produced four models and hopes it will be useful to the army as well as bear safety.

UPDATE, March 2025

Troy was born in 1963 and, even though his suit won him a Nobel Prize for Safety Engineering, he never lived to see his suit receive monetary success.

Features included solar powered air system, recording device, emergency and morphine compartments as well as knife and gun holsters. It was called a “Halo suit” and figured to be about $2000 per unit if mass produced. However after spending thousands of dollars on the experiment, Hurtubise was bankrupt and put the suit on sale, hoping to provide money for his family. Efforts were made to fine tune a newer suit, but all was for naught.

Troy was involved in a traffic accident in 2018, involving his vehicle and a transport truck. A fire erupted and Troy was killed in the explosion-fire. He left his wife and son.

Winter Bear

Skiers encounter young grizzly roaming Kincaid Park.

Wide-awake bruin is one of several prowling city this winter.

By Doug O' Harra, *Anchorage Daily News*, November 20, 2001

Laurie Macchello was practicing new skate ski moves at the Kincaid Park stadium with her husband and a ski instructor Sunday morning when she heard a deep, breathy grunt behind her back. She thought it was a moose.

"Then I saw the reaction on our instructor's face," she said. "My husband said, Oh, my god, there's a bear.' "

Macchello turned to face an agitated grizzly standing only about 25 yards away. It looked as though it had just emerged from the beginner-oriented Mize Loop ski trail and was dismayed to find a knot of humans blocking the home stretch.

It was close enough to clearly see the features of its round, brown-furred face, Macchello said.

"We basically could not speak," she said. "It was shaking its head and grunting, and then it looked over toward us and it hurried up toward the parking lot."

In what may be the most startling bear encounter of a season that saw almost daily sightings of black bears by summer bikers and runners, a young brown bear toured Kincaid's core trail system Sunday morning, leaving distinctive prints and claw marks in the packed surface of prime ski routes.

After surprising skiers at the stadium around 11 a.m., the animal loped across the road toward the snowy woods to the south, prompting a van carrying young sledders to brake, according to several witnesses. By midday, warnings about the sightings had been posted at the Kincaid visitors center and along several trails as hundreds of skiers scattered throughout the park.

"It was very, very odd to see a bear in the middle of November in the middle of the stadium," Macchello said. "I mean, it had a hump, it was brown, it was big."

State biologist Rick Sinnott examined some of the 6 1/2-inch-wide prints Monday and concluded that they had been made by an adolescent bear about 3 years old.

"It's not rare for a bear to be up this late," Sinnott said. "But it is a little unusual for people to be seeing bears in Kincaid Park this late, and I've never heard of a brown bear being in Kincaid Park this late in the year.

"Who knows what this one was thinking?"

In theory, most bears hunker down for a winter's snooze after they fatten up or can't find any more easy food, Sinnott said. But the animals will emerge from their dens if disturbed, and they will stay out late if they're still hungry.

"They're fully capable of waking up in an instant," he said.

A brown bear was reported scarfing down spawned-out salmon along Campbell Creek in Far North Bicentennial Park in East Anchorage only a few days ago, and a black bear with a yellow ear tag was nosing around homes off West Dimond Boulevard within the past two weeks, Sinnott said.

Yet another black bear, in Girdwood, has been misbehaving over the past couple of weeks, looking for garbage around people's homes along the Alyeska Highway.

"Apparently last night, people were cooking fried chicken and (the bear) tried to rip the stove vent out of the wall trying to get at that smell," Sinnott said.

Still, a brown bear meandering around Kincaid Park miles from any salmon run or stash of garbage was more difficult to explain, especially weeks into the ski season.

"I'll just monitor it," Sinnott said. "If it starts following people or acting aggressive, I'll have to do something. But for right now, it's just an interesting story."

When Macchello saw the bear, she was alone in the stadium with husband Alec Kay and ski instructor Amy Crawford. As the animal bolted up the hill, it surprised some other skiers and then disappeared toward the woods.

"It didn't look like it was aggressive or like it was chasing after somebody," she said. "But it definitely looked like it was spooked."

Macchello, a physical therapist and trail runner who has seen brown bears in the Chugach Mountains, said she and her husband later had trouble convincing friends of what they had seen.

"Nobody believed me," she said. "Everybody was like: No, it couldn't have been a grizzly. It had to be a black bear.' . . . My husband said, I'm glad there's three of us so they don't think we're crazy.'"

Man Shoots Self

Alaska Digest, Sunday, July 7, 2002

ALEXANDER CREEK

Man shoots himself in thigh while checking out bear sounds at cabin. A Palmer man shot himself in the thigh investigating what he thought was a bear outside his cabin, Alaska State Troopers said.

Dustin M. Mason, 19, was staying alone at his cabin near Alexander Creek when he thought he heard a bear Friday afternoon, troopers said. A bear had been seen in the area. Mason went out on the porch and drew his .357-caliber revolver but didn't see a bear and went back inside. A little later, he again thought he heard a bear and went out on the porch to investigate. This time, when he took the revolver from its holster, it went off and a bullet hit him in the thigh, troopers said.

Mason drove himself on a four-wheeler to a fishing lodge about four miles away.

Troopers in Talkeetna received a report of the shooting at 3:13 p.m. Friday.

The Alaska Rescue Coordination Center dispatched a helicopter from the 210th Rescue Squadron at Kulis Air National Guard Base. Mason was taken to Alaska Regional Hospital, where he was in stable condition Saturday, a nursing supervisor said.

An investigation continues.

Bear Management for Kodiak

Kodiak drafts bear plan.

MANAGEMENT Group makes 270 recommendations for handling 3,000 animals.

By Mary Pemberton, *The Associated Press*, April 22, 2002

After 20 years of trying, the state has come up with the first comprehensive plan for managing the world's largest brown bears.

The plan makes 270 recommendations for managing the approximately 3,000 brown bears that roam the 5,000 square miles of the Kodiak archipelago, a group of three large islands and numerous smaller ones stretching southwest of Anchorage, said Larry Van Daele, an Alaska Department of Fish and Game wildlife biologist.

Kodiak not only has the largest brown bears in the world but has one of the densest populations. Only a few other remote areas of Alaska and Russia have similar numbers of bears.

About a year ago state officials decided to tackle bear management again, in part out of concern that conflicts were increasing between hunters hoping to bag a record bruin and non-hunters interested in bear viewing.

Fish and Game changed its approach this time. Instead of telling the interested parties it knew what was best, it asked them what they thought was needed.

Calling themselves the Citizens Advisory Council, representatives of 12 groups met for five months. The council included state and federal wildlife officials, as well representatives for Alaska Natives, environmentalists, hunting guides, commercial fishermen, tourism, ranchers, air taxi operators and wildlife photographers.

A professional facilitator guided discussions.

The council's 270 recommendations could require changes in federal, state and local laws. Van Daele said a meeting will be held within a month to discuss implementation of the plan with the different agencies, which already are committed to supporting the plan.

Bear hunting traditionally has been a huge economic resource for Kodiak Island, where food is plentiful and the bears grow big on salmon. Nonresident hunters spend $20,000 to $23,000 per hunting trip, Van Daele said.

Hunters looking for a trophy kill find the cost worth it. Sixteen of the top 20 record holders are Kodiak bears, according to the Boone and Crockett Club. The record is a Kodiak bear killed in 1952 with a skull size of 30 3/4 inches, Van Daele said.

Bear viewing, while not generating the same big dollars yet, has gained in popularity in the past decade. "We have had a culture shift," Van Daele said. "People are much more interested in looking at bears than hunting them."

Pam Foreman, executive director of the Kodiak Island Convention and Visitors Center, said tourists increasingly are asking the same question: "How can I see those bears?"

Over three months last year, approximately 10,000 non-Alaskans and 9,000 state residents visited Kodiak, Foreman said. Of those making tourism inquiries, 64 percent asked about wildlife viewing opportunities. Of those, 95 percent were interested in seeing bears.

"Fortunately the bears here in Kodiak are pretty darn well

behaved. The reason they are so big is that they have so much darn food to eat. They are fat and happy," Van Daele said.

The plan was finalized in February, in time to be considered by the federal government in updating its management plan for the Kodiak National Wildlife Refuge. The refuge takes up about two-thirds of Kodiak Island.

Van Daele said the council's recommendations include keeping the annual bear harvest of approximately 160 bears the same but reducing populations along the road system in northeast Kodiak -- where nearly all the people live -- by 10 percent.

Cattle ranchers under the plan would be allowed permits to hunt problem bears that kill livestock. Current regulations require ranchers to catch bears in the act.

Bear education for visitors and the archipelago's approximately 14,000 residents is an important component of the plan, Van Daele said.

It recommends that all the landfills and dumps have electric fences to keep bears out. Island residents would be educated about the proper handling of chicken pens, fish-drying sheds, food storage and pet food to minimize bear-human encounters. Outdoor recreationists would receive information on proper food handling and trash disposal. And visitors would get a crash course on keeping bears away from food and garbage.

The plan also includes educating people on bear behavior to "dispel rumors that bears are unpredictable," Van Daele said.

Several council members said a key part of the plan is the finding that bear viewing and bear hunting are not natural enemies.

Council members realized from talking to one another and looking at scientific data that there is no need to shut one activity down for the sake of the other.

"Kodiak has proven that the two can coexist. They happen in different seasons of the year. There's no conflict in the field between user groups," said Dick Rohrer, a licensed master guide who has lived on Kodiak Island for 32 years.

Hunters looking for a trophy bear will be interested in big males, not the sows with cubs that tourists view feeding at salmon streams in summer. Bear hunting is allowed in spring and fall, Van Daele said.

The plan also asks that the refuge consider reopening O'Malley Creek from June through September to allow for guided day-use bear viewing. The area currently is closed to the public but is considered best on the island for bear viewing.

Cat vs. Bear

The Associated Press carried a story in early June 2006 re: Jack, the orange Tabby cat that chased a black bear up a tree in its back yard in West Milford, N.J. on June 4. The bear climbed down and the cat re-chased it up another tree.

Jack is a 15—pound cat that obviously prides himself in ruling his yard. Donna Dickey, owner of the bear chaser told the Star-Ledger of Newark that they referred to Jack as being "on duty" never realizing that he'd chase a bear.

Bear in the Outhouse

KTOO NEWS 104.3 FM in Juneau

'Something just immediately bit me in the butt': Haines woman survives outhouse bear

February 17, 2021 by Henry Leasia, KHNS - Haines

A group of Haines residents had a bizarre encounter with a bear near Chilkat Lake on Saturday. Shannon Stevens said she was using an outhouse when she felt something bite her bottom.

Shannon Stevens spent the weekend with her brother and his girlfriend at a remote yurt on Chilkat Lake, 17 miles from Haines.

After traveling across the frozen lake by snowmachine on Saturday, they cooked sausages over an outdoor firepit. Later that evening, Stevens left the yurt to use the outhouse.

"Normally, when we are out there in the summer or the fall I'm used to shouting 'Hey, bear!' the whole way. It was the dead of winter, so I didn't think to do that this time," Stevens said. "I got in there and sat down on the toilet seat, and something just immediately bit me in the butt. I jumped up and screamed."

She called for her brother Erik Stevens who came running to investigate.

"I'm like, 'Okay, I'm going to open the lid and look.' I take the headlamp and I grab the lid of the toilet seat and I lift it up," Erik Stevens said. "Right at the level of the toilet seat, maybe an inch or two below, is a gigantic bear face looking right back up at me."

He closed the lid and they ran back to the yurt as fast as they could. Shannon Stevens was bleeding, so they cleaned the wound and bandaged it up.

She said she was shocked, but not seriously injured.

"It felt like just a single puncture. Maybe it wasn't even a bite. It might have been a swipe with his claw potentially. I don't think we'll ever really know that part," Shannon Stevens said.

They stayed in the yurt the rest of the night and waited till morning to take a look around. The next day, the bear was gone. The fire pit had been knocked over and there were tracks running towards the outhouse.

Erik Stevens said he believes the bear was attracted by the smell of cooking, then entered the hole below the outhouse through an opening downhill.

"There's a way out in the back of the outhouse, there's a rock wall and there's a way for a creature to get in through that rock wall. He probably just pushed the rocks over and got down into the hole," Erik Stevens said.

Alaska Department of Fish and Game biologist Carl Koch conducted a brief investigation after learning about the incident. He believes it was a black bear based on photos of the tracks and other recent reports of bear activity in the area.

"[She] might be the only person this has ever happened to," Koch said. "I wouldn't be surprised over the years if other folks have had bizarre things — but during February to sit down in an outhouse and have something like that happen is very unusual."

Koch said he has heard of bears damaging outhouses after being drawn to their smell. In general, bears are less active during the winter as they tend to stay in their dens for a long period of time. That's not always the case.

"Some bears will stay out a long time if there is food, maybe almost never den up," Koch said. "We get calls year round in Juneau and all sorts of places, just not nearly as many as we do in the summertime."

This is not the first close encounter with a bear in Haines this winter. Earlier this month, a Haines man was mauled by a brown bear while backcountry snowboarding with a group of friends. The attack left him with a broken arm, puncture wounds and other injuries. He has since been released from the hospital and is recovering at home.

Shannon Stevens said her experience was not nearly as traumatic, but she has learned a valuable lesson.

"I mean, I'm definitely going to look down in the hole next time," she said.

Watching the Game

Football players find a fan in brown bear.

MOOSE KILL: A sow and her cubs hang out at Soldotna practice field.

The Associated Press, August 2, 2001

Kenai -- Football players had just finished practicing the "bear crawl" at Skyview High School in Soldotna when they got a glimpse of the real thing.

The day before Monday's incident, the brown bear had killed a moose near the gate to the high school driveway.

"It didn't stand up until it got to the top of the hill, but it stopped and looked at us through the fence. I kind of wondered, what if the fence was not there?" said Greg Zorbas, assistant Skyview football coach. "She loped up to the top of the hill close to the birch trees, stood up, tore down a stump, and then she was gone."

But not far. Since its moose kill, the bear -- actually a sow with two cubs -- has been seen several times in the area south of the driveway from the Sterling Highway to the woods behind the football and soccer fields. So have her cubs.

Mike Crawford, a visitor from Kent, Wash., said he was talking to an Alaska state trooper when a report of the bear came over the officer's radio Sunday. He followed the trooper to the school, then watched one of the bears.

"I stayed until it got dark and watched the bear eating (the moose)," Crawford told the Peninsula Clarion.

Crawford said that bear looked like a 2-year-old cub. Shortly after it disappeared into the trees, he saw a sow and a cub in a meadow just west of the moose.

Coach Wade Marcuson said the bear showed up for football practice about 9:30 a.m. Monday.

"The bear was milling around, tearing down stumps. It looked like she was having a good time," he said. The players had just finished the bear crawl drill, and Zorbas noted the bear's presence.

"He said, 'We're going to stop for a moment. We've got a demonstration going on over here. That's what I want you to be -- low to the ground,"' Marcuson said.

Athletic director Dan Creel said school officials met with Fish and Game biologists, who advised that trapping and relocating the bears would do little good, since relocated bears generally return quickly to their original stomping grounds.

Marcuson said he told the football players, about 70 students, that they have a special opportunity.

"We told the kids, 'You don't have too many football camps where you see a brown bear,"' he said. "We told the kids not to be over there, not to go looking for the kill, to stay together and to stay close to the building. I think as long as we're together and by the building we're OK."

Advice

FIGHTING BACK

Kenai fire chief battles bruin with fists, stick.

SCUFFLE: Hunters fight back while grizzly sow decides which one to bite.

By Jon Little, *Anchorage Daily News*, September 16, 2001

Soldotna -- Scott Walden, the city of Kenai's fire chief, rabbit-punched a charging brown bear last weekend and lived to tell about it.

Nobody even got hurt, apart from some minor shock after the fact.

"I never want to see this again. It was probably one of the most unnerving things I've ever seen," said Walden, a 16-year firefighter.

He and two other men stood their ground and made noise, as experts recommend, while a sow bear bluff-charged them. But instead of following the usual script by playing dead when the bruin roared back a second time, two of them shoved and whacked at her for a few seconds until the third man fired his hunting rifle, startling her away.

Wildlife biologists are astonished no one was bitten or killed.

"I am too," Walden said. "That was a real topic of conversation afterwards. One of us should be in the hospital right now."

Walden, 44, was taking his two cousins from rural northern Idaho, Justin and Rocky Sauer, on a morning moose hunt Sept. 8 in the mixed tundra and patchy spruce thickets just east of downtown Kenai.

Justin, 21, and Rocky, 45, had .30-06 rifles. But Walden was unarmed as they set off on foot down a dirt road that leads to the Snowshoe Gun Club, a target range just outside the Kenai city limits.

Near the target-shooting range, they saw a scrawny grizzly sow with one cub cross the road, but they kept hiking along a game trail on a low ridge bordering Beaver Creek, a salmon stream that feeds the Kenai River.

They saw no moose and turned back. About a half mile from the gun range, the three heard the telltale popping of an agitated brown bear snapping her jaws, Walden said.

"I told them, 'Uh-oh, there's a bear.' She was probably 50 feet up the ridge from us," he said.

Walden said he's no expert on bears but had more experience than either of his cousins, who are accustomed to hunting deer. He told them to bunch together and yell as the sow appeared out of the brush and looked at them.

This one was different from the thin bear they'd seen earlier. She was fat and healthy, about 5 or 6 feet long, and accompanied by two cubs, Walden said.

She charged once but stopped about 20 feet away after the hunters fired warning shots.

She ambled back. With her back to the men, she looked at her cubs, her head bobbed, and she turned to look back over her left shoulder. "She whirled straight at us and came four times faster than she did the first time," Walden said. "She was in a full-bore run straight toward us."

The bear covered the 50 feet at an unimaginably fast pace, Walden said. The men couldn't react.

"I said, 'She's coming and she's not stopping -- just kill her!' "Walden said. "Justin pulled his gun up, and she skidded to within 18 inches or two feet of us."

The bear was too close for Justin to get a shot off, he said. Besides, she was pawing and mouthing at the younger hunter's thigh, and his rifle butt and scope were the only barriers in her way. He jabbed at her with the gun.

Walden, meanwhile, had grabbed the only weapon at hand, a scrawny birch sapling, which he bent over and waved at the bellowing sow bear.

So there they were. Walden and his cousin Justin were side by side, boot to paw with the roaring, mouth-snapping sow for four or five seconds, Justin shoving at her with his rifle and Walden, to his right, waving the bent-over birch sapling in her face and swinging his right fist at her. Rocky was on Justin's left side.

Several times she appeared poised to bite Justin's leg but would lose focus when Walden swung at her. His blows barely grazed the sow's ear, but she would watch his fist. Her gaze followed his hand the way a retriever watches a ball taken from its mouth, he said.

"I kept yelling, 'Stand your ground, shoot her, shoot her!'" Walden said.

"She was just kind of going back and forth between Justin and I, him with a gun and me with a little branch," Walden said. "Her head was bobbing. She was mouthing. It was almost as if she couldn't focus on which one of us she wanted to grab. She was making an ungodly roar. It just sent chills up my neck."

Finally, Rocky fired a shot at her head. It missed or maybe

grazed an ear.

"She got as bad a look on her face as we had on ours and did a quick U-turn back to her cubs," Walden said.

The hunters reloaded their rifles and slowly backed away until they were out of view. They swung wide around the bear, all the time hearing the popping and rustling in the brush as they skirted her.

Later they called the state Division of Fish and Wildlife Protection to report the incident.

Walden said he has no explanation for why nobody got hurt. His best guess is that the bear hesitated because there were three targets instead of one and none of the men ran, which would have triggered her chase instinct.

"She was more aggressive towards Justin than she was with me, and I was really concerned she was going to get him in the thigh," he said. "The poor kid, he never swears. He's a religious kid. I told him, 'Justin, for as religious a kid as you are, it sounded like you'd just been discharged from the Navy.'"

Justin's father refused to believe the story at first, and wildlife biologists say the account is highly unusual.

A sow with two cubs would be at least 5 years old, and bears that age usually react swiftly with deadly force rather than dither over where to bite, said Ted Spraker, area management biologist on the Kenai Peninsula.

"I'm clearly baffled that the bear didn't grab him when she was that close, and especially since he fought back. That usually elicits an aggressive response from the bear," Spraker said.

"If he was laying down motionless and the bear sniffed him, stepped on him and turned around and walked away, that would be normal," Spraker added. "But when you stand there toe to toe and duke it out with a bear and she doesn't do anything --

and a young adult sow -- I don't know. That's a new one for the books."

Shocking

Bears in for a shock at one man's set net cabin

ELECTRIC FENCE: Bruins are a problem for folks in Egegik Bay.

The Associated Press, June 16, 2003

KODIAK -- Kodiak teacher Steve Steffensen is packing something new in with supplies destined for the family's setnet site in Egegik: a solar-powered electric fence.

The fence is the same as ones used by farmers to corral livestock. But Steffensen bought his fence to keep the wildlife out, particularly brown bears that have repeatedly broken into the family cabin, destroyed belongings and made a mess.

During winter, while the family is away from the Alaska Peninsula, brown bears have climbed in through windows of their plywood cabin and wreaked chaos, Steffensen said. They've eaten food, torn up sleeping bags, clothes and packages of soap, and clawed equipment. They've urinated and defecated in corners before "blasting their way out through the walls like bulldozers," he said.

"They're insatiable," said Steffensen, who estimates the damage at $1,300.

"They broke every window in the cabin," said Steffensen's wife, Carol. "I think they're having fun in there."

Bears have busted into an estimated 22 setnetters' cabins along seven miles of beach in Egegik Bay, according to year-round watchmen employed by the canneries. The problem has become so bad that even the canneries aren't safe. Bears broke into the ISA cannery and trashed the store.

"I heard the cook camp just got mauled," Steve Steffensen said.

The problem is especially frustrating for setnetters who don't live year-round in Egegik. Kodiak setnetters Stosh Anderson, Cecil Ranney and Judy Phillips have all had cabins broken into by bears.

"It makes packing difficult," Carol Steffensen said. "You say to yourself, 'Do I have any pots and pans left?'"

"It really bums you out when someone sends you a picture of your cabin and you look at it and see your sleeping bags and clothes lying on the tundra," Steve Steffensen said.

Then there are the added cost and trouble of shipping new windows and plywood to Egegik.

Steffensen said the first year was the worst. Bears ate about $600 worth of groceries. He suspects the bears have come to associate cabins with food.

Steffensen, who grew up on a farm with miles and miles of electric fence to keep pigs and cattle inside, plans to coil wire around his house, held inches off the walls by insulators.

Any bears attempting to crawl through the cabin's windows will immediately be zapped with 40-plus volts.

Past efforts at warding off the bears by Egegik setnetters have met with less than satisfactory results. One setnetter, a carpenter, planed down all of his window frames so bears couldn't gain purchase. Instead, the bears rammed inside through his half-inch plywood walls.

Another neighbor surrounded his cabin with boards studded with nails. The bears walked over them.

"Short of a 20-foot steel van, the term bear-proof cabin might be an oxymoron," Steffensen said.

Solar-powered fence thwarts bears.

Smokehouse

SMOKEHOUSE: The apparatus was installed as a model two years ago.

By Erik Hillstrom, ***Bristol Bay Times***, July 15, 2002

Dillingham -- While the sight of a brown bear in the wild can be awe-inspiring, the sight of a furry thief in your smokehouse filled with drying salmon can be downright discouraging.

Just ask Anuska Olson. She and her husband, Hjalmar, have spent their entire lives in the Dillingham area, and too many times have unwillingly donated their family's fish to an ursine robber.

One year I had over 200 fish in the smokehouse," Anuska said. "I went and opened the door one day, and there was a big hole in the back of the smokehouse. All my fish were gone but about 20, and those were sour. That bear ate the good ones and left the sour ones."

Rather than be forced into a situation where a bear must be shot, the Olsons agreed to be part of a local experiment pitting a solar-powered electric fence against the wily and powerful thieves. Alaska Department of Fish and Game wildlife biologist Jim Woolington installed the apparatus as a model two years ago.

"We put this up with the idea that the public could actually come see how it works," Woolington said.

Designed and built with the same tools used by livestock farmers, the fence at the Olsons is powered by a solar panel roughly the size of a three-ring binder found in any middle school. Systems also were available using standard house current or car batteries.

"What we are trying to do is prevent problems from happening," Woolington said. "These are basically the same materials used by ranchers, and while we don't do installation, and we don't actually get materials for people, we will definitely give them good ideas and good information if they are interested."

The fence is working.

Hjalmar said that he had not seen a better way for keep bears away, other than a rifle. He said the versatile system could be used in many locations.

"The bears don't come around anymore," Olson said. "And it has been pretty bad the last 15 years. It's a great system, and it's for people to come see for themselves. It uses no electricity, and with it being solar powered, it could be used at a subsistence camp or fishing camp upriver. They could use one of these at Lewis Point or at Ekuk to protect their fish. If enough people were interested, we might even be able to get a price break on materials."

So enticing was the smell of Anuska's fish that before Woolington had a chance to install the fence this year, the Olsons were visited three times by a nosey bear.

"The last time he came, we had another little fence up, but he was getting through that," Anuska said. "So we came out hollering and making a bunch of noise, and he didn't get any of our fish. The next day we put up the electric fence. That's a whole lot of work just so the bears can't get it."

Though they don't reach the smokehouse, ursine prowlers continue to visit the Olsons. One took the time to inspect a small pickup truck and the Olsons' 32-foot commercial fishing boat that was readying for the next salmon opener.

"Boy, you missed a million-dollar picture this morning," Hjalmar said. "My son was on his way to work and he looked over as he was going down the driveway and saw a bear on the bow of the boat. We looked for tracks, and it climbed the ladder, and walked all over the boat to the bow. It just stood there, having a good time."

Dog to Rescue

Man's Shadow scares off charging grizzly that was closing too fast

SAVED: Dog comes to rescue of camper who got between mother and cub.

By Nicole Tsong, ***Anchorage Daily News***, August 15, 2002

Bears have bluffed Don Mobley before. Usually, he stands his ground. But when a female grizzly growled and charged him last weekend, its cub 15 feet away, instinct and experience told him one thing: run.

"I don't think I had any choice," said Mobley, who at the time was gathering firewood for a night on a sandbar along the Nakochna River. With the cub so close, "I was going to get mauled."

Mobley hot-footed it toward the river, thinking the deep water might turn the grizzly off the chase. But he knew the bear would overtake him in the 50 yards to the water's edge.

The sow was about 10 feet behind Mobley when a black-and-tan savior zipped out of the woods and lunged at the bear. It was Mobley's dog, Shadow.

Mobley heard the dog and soon realized that the bear and its cub had disappeared with 3-year-old Shadow barking madly in hot pursuit.

The only thing that saved me was my dog," he said Wednesday of the German shepherd mix.

Don Mobley figures he owes his life to his dog Shadow. The 3-year-old German shepherd mix took on a charging grizzly to protect his master on the Nakochna River last weekend. (Photo by Jim Lavrakas)

Shadow came through Saturday's ordeal with minor injury, raw spots behind his floppy black ears. Mobley isn't sure if the bear bit the dog or clawed it. He also doesn't know if Shadow bit back. But he's fine and so is Mobley, who is in Anchorage this week for an appointment.

Mobley and a friend, Cheryl Milline, were hiking up the Nakochna River over the weekend when they decided to camp on a sandbar. The Nakochna runs into the Kichatna River, a tributary of the Yentna River, and sits in a sparsely populated area between the Yentna and Rainy Pass, a checkpoint on the Iditarod Trail.

Two or three days earlier, they had traveled by boat from his homestead on the Kichatna River to the mouth of the Nakochna. From there, they had planned to spend time at his base camp about 10 miles upriver.

The 56-year-old retired Army air traffic controller knew there were plenty of bears in the area. He and Milline hollered during the hike to ward them off, and he carried his .30-06-caliber semi-automatic rifle.

But as they began gathering wood for a fire, Mobley did something he won't do again -- leave the rifle next to his hiking pack.

"On that island I lost concentration," he said. "I went looking for wood and forgot about being in a situation with so many bears around."

Mobley had his head down, collecting brush, when he looked up and saw a grizzly cub close by. It was staring curiously at him, he said.

And "before I even seen her, I started to look for her," he said. And the mama bear was right there, clambering over a log heading straight toward him. Mobley was between the two animals.

"She growled and came at me," he said. "She was so close -- I knew it wasn't a false charge."

Mobley yelled, "Run, Cheryl!" and took off for deep water, hoping that if he made it into the stream, the bear would give up.

As the sow closed in, Mobley heard Shadow barking. He sensed that the bears had fled and eventually had to call the dog back from the woods, he said.

Shadow usually follows Mobley everywhere he goes, but that day the dog was lying at their camp when Mobley encountered the grizzlies. Shadow is very protective and has chased a few bears from the homestead, Mobley said, fondly rubbing the dog's head Wednesday in front of an Anchorage hotel.

"He's a really tough dog," the man said. "He's just fast enough he can harass them."

And because the dog saved his life, Shadow gets to eat what he wants. On Tuesday night, Shadow ate pizza. On Wednesday night, Mobley's daughter Shawna Murray was planning a special meal of chicken and twice-baked potatoes for the family and for Shadow. "He's our hero," Murray said. "My dad survived what could have been his death."

Generated Stories

Brad Risch

How it all began... Sometime between 2000 and 2001 (I think) my son-in-law Brad Risch told me that as a child he read ***Alaska Bear Tales*** under the covers at night with the aid of a flashlight, while he was supposed to be sleeping. And some time prior to that I believe I was at a book signing when someone told me about his experience with ***Alaska Bear Tales***. After hearing his story and Brad's, I got the idea that it would be neat to feature stories generated by our books in a chapter in order to showcase others' experiences. I'll start with Brad's version.

The year was 1983, I was 13 and an avid reader. I loved to read science fiction and ate westerns as snacks between the sci fi titles I found. Then, I came across ***Alaska Bear Tales*** at the grocery store. This was my first real *true-life* nonfiction book that I had read. I purchased the brown eyes that looked at me from the cover and took it home. It was then put into the lineup that was on my nightstand table; western, sci fi, ***Alaska Bear Tales***, western. Little did I know that this book not only would change my reading habits but its content made me much more aware in the coming years while camping and hiking. Its author would surprisingly come into my life unexpectedly, blessing me with not only friendship, life mentorship, accepting me into his family and truly blessing me as my father-in-law.

When I start to read I may not be the fastest reader but I am a thorough reader and as I read the pages of ***Alaska Bear Tales***, the movie of the stories started to play. To say that these pages playing before my eyes made a big hairy impression is to say the least. For three days I would get up for school and live life as normal but at 9 P.M. it was bedtime and lights out! So as not to disturb my parents that so dutifully patrolled for light emanations from the crack of my bedroom door, I, a flashlight and ***Alaska Bear Tales*** crawled under my thick comforter. I read ***Alaska Bear Tales*** in three nights, getting very little sleep. When finished, it went right back into the rotation; western, ***Alaska Bear Tales***, science fiction. I read ***Alaska Bear Tales*** two times that month.

I have been very fortunate and honored to go on several interviews with Larry. To hear the contributors in their own words the Alaskan adventure, plane crash survived or mauling they endured and prevailed from. It is absolutely amazing to me the strength of the human spirit that is displayed between Larry Kaniut's written pages.

SHEEP HUNTER

The sheep hunter's story was pretty funny. He and a partner had packed into Dall sheep country for rams. After dinner the first night they crawled into their sleeping bags in their tent, but the story teller couldn't get to sleep because his partner snored. He told me that they hunted hard the next day and after dinner, "I took out a copy of my ***Alaska Bear Tales***." I thought anyone who packed a book into sheep country was either pretty tough, not too bright or loved to read.

He continued, "I read some bear stories and went to sleep. My partner didn't snore the rest of the hunt." (But, of course, he didn't sleep either).

JEFF DAVIS Author Jeff Davis sent me this email.

Bears were on my mind when I first arrived in Alaska in

1983. So much so that the first book I bought in Alaska was Larry's recently released "***Alaska Bear Tales***."

I knew about bears. My first year out of high school, I worked at a National Park. This was back in the days of open garbage dumps. My free time was quite often spent watching and photographing the freeloaders. The park service even appointed me unofficial guide to a Canadian researcher who was interested in our local population. Years later, Dr. Herrera and I laughed about that summer of '69 when we realized we'd met so long ago.

After a couple of close calls which turned out to be bluff charges, and one more serious adventure that luckily ended up with no more damage than a large bear-head dent in the side of my car, I came away from that summer with a healthy respect for anything with hair, teeth and claws.

Despite my ursine experiences, Larry's first bear book was an eye-opener as I nervously read through it that first spring, waiting on warmer weather, salmon runs and hunting season.

Over the next 19 summers, I had reason to reflect on the experiences chronicled in the book. Every spring I faithfully pulled the book off my book shelf and reread it, knowing how important it would be to keep those unfortunate incidents fresh in mind every time I left Anchorage. (And today – even for those of you in Anchorage!) Often over the years, I'd crawl out of a tent on a distant stream and find huge, deep, clawed impressions in the mud around my tent. I saw many bears on distant hillsides. A couple even inadvertently wandered into rifle range so that I have two nice wall-rugs.

The book became a classic. More adventures followed in succeeding years. The definition of "a Real Alaskan" changed from something to do with the Yukon River, grizzly bears, etc., to having your own chapter in one of Larry's books. I have mixed emotions about not reaching that exalted status. Probably best to leave well enough alone. And hope for another collection of bear stories from Larry Kaniut, Alaska's best known spinner of bear tales!

Jeff Davis, Oregon City, May 2010

Author: ***Return To Toonaklut*** (Safaripress)

Fifty-Five Years in the Alaskan Bush (iUniverse)

Northern Lights, Frozen Nights (iUniverse)

KANIUT REFERRED TO KANIUT

In the search for more good bear stories for ***Some Bears Kill***, I stopped by B Detachment State Troopers on Tudor in Anchorage. I had hoped to find the folder that Capt. Robert Penman had in the mid-1970's when I interviewed him and saw the story of Mc Edwards and Roberts on Burma Road. The person I spoke with at the Troopers said their bear stuff had been turned over to ADFG. That person suggested that I call ADFG, offering me the use of their phone.

When I reached ADFG, I told them that I was attempting to locate the folder which the Troopers previously had. The person said that the Troopers—not ADFG— had the folder. I asked if the person had any other suggestions to which she replied, "You could contact Larry Kaniut; he's written several books about bears in Alaska."

Not having the heart to tell her she was speaking to him, I thanked her.

WILLIAM CHAPPELL

July 8, 2001

Dear Larry,

Sorry for the delay, but the computer thing just isn't so simple for those of us still living in caves (culverts, underpasses, and/or abandoned cars).

You don't know how great it was to meet you at Wal-Mart in Wasilla (06-14-01). Our conversation caused me to think back to 1984 when I was preparing to attend my 20th high school reunion (Savannah High School) in Anaheim, California. I had wanted to prepare a couple of packages from Alaska to be given as door prizes. I had purchased two boxes of Wildberry candy and two very nicely, hand-painted tree fungi, both bearing a scene of a cabin in mountain wilderness. Yet I wanted something else as well, one more thing (rustic spice) for each of the packages. As I walked past the Book Cache, my eyes lit upon your ***Alaska Bear Tales***, and I knew, there it was! At that moment, your first book was all the rage up here, and I bought three of them...two to give and one to read.

After having the two bundles gift-wrapped, I was off, not being able to investigate your bear tales just then.

Later, at the reunion, the presents were very well received, and both winners hunted me up to thank me.

One beautiful lady from Laguna Beach, California, who remembered me, but I couldn't place her (I felt like a beet), asked of me, "Can a person still live this simple kind of life in Alaska?" I thought for a second, and then responded, "Yes, as much as anywhere."

The other recipient, an old rediscovered buddy, grimaced a bit and then said, "I've been reading about the simple life," then held up your book and grinned, stating, "Simple, maybe, but, oh, what a grizzly neighborhood!"

We all had a good laugh and I couldn't help but feel there were at least two more coming up to look around.

Truly,

William S. (Chaparral) Chappell

KIM BLANAS

This morning August 22, 2001, I visited Dr. Robin Robbins at Advance Chiropractic in Anchorage for an adjustment. After my meeting, Kim Blanas, office receptionist, told me that they had recently taken their pooch, a microscopic member of the canine community, to their vet. There they encountered a huge yellow lab tipping the scales at 120 pounds. The dog's name was Kaniut. Kim's husband Peter, a former student of mine, asked the lab's owners how they came to name their dog Kaniut to which they replied, "We named it after the guy who writes the bear books."

I've fulfilled my life's goals—I have a dog named for me.

MARC TAYLOR

While selling our first self-published book ***Bear Tales for the Ages*** at the Great Alaska Sportsman's Show in April 2001, a man approached and said, "I'd like to shake your hand." I was somewhat surprised and wondered why. He responded that "you are one of the reasons that I moved to Alaska. I read ***Alaska Bear Tales*** and decided to move here from Kansas... and I read Michener's ***Alaska***." Marc agreed to write for this section... neither of us realizing that within two years he'd ask me to write an intro to his own book, ***Hunting Hard...in Alaska***.

From June 8, 2003 email from Marc:

What you read in this book may change your life forever.

Back in 1993 I picked up a paperback book called "*Alaska Bear Tales*." I don't remember specifically why I bought it, but I remember that I was drawn to the romantic notion that there was a state that produced stories about encounters with bears that were worthy of an author documenting them. Of course, that book was written by a man whose name I could not pronounce, but it sounded like an "Alaskan" name, so that made it all the better.

As a reader, I was drawn into that place called Alaska, so I actively sought to read more about the so-called "Last Frontier". Being a hunter, I began to dream of someday venturing to the state where bears roam wild and can be experienced in their natural environment. Of course, nearly everyone has glimpsed a bear as it paces back and forth in the confines of a zoo, but I wanted to view a bear that had never seen steel bars and gawking spectators; one that might decide to stalk a hunter under the right (wrong) conditions. I was not attracted by the danger; I was attracted by the untamed wilderness that produces such beasts.

One thing I know for certain – If you truly want something bad enough, you will find a way to make it happen, so I was fortunate enough to accompany some good friends on a caribou hunt in the Alaska interior. And yes, I watched a huge grizzly bear as it "stalked" our meat bags on the fourth day of the hunt.

The experience was so overwhelming that I then made a way to move my family and I to Alaska.

Although the largest state, Alaska is the least populated, so it wasn't long before I bumped into the man whose book lit the tinder in this now blazing inferno. I learned to pronounce his name, although I misspell it every once in a while, and not quite a year later he and I shared the meat of my first bull moose.

Nothing is free in this world, especially moose meat. Therefore, much later, Larry Kaniut got to help me publish a book about my hunting experiences since moving to Alaska.

Think about it – After reading a book, much like the one you hold in your hand, I was able to create a new life for myself in a land that once only existed in my dreams; and of course in the book that you hold.

Read on. Dream on. Then turn those dreams into *your* reality!

PAT HANLEY (spring 2004)

Hi Mr. Kaniut,

I saw you a few days ago at Kimsey Eller's funeral and we spoke about unique settings for bear tale readings.

When I was a Resident Assistant in the dorm at Pacific Lutheran University, I was tasked with sponsoring events and generally providing entertainment to the residents. We had two stalls in the men's bathroom on my floor, and I would post one bear tale per week. The response was mixed: most loved them, a few were appalled at the tales documenting the death of a bear. To accommodate both, I made one stall the "happy bear stall" and the other the "gory bear stall." In the former I would post cheerful, uplifting stories of bears, and in the latter, stories demonstrating the brutal side of bears and man's survival responses. Then, the residents could choose their stall, depending on their philosophy and mood at the moment. It was an interesting way to pass a few moments while letting nature take its course.

It was good seeing you the other day. Enjoy your writing and other pursuits.

TOM DUBRANSKY

Having been Ben Kaniut's roommate in college, it was not unusual for remarkable, and somehow strangely unique, things to happen in his presence. Meeting Heather for the first time was no different.

One afternoon, with no forewarning, I received a phone call from Ben asking me if he could come over for a visit so that I might be able to meet his girlfriend, Heather. I had heard stories of Heather at that time, but had never gotten the chance to meet her.

I work out of my house and so was already home. I agreed to meet them just as soon as they could get to my house, which happened to be in a couple of minutes considering they were already right around the corner. That is the epitome of "Ben's Way." The process goes like this: Be at a place. That place is close to someplace else. Remember where the someplace else is. Go to that place.

When Ben and Heather arrived, Ben, the Good Samaritan, was carrying a UPS box of medium size that he picked up from off of my front porch. We noticed that it was from Amazon.com, deduced that it was my wife who had made the purchase and plopped the box down on the kitchen table, proceeding then on to introductions and current events.

When the curiosity of the UPS box finally got the best of Ben, as it usually does, he snapped out his pocket knife (which he always has hidden away in there) and sliced open the box. The looks on our faces were those of the perplexed, but then again, because it was Ben, I should not have been surprised. My wife and I were going to Alaska later that year to witness Ben and Heather's wedding, and in preparation, my wife bought a copy of as many of Ben's dad, Larry's books as Amazon had in their catalog.

So there was Ben opening a box of his dads' books in somebody else's house whom he had not seen in person in over eight months. Typical Ben. After laughing about it and wondering why cosmic powers revolve so strangely around Ben, we went and had lunch.

Tom DuBransky, August 4, 2003 e-mail

ERIC BADGER

I was in the M Bar D fetching 2 bales of Timothy hay, 3 Don's complete horse grain and an apple picker for Pam's horse Prince today (Nov. 29, 2005). Joined conversation with Scott and a guy from Alaska Marine Lines. We talked a bit then the guy left with a wave to Scott who had to answer the phone. The guy shook my hand and said "Eric Badger." I said, "Larry Kaniut." Didn't know if the Kaniut was necessary but I thought polite.

Eric nearly did a back flip returning from his departure toward the door and stated in a question, "The writer?"

"Yes."

"Oh, I've read all your books. Well, maybe not all...but the bear books. I've been reading one about the hardships and dangers people face."

"*Danger Stalks the Land*?"

"Yes."

BEN FORBES

November 5, 1987 from Ben Forbes of Forbes Marine Service, Sitka, Alaska

Dear Larry;

I was mad at you—you cost me $10,000 last year. Here is the story—I spend the winter in Mesa and met a young doctor who was all fired up to go hunt the big Brown bears, and he had a friend that wanted to go and get one too, so I booked him and his friend for a hunt

The next time I saw him, a couple months later he had read your book, ***Bear Tales of Alaska***, and cancelled the hunt, said: those things are dangerous: a fellow could get killed messing around with them. I assured him that I never had a bear lay a claw on one of my hunters, but he still backed out, as it worked out I replaced the two chickens with a pair of hawks and we had a grand hunt—so I got over my mad.

I have read your book and am familiar with several of the episodes, in fact as head of the Sitka search group I ran the search for Mark Rigling, the deer hunter lost on Chichagof near Salisbury Sound. I had a broken foot so set up the search operation base on my cruiser in the Sitka harbor, had one of my men run a phone line down so I had complete communications. I thought that much had been left out of a good story, or perhaps Mrs. Rigling objected?

I had a Texas hunter this spring who became interested in your book after I told him about the cancellation and he bought the book in Sitka, then had it swiped on the way home, he wrote and had me get two more, one of which I added some stick in notes on some of the stories I knew something about, he wrote and said it made the book far more valuable to him. He was giving one to his son-in-law—hope it won't scare him off.

Your proposal is interesting, I am considering doing some story writing, I've been guiding for 40 years and am getting a bit old for the game, so I would like to profit from what tales I have to tell. Would appreciate hearing from you, perhaps should have tried to see you when in Seattle Oct. 23, 24, 25 when we were migrating to Arizona.

Sincerely,

Ben H. Forbes

AVRIL

My wife Pam and I attended a meeting with Kay Stevens of Thompson-Shore of Michigan at the Windbreak Restaurant in Wasilla where we met Avril Johannes. Avril shared her story with us and I asked her to email it to me...which follows.

Larry,

Is this what you had in Mind?

Used to seeing Larry Kaniut books in local stores in Alaska where I live, I was delighted to find his book, "***More Alaska Bear Tales***," while vacationing in a tiny village in Mexico.

This was the second time I'd come across one of his books while far from home. Earlier I found one while staying at a remote jungle resort in Belize.

Congratulations, Larry. Your books are obviously internationally read.

Avril Johannes
3/30/2003

An avid reader, I always look for books while on vacation. In Mexico, I scrounged through the books available to visitors and found your book. In Bleize a friend asked me if I knew who you were. I told her I had bought all your books for my son-in-law and that you had signed them, so, yes, I was familiar with you and all your books.

By the way, I have an exceptional photo of a jaguar, which I took while on a jungle hike in Bleize. Next time I see you (maybe at the Book Bonanza in October) I'll try to remember to show it to you. It really is spectacular. (4-1-2003)

Avril

SHARON CARTER

My son-in-law Brad Risch and I were at the Anchorage Alaska Railroad train station when a young lady appeared with a pretty discombobulated copy of ***Danger Stalks the Land***. She offered to submit an account of her experience with the book for our "possible chapter on stories that our books have generated in order to showcase others' stories."

From: sharon carter

Sent: Monday, June 19, 2006 3:34 PM

To: beartales@kaniut.com

Subject: Hi!

Hi,

You probably don't remember me, I was at the book signing at the Alaska Railroad on Easter. I work as a tour guide for the railroad and I remember you were telling me about a story that someone wrote you after reading your book. So I put together a very short story about my reading ***Danger Stalks the Land***, out in the wilderness. I also attached some pics from that trip.

How to Quiet an Annoying Little Brother on a Rainy Day

by Sharon Carter

A cold breeze flew into the tent along with a group of hungry mosquitoes, when I unzipped the door. I quickly took off my muddy hiking boots before entering, and made sure they wouldn't get wet if I left them outside. Inside was my little brother, Jordan, all curled up in his lightweight sleeping bag. He wasn't asleep. He always seemed to be in the tent when he wasn't shooting his .22.

"I see you came in here right in time to collect fire wood," I said sarcastically.

Jordan laughed, "Well I was getting eaten alive out there."

"Looks like it's not much better in here," I smashed the back of my hand against the ceiling and it killed about six mosquitoes.

I looked out the screen window and it was still pretty bright outside for 7:00 P.M., but then again in an Alaskan summer it always is.

"Sharon, when's dad coming in?" Jordan asked curiously while pushing his glasses up.

I opened my sleeping bag and crawled in, then I grabbed my backpack and pulled a book out of it, "You'll know when you can hear the four wheeler. Probably not much longer with the rain pouring down like this."

I opened the book and tried to read but the loud spatter of rain drops hitting the rain fly slightly distracted me. I just knew my fire outside would be going out soon in another hour or so and I would either have to build it again or figure out how to use the Coleman's Gas stove to heat up some food and coffee for Dad, whenever he came in.

"Where's JJ?" Jordan asked?

"Outside," I said quickly, trying to get back to reading. JJ, our dog that we found on the street, some years back was half Pomeranian and half Chow was bright orange and a medium size dog. He was outside sitting in a cardboard box with a grocery bag tucked on the sides with his head sticking out. He was just sitting in the rain though. We constructed a large tarp that covered our little campsite that consisted of fold out chairs, a little table that held most of the food on it and the stove, the dying camp fire, and the bright orange dog.

"Whatcha readin?" I heard the voice that came out of my annoying brother once again.

"*Danger Stalks the Land*, by Larry Kaniut."

"Will you read me some? I'm kind of bored."

I sighed to show my frustration," I guess, but will you promise to leave me alone after one story?"

"Yup."

I started reading the "*Heroes, One and All.*" The reading worked, he was so interested he finally shut his mouth and listened. Even when I was finished he asked me to read another. Before I knew it, there were no more pages to read. About that time we heard the four-wheeler making its way back into camp. I glanced at my watch; it was passed ten!

"Dad's back," I said closing the book and putting it away. Jordan wrinkled up his nose in disappointment, not because dad was back, but because we already finished the book.
"Jordan, I read for over 3 hours!" He just shrugged," Too bad you didn't bring another one."

We heard some steps getting closer to the tent, and when it stopped, the tent door was unzipped. My dad poked his head in, a big smile on his face, "Where's supper?"

JEFF WILLIAMS

Date: Tue Oct 23 05:31:45 PDT 2007

Sender: "Jeff Williams"

To: "kaniut@alaska.net"<kaniut@spamarrest.com>

CC:

Subject: ***Alaskan Bear Tales***

Larry,

Hey, how are ya? Sorry, again, that it's taken me so long

to get back to you. I've had a lot going on over with here with broken down vehicles, home improvement projects before the snow flies...you know how it is! Anyway, here's a short recap of what I told you at the men's retreat here in PA.

"I hate to admit this, but I am 45 years old and have read only two books, cover to cover, in my lifetime; ***Old Yeller***, which was a seventh grade school assignment, and ***Alaskan Bear Tales***. I was so into the stories in this book that it felt like I was there, seeing and hearing the events as they took place! You really make things come alive and seem real."

Does that sound okay? I know it's short. Let me know if it's not exactly what you're looking for!

Thanks,

Jeff

HAILEY

One of the bride's maids for our new daughter-in-law Heather is a best friend from childhood. At the wedding rehearsal Friday, May 9, 2003, she told me that her last name is Lindow and that her uncles graduated about 30 years ago from A. J. Dimond, where I taught for 26 years.

I said, "You mean Tony?" I was dip netting salmon about 6 or 8 years ago and bumped into him and his son Auggie, who was about 10 or so."

Hailey said, "That's Uncle Eric. Auggie graduates this year."

"You're right; it was Eric, not Tony. I sent Auggie one of my books because I enjoyed our time together and thought he'd like a little reading material from a former teacher of his father's."

As we visited, it was fun to learn that Hailey was from a long line of my former students. The next night when my wife and I prepared to leave the wedding reception, I told Hailey, "It was nice meeting you. Please send us a wedding announcement for your August 16th wedding and we'll stay in touch. Say hello to the Lindow's."

She said, "When my mother and I were talking, she told me that she was one of your students, graduating with the first class from Dimond in 1969."

"What was her maiden name?"

"Kitty Dixon."

I turned a complete circle before saying, "No way! She was one of my favorite students. Be sure to tell her 'hi' for me."

DAVE HEMRY

Ben's fiancee Heather's father Dave had a 70-80 year old patient recommend a good book and brought it in for Dave, ***Cheating Death***.

DR. MC LAUGHLIN

Dr. McLaughlin told me that he was moose hunting when he encountered a sow grizzly's tracks in the snow and her two cubs. He turned around and headed back for his vehicle, placing surveyor's tape along the way. She followed him for a mile and charged while he stopped to place surveyor's tape on a branch.

Dr. McLaughlin had a patient from a Yukon village who walked his lab, ran into a black sow with cubs. She charged. He stood tall, raised his arms and the bear stood up, looked at him and left. He climbed a tree then noticed pain in his arms and saw blood. The bear had bitten both arms and small of his back and he didn't even know it.

Heads up for archers...be careful in grizzly country with

moose scent on your clothing or near you.

CATHERIN

In mid-February 2015 my son-in-law Brad Risch and I enjoyed a meal at AJ's Old Town Steakhouse and Tavern in Homer. Our server, "Cathrine without an 'e'," regaled us with stories of playing soccer in Kenai and going to college in Bakersfield, returning home, getting married and working in Homer. During the evening Brad asked if she had a favorite Alaskan author and followed it up with, "Have you read any Alaska bear books?" She said she read a red and yellow covered one with a dozen stories in it that scared what bears do in the woods out of her. Although I have a hundred different bear books, I couldn't put a finger on one with a red and yellow cover.

Remembering I had a copy or two of our ***Bear Tales for the Ages*** in our car, I decided to fetch one as a gift for our efficient and fun server. I returned and asked her if she wanted me to personalize it to her or her family. She turned it over and saw the book with the red and yellow cover—my first book with a second cover (which I'd forgotten)—and said, "My dad will be so jealous I'm talking with the author."

KAREN TIMBLIN

Karen Timblin shared with us her "discovery" in Canada and I asked her to write a blurb about it. She is compiling a bunch of stories about their vehicle transporting business and she graciously sent me this piece June 15, 2021…and called at the same time asking me to read it. So, here, again is a blurb showcasing another "stories generated by our books."

Thanks, Karen.

I Think I Recognize That Name!

We usually only have two meals a day...so we are having "linner" at Sasquatch Crossing which is a little over 100 miles west of Charlie Lake in British Columbia. I always like stopping at this little stop as I am a believer in Sasquatch. After we get done eating, Phil goes back to the truck and I am waiting to pay the bill. While waiting, I am browsing through the book rack... Hummmm...I notice a book about "Bears", the author is Larry Kaniut...I think we are transporting a 1930's Model A panel wagon for a person with that name????

This person contacted our company about a year earlier, inquiring about transport to Alaska from Tennessee. Often customers inquire about transport trying to determine whether or not they may wish to purchase a specific vehicle. I never gave it much thought as I just figured it was someone who was just shopping. Then about a year later, a man named "Larry Kaniut" called again requesting transport of this older panel wagon for our enclosed transport. There were several hitches to getting this vehicle—among them, we needed to deliver the funds for him and wait until funds cleared before securing the vehicle. This is not totally uncommon in our business, but after talking the situation out, we came to a resolution/ wire transfer funds and the driver would do his delivery about two days away, come back and retrieve "Mr. Kaniut's" vehicle.

Now I don't know anything about the "Mr. Kaniut" whose panel Ford we have on board, but it struck me that it isn't a very common name--like I've never heard of that last name. As I look at the cover of this book on the rack before me, I read the preface which explains that author Larry Kaniut is from Anchorage, Alaska. Now my curiosity is getting the best of me! I'm dying to ask the Larry Kaniut if, in fact, he is the same as the author of the book at Sasquatch Crossing. My husband Phil spills the beans to Larry's wife, Pam, letting her know what I had found along our route. Yes, in fact, author Larry Kaniut is the same owner of the panel Ford we are transporting from Tennessee. God has placed so many fellow believers in our path! I'm forever grateful! It truly is a "small world"!

MELISSA COOK

I suggested to Melissa that a comment from her for this section might be neat. On December 9, 2021, she responded with the following after I emailed her that I was looking forward to reading her lies.

Larry Kaniut: The Almighty Bear Story Writer

As a tenderfoot in Alaska, I curled up on the couch in the tiny Nelson Lagoon teacherage that I called home to read the ***Alaska Bear Tales*** by Larry Kaniut. Bering Sea waves crashed onto the beach outside my window as the wind howled throughout the evening. I snuggled under a flannel blanket, shivering from the constant feeling of being cold.

Earlier that day, I knew I would be bored with no television reception, and it was the boys' night to play on the family computer. That meant I required my own source of entertainment, at least until the kids' bedtime. That's when my husband and I would fight it out for a seat at our latest, greatest computer – a dinosaur by today's standards, but back in 1995, it was a godsend. Since I won the last computer time battle, I knew I probably needed a book that night. Looking through the school library, a bright red book with a growling bear on the front jumped off the shelf and into my hands.

Alaska Bear Tales kept me glued to its pages every night until I finished it. Looking back, I suspect the bright red color was probably indicative of the bloody stories awaiting me. You don't think that could have been just a coincidence? Probably not.

I was reading this bear tales book because Alaska brown bear prints were all over my front porch, and I was terrified each morning getting into the school Suburban because I couldn't see a thing – not one thing! But I could see the prints in my driveway and on my doorsteps when the sun came up, and they proved we were *not* alone out there.

You would think reading a book about bear attacks would strike fear into my heart, and then I would be stuck in the house, unable or unwilling to exit in the morning to drive to work. I won't lie; I always feared the bears when I couldn't see. However, the ***Alaska Bear Tales*** helped me understand bears and how people ended up victims of attacks. Knowledge is power. By understanding, I had a better grasp of my situation. In the end, I stopped walking around the Suburban to get in; I climbed in the driver's side instead and slid over to the passenger seat. Now that I think about it, maybe I should have driven, and my husband could have walked around the beach side of the vehicle every morning. Ha, ha.

Fast forward 25 years. A tenderfoot no more, I wrote a book about my twenty-year Alaska adventure. As I finished my manuscript, I scanned the bookshelf, searching for a potential endorser. Larry Kaniut's name was all over my shelf. ***Alaska Bear Tales. More Alaska Bear Tales. Cheating Death. Alaska Bear Tales for the Ages.*** Well, that was easy; I penned a letter and mailed it straight away. Then I waited. And waited. And waited. Darn. *Larry isn't interested*, I thought. I moved on and found two other best-selling authors to read and endorse my book.

Weeks before the manuscript went to print, my phone rang. "This is Larry Kaniut. I don't know if you know who I am, but I received a letter from you today and thought I better call since you wrote it a year ago!"

"I **absolutely** know who you are!!" I danced around the

house, smiling ear-to-ear, whispering with my hand over the phone to my husband, "It's Larry Kaniut. The ***Alaska Bear Tales*** author." He nodded in excitement with me.

Larry and I went on to have a lengthy conversation about Alaska, our writing, our teaching, and our books. Two days later, my inbox was overflowing with notes, edits, and several options for endorsements. I still pinch myself when I think about it or see his name on my cover! *His name is on MY cover! Can you believe it?* I still can't!

Today, I call Larry my friend. We send occasional emails back and forth. He has quite the sense of humor and way with words. I can tell through our correspondence that there is never a dull moment when he is around. I have no doubt Mr. Kaniut is beloved by his many students and loads of Alaska fans to boot.

And just for the record, Larry… No lies here. Not one! LOL (re: "I look forward to seeing your lies." – Larry Kaniut in reference to this piece, 12/9/21)

Melissa L. Cook

Author of ***The Call of the Last Frontier:***

The True Story of a Woman's Twenty-Year

Alaska Adventure

TED GORSLINE

Ted contacted me a few years ago for permission to incorporate a few of my stories into his bear book trilogy. I told Ted to "go for it." Next thing I knew he had written not 3 but 9 books titled ***Man-eating Black Bears.*** They are heavily researched, awesome books. I emailed him to see if he'd consent to write something for this section. Ted wrote me a series of emails in late October 2021 and the following is the result.

Dear Larry,

It was your book ***Alaska Bear Tales*** that encouraged me to think there might be a market for bear attack books.

Before I went to university, I quit high school and went to British Guiana, South America, on a bauxite boat, to hunt jaguars. I did not get the chance to shoot any but ended up working as a dog handler on jaguar hunts and also helped to raise several jaguars and many other South American animals, like tapir in captivity. This menagerie attracted the film company of Don Meier Productions to produce ***Wild Kingdom*** advertised by Mutual of Omaha and eventually I ended up working for them as an animal handler.

I left British Guiana on independence day because I thought there was going to be a civil war. In some places things had gotten a bit tense. Although I holed up at sugar plantations and British army posts whenever possible to keep from getting hacked up, I did get a knife slash on one arm.

Back in Canada, I attended the University of Guelph which had a semester system. I attended school for three months and worked for three months to get money to pay school fees. Since most films took from one to five months to make, I attended school, then did some animal handling for a few months.

After graduation I began freelance writing at first for government agencies and eventually I got a newspaper column. It was fun and I met some interesting people. The lady at the desk next to me was actress Lois Maxwell who played Miss Moneypenny in the original James Bond films. She thought Sean Connery made a better Bond than Roger Moore. She said she made peanuts on the films, not more than $200 a film if I remember correctly. I also got to spend a day shooting with the actor Slim Pickens who loved elk hunting.

A lot of the government writing was designed not to tell the truth but rather to bury it...and to make the ministers look as good as possible. One such story involved a huge tank of poisonous chlorine gas that had exploded west of Toronto. If there had been a weather inversion an estimated 350,000 to 450,000 people would have died. The Ministry of Environment was tasked with solving the problem since the government had to appear to be acting to solve the problem. A press release stated a man had been rushed to the scene and was standing by in case of emergency.

After I got a newspaper column, I found the newspaper life of sitting on my butt and typing to be very unhealthy. Just about all of the deadline stressed people I worked with at the ***Toronto Sun*** have died and most died young.

So I longed to get back into the field. Also I detested the managing editor, known as "The Boy Lester."

Since I had already gotten a chance to work at the Nazinga Game Ranch in Burkina Faso, Africa I began working in the field for them. I sold all of their original hunting safaris. They had developed a photo safari business but a Quebec based university study showed that the trophy hunting money I brought in, made the ranch more viable than the photo safaris. Based solely on clients I booked, the ranch made a profit in its very first official year of operation. Unfortunately, the money attracted the attention of the Minister of Tourism so he took the ranch over for his own personal use and I left. Africa had won again.

I went to Tanzania and one of my clients from Burkina Faso loaned me the money to start a hunting safari company. I created Kilombero North Safaris and leased the largest hunting concession in Tanzania, essentially the whole 200-mile-long north side of the Kilombero River. I had a quota of 120 buffalo bulls and 4 lions per year.

Although I did not know it when I went there, man-eating lions were endemic and crocs, hyenas, buffalo and hippos added substantially to the human death toll. I am sure that an absolute minimum of 120 people were killed by wild animals while I was there and believe the real total was two or three times higher. All kinds of people ended up as blood smears in the grass and were not recorded.

I found the environment intoxicating. The only thing that has ever made me tremble with fear was old Simba roaring at me in total darkness from the far side of a 3-inch-thick grass blind that I could stick my fingers through.

Larry Kaniut's bear books, and I have read the first four, brought the experiences of those who met the bear, and paid the price, to the fore, as a kind of counter balance to official government reports where everyone is trying to smooth over troubled waters to save their cash for life in the form of salaries and pensions because that is what is at stake.

You will notice that nowadays whenever there is a bear attack, general interest reporters, always go to government officials to get the party line, and then rush into print with stories carrying headlines about "rare" bear attacks. The word "rare" is now the official government party line everywhere in North America. However I came across one study that said there are 44,000 bear incidents in North America every year. There was no breakdown of what they were but many of people are being dragged out of their tents by the head in campgrounds leading to thousands of nuisance bears, really man-eating bears in training, being shot every year.

My guess is that it is about 2,000 or more attacks a year because that is how many park officials have been recorded as killing in campgrounds alone and in protected parks they only kill dangerous bears.

Larry Kaniut's bear books, to a large extent, were the spark plug that encouraged me to look into the issue. His books are now best selling classics, and he helped me considerably with my Alaska research. In 1963 black bears attacked six people in Alaska and killed or ate three. Larry had them documented.

His books ignited the spark that led me to take a detailed look at the black bear because they are increasing steadily in numbers all across North America and more conflicts are to be expected. The naturalist Ernest Thompson Seton once estimated that the black bear population in North America was 500,000 before the European invasion. Nowadays there are at least 700,000 black bears in Canada, the United States and Mexico and the population is heading for a million

I accumulated so much new material and unpublished material and ideas looking at the issue that I decided to break my books down into nine volumes because modern people seem to have short attention spans and the work in total began approaching the length of Gibbon's ***Rise And Fall Of The Roman Empire.***

Ted

When I'd received copies of Ted's nine books, I sent him a copy of my ***SAFE with Bears***, into which I'd written, "From the Dean of bear book writers to the King of bear book writers."

Rest of the Story

THE REST OF THE STORY

Over the years since our books were published, I've had the good fortune of having participants in those events contact me. One such was from ***Cheating Death*** wherein Mike Harbaugh slammed into and skidded across the slope of Merrill Pass, pockmarked with fuselages of other planes where the pilots weren't prepared to leave the bone yard. Some of the stories in my books were finished...until years later when the following information emerged regarding those "finished" stories.

KEN E. GRIFFIN

I received an email from Ken E. Griffin in June 2005 about his participation in that event. He wrote:

I realize the book has been out for over 10 years but I just read an excerpt regarding the rescue of mike Harbaugh from Merrill Pass in the chapter titled "Jaws of Death."

I was the radio operator onboard the HC-130 aircraft that initially located and then directed the rescue operation on scene. You'll never know how close Mike came to remaining there overnight if not permanently. Snippets of a conversation I overheard over monitored radio frequencies between the civilian aircraft which spotted him and a Flight Service Station he was communicating with clued us in as to his whereabouts which subsequently led to his rescue that evening.

I say it was a close call because we had already sent the various search aircraft home for the day and were ourselves heading back to Elmendorf. We decided to drop a flare in order for Mike to know he had been spotted and that help was on the way.

I radioed the RCC at Elmendorf and requested our needed supplies including fuel because there was no way we were leaving him there for another night. We also requested the launching of the helicopters noted in your story.

We returned to Elmendorf and took flight again as soon as we were provisioned. We caught up with the Jolly's on the way and led them to the location.

Everything else is in the story except our crew had put in a 14 ½ hour flying day but to a man agreed we had a job to do and we did it.

Just another insight into the story. Just file it away.

Thanks for your attention.

Ken Griffin

CYNTHIA DUSEL-BACON

Call me clown, nuisance, panhandler, habituated, menace, killer, man-eater. I could be any of these. Or all of them. I'm your average North American bear and I come in three flavors—black, grizzly or polar. Most of the time I mind my own business, making my living scrounging grub, resting, protecting my cubs, looking over my pecking order shoulder or finding a mate. I'm not interested in people...usually. However every once in a while I rock your world and things get ugly.

While listening to the radio in 1977, I learned about a lady who had been frightfully mauled by a bear. I hoped to acquire the details of the event. Her tale of confrontation and survival is one of the most amazing I've ever heard...so much so that other authors have included it in their books or magazines.

I wrote Cynthia at the Stanford University Medical Center to which she'd been transferred and suggested if she were willing to share her story, that she call me collect. After all, how could a person without arms write?

Imagine my surprise when a short time later I received her cassette taped story and a letter. She had typed her letter with a stylus between her jaws. She was eager to share her story in hopes of sparing others the dilemma similar to hers. And she stated, "I couldn't be more pleased about your efforts to amass all available information about bear maulings in Alaska. I can't think of a greater contribution one could make to educate people about the potential danger of a bear encounter. I believe very strongly in what you are doing."

Cynthia decided that her tape recorded, off-the-cuff, account of her experience needed to be written up as a complete article so she, helped by her father, wrote it up and sent it to me to include in ***Alaska Bear Tales***, which took me five years to research and write.

Subsequently we met on a couple of occasions. The first time our family met her was a couple of years later when I was on my way to commercial fish Bristol Bay...so I missed Cynthia. Our 6-year-old son was most impressed that she could squash a paper cup with her artificial split-hook, which she chose as the most functional replacements for her hands.

We met about five years after when Cyn travelled to Alaska with an assistant and I drove them to Girdwood. I told her that she and her assistant could come to our home for dinner instead of staring at the four walls of the hotel. She agreed; I called my wife and we headed home.

Once inside our house, Cyn told me that her shoulders and neck were sore from wearing her artificial arms and wondered if it would be okay to remove them. I told her that we did not normally allow it but that we would make an exception in her case. Her assistant helped her remove her prosthetic devices and she put on a poncho.

I had some concern that our children might have a negative reaction to a handicapped person, but it was one of our most awesome experiences. My brother-in-law and sister Lester and Laura Lee Smothers were visiting and while Les ate peanuts at the kitchen table, he asked Cynthia if she wanted some. She assented and Les removed peanuts from shells, placed them on a napkin and slid it across the table to her. She bent at the waist and ate the peanuts, much like a cat or dog would do. Amazingly beautiful.

We receive Christmas cards every year from Cyn and Charlie, usually with their son Ian and his wife included. They live very productive lives. In 2017 when Ted Gorsline, former animal handler for Mutual of Omaha's TV show "Wild Kingdom," contacted me about his plans to write three bear books, he requested usage of some of my Alaska stories. He later provided a cover quote for ***SAFE with Bears*** in which he claimed "Larry Kaniut is the dean of bear book writers…" When I realized he was writing not three books but a nine volume set, I sent him his complimentary copy of ***SAFE with Bears*** to Germany, I inscribed it "From the Dean of bear book writers to the King of bear book writers."

I've just finished his volume number nine. On page 24 Ted has a picture of Cynthia Dusel-Bacon which I've never seen. He includes her story from my ***Alaska Bear Tales*** AND Cynthia's comments. From her "How my accident could have been prevented," I've cherry-picked three paragraphs:

…"I believe what would have prevented my accident from happening was to have had a gun and not been alone. Had I been with another person, we might have been more intimidating to the bear or one of us could have been on the radio calling for help while the other tried to scare off the bear…

"My boss had a strong belief that guns were more dangerous than they were helpful, and I was talked out of my original request to carry a gun. I should have insisted and proactively got firearms training. As a result of my accident, the U.S.G.S. subsequently provided firearms and bear-behavior training annually and made a firearm available for anyone working in Alaska.

"I can't say that I would've chosen the exact right moment to shoot the bear, which maintained a 10 foot distance from me prior to attacking, but if I had been trained in bear behavior, I would've recognized the bear's raised hair and chomping teeth as sure signs that the bear was going to attack. It would've been an easy shot."

Ted has done an incredible job 'researching bears and the need for protection against them. His website is Ted-Gorsline.com. I suggest you buy his books.

The day after Thanksgiving 2021 Cynthia responded to my request for an update with the following e-mail:

Summary of post accident for Larry K.

Since my losing my arms to the bear in 1977, I have been able to live the happy and lucky life to which I had aspired as a newlywed. My husband, Charlie, took my lack of arms in stride and saw me as the same woman he married. Being an outstandingly competent husband, who always enjoyed cooking, he took it over full-time, along with grocery shopping, which he also enjoys and looks forward to seeing his cashier friends during his weekly shopping excursions. Being a go-getter myself, I had to get used to being taken care of and have done very well at accepting and enjoying being a "kept woman". Charlie refers to me as "management", which I try to do well. Such duties have been managing our son's care, driving him everywhere before he turned 16, planning vacations, dealing with home improvement projects, etc.

I'm also happy to report that I was able to continue my career as a USGS Research Geologist specializing in the geology and mineral deposit potential of east-central Alaska. Having my husband come with me as an exemplary (overqualified) field assistant made all of this possible. I planned and supervised fieldwork, but my husband was the gun-bearer and sample collector. I've published almost 70 scientific papers and maps, starting out by typing one key at a time with my left hook, then, since 1995 dictating everything with voice recognition software. Because my managers at the USGS gave me a chance to see what I can do using my brain, and with my husband's support in the field, and my own publication record, I was able to be promoted through the years to the top of the Research Geology grade hierarchy. I retired in 2014 and still am writing scientific papers and working with the next generation of geologists working in Alaska as a volunteer (Scientist Emerita).

As far as my hobbies go, losing my arms caused me to have to look elsewhere for my musical passion, since playing the guitar was no longer an option. Instead, I took up playing the chromatic harmonica and learned to play jazz standards, which I have enjoyed since childhood hearing them played by my musical father. After evolving to a modified hands-free harmonica in a neck rack, I was able to join a jazz quintet and play that kind of music for senior groups – even for money! I've regularly attended and occasionally played at the annual international convention of the Society for the Preservation and Advancement of the Harmonica (SPAH) and am the Chair of the

Youth Committee, which gives scholarships for young players to come to the convention. For the past year, I've been taking harmonica lessons on Skype to learn to improvise in jazz – not an easy task, but I'm really enjoying the journey.

I stay in shape through hiking and swimming and have enjoyed backpacking in the High Sierra of California with my husband and son. At 75, we've evolved to staying in mountain cabins and doing day hikes. In addition to geology, all aspects of nature interest me, especially butterflies and birds. Every year on "bear day", August 13, I thank my lucky stars that I've been able to have another year that I almost didn't get to have.

ALLEN LEE PRECUP

I contacted Bob Brown, brown shirt Alaska State Troopers employee (game warden) who steered me to many bear episodes, one of which was the Alan Lee Precup mauling on White Thunder Ridge at Glacier Bay National Monument. Anticipating I'd like pictures for the book, Bob showed me photos of the victim, one a novel covering a severed hand and another the bare leg bone from the hip socket to the bottom of the boot, including a wool sock. I chose NOT to use those photos.

Bob also gave me some sobering information about Ron Cole and his misnomered encounter with a bear.

While visiting one day with my friend and insurance agent Jack Gwaltney, we discussed various stories. It came to my attention that he'd worked with Jay B.L. Reeves, one of the victims in my first book ***Alaska Bear Tales***. In that tragic story I told about Jay's decision to photograph bears. He visited the Izembek National Wildlife office and discussed the need for a firearm; Robert Jones offered him a .357 magnum. Jay did not own a firearm and felt the bears were sated with salmon and of no danger. He hitched a ride to his camp area, set up his tent and ate an evening meal before turning in. During the night a bear showed up at his tent and Jay slipped from his sleeping bag and fled into the night. Scared is putting it mildly. He did not outrun the bear which took him down and proceeded to eat Jay. The next day Frank Snodgrass observed the downed tent and reported to the headquarters. Refuge manager John Sarvis wrote that he felt Jay made two mistakes: 1) he had food in his tent and 2) he placed his tent on a bear trail.

Below Jack commented on the late insurance customer.

Jay B.L. Reeves came into my office, I am guessing in the mid-seventies. He said he was going down to the Alaska Peninsula on one of the bear filming rivers and shoot a bunch of bear pictures. He fancied himself a wildlife photographer.

He wanted to buy a $25,000 life insurance policy. I asked him why, because in those days there had to be an insurable interest between the insured and the beneficiary of the policy being purchased. He said he wanted the policy for his parents. They were to be the beneficiaries of the policy.

As a matter of curiosity, I asked if he was taking a large caliber rifle with him for protection, since he was going to be on bear streams filming their activity. His reply was no, he didn't believe in guns, and besides he had been told by experts, all the bears in that area had plenty of food since he was going to be there during the salmon season and they had plenty to eat. I realized, whatever I may have said at that point would not make any difference, so I said no more about it.

I wrote the application with his parents being the beneficiaries. After I completed the application I asked him for the first month's premium. He said no, he would pay the premium after the policy was issued and he was back in town. I then reminded him if he did not pay the premium with the application, there would be no insurance in force until the policy was issued and the premium had been paid. I reminded him, he would be flying by bush plane, in addition to being close to bears that were having lunch along the rivers.

As he had said before, being close to the bears was not a big deal, but flying in a small aircraft was a big deal, so he paid one month's premium, which in this case put the policy in force at that moment, even though the policy had not yet been issued.

He was a very pleasant fellow and seemed excited to be able to photograph bears while they were fishing along the river. He said he had plenty of food and camping gear, and had been schooled about not leaving food around, near his tent.

As I recall, he said he was going to be gone for a couple of weeks, and then when he got back to town he would stop by and pick up his new policy which would have been issued by them, and show me his new bear pictures.

A couple of weeks came and went, when somebody, I don't remember who, came into my office and asked me if I had insured this same follow. I said "yes," he replied, "Well, he won't be coming back in to see you." He then showed me the article in the newspaper about his death and having been eaten by a bear on the trail near his tent.

As I recall, I later learned after they shot the bear and found human remains in the stomach, the bear was a very old boar, had lost several teeth and could not compete for salmon on the stream, so he naturally killed and ate what he could, and that was a human that had nothing with which to defend himself.

At that point, I called the John Hancock home office and told them what had taken place, and then sent them a copy of the article in the newspaper. By that time the parents had been informed. Of course, they were in shock and devastated. As I recall, they got on a plane and came to the location to see for themselves what had taken place.

The insurance claim was paid to them even though the policy had not been issued. That was because the premium had been paid with the application when it was written.

Larry, this has been a long time ago and as I have gotten older, I realize my memory isn't foolproof. But, this is the general essence of the story. What a shame. In this case, how can one blame the bear?

NORM CARSON

I became friends with Norm Carson of Pelican, Alaska, several years ago. He's a retired Alaska State Trooper. It's a follow up "rest of the story" regarding Alan Lee Precup, a victim in ***Alaska Bear Tales***. Having been one of the searchers for the missing Precup, Norm emailed me this report June 27, 2016.

June 24, 2016

Case Reflection:

Bear Attack and Death of Alan Precup, September 13, 1976 at Glacier Bay National Monument.

Alaska State Trooper Case Report: B76-4081, F/Sgt. Norm Carson and Inv. John Glass.

By: Norm Carson, AST Retired.

It has been nearly 40 years since this incident occurred; it is one of those cases a trooper reflects on throughout his retirement. At the time of this incident I was the Juneau Post Commander working out of our office at three mile Glacier Highway.

The Division of Alaska State Troopers responded to and coordinated all land based search and rescue incidents.

Summary of Events:

9/14/76, Tuesday, Chuck Janda, Chief Ranger, Glacier Bay National Monument, (GBNM), reported a hiker was overdue. The hiker had been dropped off by a GBNM boat at Wolf's Point the previous Friday at noon for a hike up White Thunder Ridge. The hiker was due to be picked up on Monday, 9/13, noon, at the same location; he did not return. Identity of the hiker was not known. AST assistance was not requested; the GBNM Ranger staff would handle the situation. Janda was informed that AST had jurisdiction within the GBNM and if requested would take command and control of the search effort.

Hiker is still overdue.

9/15/76, Wednesday. Janda requested AST assistance identifying hiker through a Master Card transaction receipt. AST confirmed identity as Alan Lee Precup. Precup's vehicle was located at the Juneau Municipal Airport.

A GBNM Ranger flew over White Thunder Ridge in chartered fixed wing aircraft with negative results. A US Coast Guard helicopter attempted to search the area in the afternoon; this was aborted due to weather issues.

Hiker is still overdue.

9/16/76, Thursday. At 10:00 AM a GBNM boat dropped a hiking party of 4 and another party of 2 off at Wolf's Point for a hike up White Thunder Ridge. The hikers were aware of a hiker missing in the area; description of their clothing and gear was noted so that search parties would not mistake them for the hiker.

(2)

9/16/76, Thursday cont'd.

11:30 AM Hikers pitched camp and were eating lunch when an aggressive brown bear approached. The bear tore up the camp and followed the group of hikers around a pond. The hikers confronted the bear with noise, sticks, and rocks. The bear moved off up the White Thunder Ridge trail and the hikers returned to the beach.

4:00 PM. Party of 4 eventually made their way out to a GBNM boat via a dinghy; the other party of 2 returned to get their gear. Radio transmissions were made to alert GBNM staff and searchers of the aggressive bear.

5:30 PM GBMN Ranger Jim Luthy was transported to White Thunder Ridge via USCG helicopter and lowered to Precup's demolished campsite. Luthy spent minutes checking the camp and saw evidence that it had been ravaged by a bear. Luthy was retrieved by the USCG; he was unarmed. The helicopter picked up the other two hikers near Wolf Point on the route back to GBNM headquarters at Bartlett Cove.

Shortly after Luthy's return to Bartlett Cove, two Rangers hiked the White Thunder Ridge Trail and as Precup's camp came in view, they were confronted by a very aggressive brown bear. The Rangers discouraged the bear with shouting and rock throwing; they were unarmed.

6:00 PM time approximate. Chief Ranger Janda requested AST search and rescue assistance. Janda told F/Sgt. Carson that any troopers traveling to GBNM are to be unarmed as it is against Monument policy for anyone to be armed within GBNM. F/Sgt. Carson reminded Janda that GBNM is within the State of Alaska and troopers have jurisdiction within Monument boundaries; they will be armed.

Inv. John Glass is dispatched to Bartlett Cove; he carried his duty revolver as well as a .350 magnum rifle. Inv. Glass interviewed Luthy and the party of 4 hikers. F/Sgt. Carson arranged for Livingston Helicopters to transport him to Bartlett Cove the next morning. It was too late in the day with limited daylight to begin a search.

Precup is still missing.

9/17/76, Friday.

8:30 AM approximate. F/Sgt Carson arrived at Bartlett Cove via helicopter, (armed with duty revolver and carrying a .458 mag rifle). After a briefing by Inv Glass, a search by helicopter of the Precup campsite was organized. Janda assigned Ranger Luthy to accompany Troopers Carson and Glass. It worth noting that Luthy is now armed with a .35 Remington rifle; generally considered a deer rifle.

(3)

9:30 AM.

Trooper search party landed at Precup campsite. Inv. Glass and Ranger Luthy searched downhill from the campsite. F/Sgt. Carson tracked uphill from the campsite and within about 60 yards found the skeletal remains of Alan Precup. All flesh had been consumed, other than the feet, (they were protected by hiking boots). Inv. Glass took photos of the scene. Precup's remains and personal effects were secured and taken to Juneau.

1:00 PM. Trooper activities were concluded at GBNM.

Weather at Gustavus 1976:

Date	Max temp	Low Temp	Events	Precip	Dew Point
9/10	55	48	fog	0	49
9/11	57	48	----	0	48
9/12	57	45	fog	0	45
9/13	50	46	fog/rain	0	47

Having looked at the weather for that period, my guess is that Precup was killed most likely on the 12th or 13th. The bear could have finished feeding on him by the 16th and then gone looking for another source of food. The hiking party was dropped off at Wolf's Pt at about 10 AM on 9/16 and within an hour were confronted by the bear. I do not think the bear would have left Precup until he was fairly well consumed.

Conclusion and opinion:

• It is likely that Precup was killed by the bear on the late afternoon of 9/12 or 13 at White Thunder Ridge.

• The GBNM acted in a very unwise manner in allowing the two parties of hikers off at Wolf's Point on 9/16 with a hiker still missing.

• This incident occurred before the advent of portable VHF radios; communications were extremely limited by hikers, GBMN staff, and law enforcement.

• This incident occurred prior to the development of bear spray.

(4)

• There was no indication that hikers were advised how to discourage aggressive bears.

• The GBNM policy prohibiting firearms within the Monument was ridiculous; this is bear country.

• In 1969 State Troopers Norm Carson and Tom Zaruba responded to the sinking of the F/V "Bull Moose" and worked out of the Glacier Bay Lodge at Bartlett Cove for several days. Both Troopers were in uniform and armed. Why did Chief Ranger Janda take it upon himself to insist that State Troopers be unarmed within the GBNM in 1976?

• The attempt by Chief Ranger Janda to prevent Troopers Carson and Glass from responding to an obvious bear attack without firearms was foolish at best.

• Had the Alaska State Troopers taken command of the search and rescue on 9/14 it is likely that Precup would have been recovered within 24 hours; he was most likely already deceased.

• There remains the possibility the bear in question, was a black bear and not a brown bear.

RON COLE

I really wanted the Ron Cole story for ***Alaska Bear Tales*** and spent two years trying to locate him. At one point I told my game warden friend Bob Brown my dilemma. He told me that Ron was a drug dealer and that the Troopers had found a dozen 55 gallon drums of dried marijuana on his boat in Whittier. They'd opened one and left a note: "We've got you now. AST." Bob said, "We busted him a while back for marijuana and three raw polar bear hides in his garage." That had to be around 1977. I blew it off and continued my search.

Tom Jolley, a Service High student dating my niece, moved into our neighborhood and told me I should interview his neighbor. I asked Tom his name but Tom didn't know.

Some time between 1978 and 1980 our dentist neighbor, Wayne Davis, told me I should get Ron Cole's story... "he's a patient of mine." Assuming the doctor-patient privacy I asked Wayne to have Ron call me. He did. He was Tom Jolley's neighbor.

We arranged a time to meet and I dragged a Dimond High reel-to-reel tape recorder to Ron's and met Darcy who was going to a movie with a girlfriend. Ron wanted to show me his house. I thought that something a woman would do—*wouldn't a man show off his new 4-wheeler, boat, garage, rifle? Hmmmm.*

First up was his master bedroom. Really? Resting on a night stand beside his bed was a sawed off shotgun… "for protection against burglars." I'm thinking *that's illegal unless he has paid to have it licensed.* Across the room was a stalk about two feet long which Ron informed me was puna bud marijuana from Hawaii. Next was a visit to the basement, wall to wall marijuana plants and grow lights. *Hmmm…it's looking like Bob Brown was right.*

Next stop cathedral ceilinged living room and couch. Ron informed me he needed a joint for medicinal reasons and asked if it were okay. "It's your house." So he trotted back to the couch with a container from which he drew and lit a joint. Before long it was "I need a second one." Okay.

Then there was the three-eighths-inch circle in the ceiling which Ron informed me was "a bullet hole, compliments of the Mexican mafia who ripped me off of $100,000 cash…but it's okay." It was looking more and more like my interview should be conducted at the local constabulary.

I started putting two and two together and realized *this is the guy the Troopers chased all over Chitina a couple years back, the survivalist.* After five hours of chit-chat, Ron told me his wife was writing a book about him. I suggested I'd drop off an outline addressing his medical costs, the pain of the experience and whatever he and Darci could detail. It was looonnng past time to make my departure. Never did get the interview…nor the medical details should he change his mind.*

About the time I re-wrote Ron's story from ***Alaska Magazine***, I received a letter dated December 1977, from one of his rescuers. Captain James Woolworth wrote "Lake Creek

Air Rescue" which I offer here...as a nice touch of the rest of the story.

We were nearing the end of a two hour training flight at Elmendorf A.F.B. when we were notified by the Rescue Coordination Center of a bear mauling at Lake Creek. We had an hour and one half of fuel left...enough to fly to Lake Creek and back (providing we didn't have to search when we got there). We didn't know how bad the mauling was but we had to assume the worst so we picked up a flight surgeon at the Elmendorf Hospital Helipad and proceeded direct without refueling.

We landed on a sand bar at Lake Creek Lodge where Dulcina Cole boarded our aircraft to direct us upstream to Ron's cabin. She was amazingly well composed considering what she had just been through. She had run miles through the woods to reach the lodge where she could radio Anchorage. We flew up Lake Creek and eventually located the cabin on top of a hill surrounded by tall trees. We landed in the only available spot, a rock bar on the creek, and shut down to conserve fuel.

Our flight surgeon, along with TSgt. Ewton, TSgt. Mulhall and Dulcina then made their way across the creek and up to the cabin with medical equipment and a stokes litter. It was about 30 minutes before TSgt. Ewton came back and said Cole was in bad shape and the doctor didn't want to chance bringing him down the steep embankment in the litter.

We decided on a rescue hoist recovery and a few minutes later we were in a hover over the trees near the cabin. We made several attempts to lift Cole off the ground but the litter would start spinning and a blanket protecting Cole's severely lacerated face kept blowing off and exposing Cole to the sever force of our rotor downwash. The litter eventually stabilized and with Cole's face protected we hoisted him into the helicopter. We then recovered the rest of our crew and Dulcina and returned to

Anchorage.

When I first saw Cole laying in the litter in the back of the helicopter, I was concerned for his life. He was covered with blankets with only his head exposed. His facial features were indistinguishable because of dried blood from the massive amount of bleeding. It appeared as if he had lost one of his eyes and the bridge of his nose. A large patch of torn flesh concealed one eye. Our flight surgeon assured us that his condition was stable and he would eventually recover.

Since that mission I have had one other mission involving a bear mauling. We recovered the body of a man who was killed when he was struck once in the head by a wounded black bear. Ron Cole had obviously taken more than one blow during his encounter and he survived.

I talked with Ron several months after the incident during his recovery and he confided that while he was laying at his cabin before our chopper arrived, he had every intention of shooting himself but due to severe shock he couldn't move a muscle to reach his rifle.

To this day I continue to be in awe of the devastating force of the animal.

Sincerely, James Woolworth

The P.S. came a couple of years later in the form of newspaper articles announcing the death of a couple off De Armoun Road on 147th…at the Cole residence. *Say, what?!*

Yep. In October 1981, local fish wrappers addressed the crime at length as details became available: "Man woman found dead in house" and "Couple described as drug dealers found shot to death." Ron, 45, and Darcelle, 25, were well established in the Alaska drug scene. (And little innocent Ol' Larry mistakenly visited and attempted to interview Ron!)

Turns out Bob Brown was *waayyy* right. Ron had a criminal record, the law having encountered him earlier in his life.

Investigation revealed that Ron was a commercial fisherman and Darci was employed at a real estate agency. When his brother and step-father went to the Cole residence after 8 PM on Thursday, they found the deceased. People had seen the Cole's as recently as Monday. Lieutenant John Lucking reported participating in the 1977 raid which revealed marijuana and polar bear hides; he kicked in the front door, got shot at and said (Cole) "was a bad Jose...not somebody you wanted to play with." During that raid officers found five fifty- gallon drums of marijuana and ten empty drums and speculated Cole's were frequent-large-scale marijuana smugglers. That caper resulted in a suspended one year sentence for Darci and a $15,000 fine for Ron.

Fast forward to 1981. During the investigation of the deaths of Ron and Darci law enforcement officials discovered among other things more than half ton of marijuana (largest in state history), 11 pounds of cocaine, hashish, Quaaludes and a bag full of some $17,00 in cashola in the home. And the spiral notebook. It listed twenty-eight customer names and amounts of money owed for drugs.

It appeared that Cole owed $299,000 to his suppliers (source being Miami, California or South America). The coke had a street value of $730,000

Seems one of Cole's "salesmen" did the deed. One of the names arousing investigators' interest was Michael T. Smith. They sought, found and questioned him about his involvement, never believing he'd fess up to the crime. He gunned down the couple because he owed Ron $18,500. Ron's drug source threatened him for payment and he pressured Smith to come up with the dough he owed as a dealer. In the end Smith was sentenced to 110 years, eligible for parole in 2016.

The story in ***Alaska Bear Tales*** is one I re-wrote from Ron's ***Alaska Magazine*** version...where Ron interrupted a boar and sow brown bear in the mating ritual. Not. I've heard a few stories from those in the know that Ron was actually trying to scare the pair from his marijuana patch on Lake Creek when they responded to his efforts. Michael Smith stated (in "What ever happened to" below,) Cole "survived a 'battle with two grizzly bears who had invaded his marijuana patch.'"

*__MEDICAL ASPECTS CHAPTER__—the outline I'd hoped Ron would address

I. Physical damage, repair, cost

A. Damage—exactly what damage was incurred? Ate off half face? Ear? Eye ripped out? Back damage? Legs? Muscles torn loose?

B. Repair (doctors?—names, number)

How many major operations

Plastic surgery—length...pain...extent

How often into hospital/bandages, etc.

How long in hospital

What medical attention did you receive (on way to hospital, while there)?

C. Cost per operations, medicine, hospital

Losses—cabin?

Physical losses (% of eye sight lost, strength/stamina, etc.)

II. Recovery—How much pain still have? (physical, mental) Bitterness?

Actual attack—what happened? Any idea of time it took? How far from cabin how you got to cabin (crawling/feeling for "trail"). Darci's help, run, your condition—lack of clothes, etc.

PEOPLES' THOUGHTS CHAPTER

I. Darci's thoughts while running for help, etc.

II. Ron's thoughts while being mauled (did you say/ask God to make it quick?), how did you feel about your chances for escape/survival, though while Darci was gone, while flying to hospital, while recuperating.

Newspaper articles:

- October 2, 1981, Steve Hansen, ***Anchorage Times***, "Man, woman found dead in house.
- Subsequently, Steve Hansen, "Troopers say couple was murdered."
- Subsequently, Andy Ryan, ***Anchorage Daily News***, "Troopers request help in murder."
- Subsequently, Maureen Blewett, "Cole death investigation continues."
- Subsequently, Andy Ryan, "Couple described as drug dealers found shot to death." Subsequently, Sheila Toomey, ***Anchorage Daily News***, "Murder victims were wheelers, dealers in drugs."
- October, 13, 1981, Sheila Toomey, ***Anchorage Daily News***, "Murder confession reported."

- June 28, 1982, Sheila Toomey, ***Anchorage Daily News***, A-1 and A-2, "Coming clean."
- May 17, 1986, ***Anchorage Times***, Whatever happened to, "Survivors of bear attack murdered in drug deal."

Michael Smith appeal (from internet april 7, 2021)

U.S. Court of Appeals for the Ninth Circuit - 860 F.2d 1528 (9th Cir. 1988)

Argued and Submitted Feb. 1, 1988. Decided Nov. 14, 1988

Peggy A. Roston, Bankston, McCollum & Fossey, Anchorage, Alaska, for petitioner-appellant.

W.H. Hawley, Asst. Atty. Gen., Office of Special Prosecutions and Appeals, Anchorage, Alaska, for respondent-appellee.

Appeal from the United States District Court for the District of Alaska.

Before BROWNING, NORRIS and O'SCANNLAIN, Circuit Judges.

JAMES R. BROWNING, Circuit Judge:

Smith was convicted in the Superior Court of the State of Alaska for the murder of Ron and Darcelle Cole. He appealed to the Alaska Court of Appeals asserting, among other claims, that the Superior Court failed, in violation of rules established in Miranda v. Arizona, 384 U.S. 436, 86 S. Ct. 1602, 16 L. Ed. 2d 694 (1966), to suppress a confession obtained in the absence of counsel through in-custody, police-initiated interrogation after Smith had requested an attorney. The Alaska Court of Appeals affirmed; the Supreme Court of Alaska denied review. The United States District Court for the District of Alaska dismissed Smith's petition for habeas corpus. This appeal followed.

* The governing law is clear. Under Miranda a person in

custody must be informed prior to interrogation that he has a right to remain silent and to have a lawyer present. Miranda v. Arizona, 384 U.S. at 479, 86 S. Ct. at 1630. If he requests counsel, interrogation must cease until an attorney is available. Id. at 474, 86 S. Ct. at 1628. Not only must all questioning stop when a suspect expresses his desire for counsel, but questioning can be resumed without a lawyer only if the suspect himself initiates further communication--waiver cannot be found from a suspect's continued response to questions, even if he is again advised of his rights. Edwards v. Arizona, 451 U.S. 477, 484-85, 101 S. Ct. 1880, 1884-85, 68 L. Ed. 2d 378 (1981).

Requests for counsel are to be given broad effect even when less than all-inclusive. Connecticut v. Barrett, 479 U.S. 523, 107 S. Ct. 828, 832, 93 L. Ed. 2d 920 (1987). A suspect's responses to further questioning cannot be used to cast doubt upon the adequacy of his initial request. Smith v. Illinois, 469 U.S. 91, 97-99, 105 S. Ct. 490, 493-94, 83 L. Ed. 2d 488 (1984) (per curiam). When the initial request is ambiguous or equivocal, all questioning must cease, except inquiry strictly limited to clarifying the request. United States v. Fouche, 776 F.2d 1398, 1405 (9th Cir. 1985), after remand, 833 F.2d 1284, 1287 (1987); United States v. Nordling, 804 F.2d 1466, 1470 (9th Cir. 1986).

The facts are undisputed. Smith was arrested for possession of cocaine and questioned by state troopers. The troopers advised Smith of his Miranda rights. Smith waived them. He discussed the drug charges with the troopers for approximately an hour, admitting he had been distributing cocaine, Ron Cole was his supplier, he owed Cole $15,000, and Cole maintained a list of persons who owed him for cocaine, one of whom was Smith. The trooper asked Smith if he shot Cole. Smith denied it. The trooper pressed the point. Smith's initial request for counsel followed:

Smith: Can I talk to a lawyer? At this point, I think maybe

you're looking at me as a suspect, and I should talk to a lawyer. Are you looking at me as a suspect?

Trooper: Well, it ... it wouldn't be fair to you to say that we weren't Mike.

2nd Trooper: Yeah.

Smith: Because if you are, it's ... it's a serious charge and I think I should have counsel, if that's where ... what you're ... where you're coming from, just tell me if you are.

The troopers reminded Smith he himself had pointed out that anyone in Cole's list of debtors who owed him money for drugs "would certainly have reason enough to kill him," to which Smith responded, "Yeah. I admitted my name is probably in it." The troopers then said:

[L]et's face it, you're a person who dealt with Ron Cole, and you're a person who owed him a lot of money.

The troopers added that if Smith still did not regard himself as a suspect:

[W]e have no choice but to say well, he's ... he's told us everything about what the suspect should look like, and we're sitting here saying, well you're ... you're right, we think that's probably what the suspect looks like too.

Smith responded, "Yeah," after which the trooper again repeated the evidence against Smith:

Okay. And if you for one minute you think that we don't think the suspect is someone who is friends with him, someone who dealt with dope and someone who was in debt to him, then absolutely, you're correct.

Smith reacted by pointing out that others were equally suspect:

I know, but I'm saying there's probably a ... at least a dozen people like me that have known him for years and in the same position. They owe him money. They're friends [ ] in the same position as I am.

The troopers responded by reminding Smith he had been advised of his right to counsel and if he wanted counsel he should not hesitate to get one, but if " [y]ou want to talk to us about Ron Cole's dealings, you want to talk about the murder and suspects, anybody, will talk with you."

Smith then made his second statement regarding representation by counsel, saying: "I don't know if I need one or not. That's why I'm trying to make my mind up, if I need to go that route for myself, you know."

A trooper responded with still another recitation of the circumstances connecting Smith with the murder:

Alright ... Well, you ... you heard what ... you heard what I said. I ... you yourself say anybody that would be in that notebook could be ... could be logical suspect, and you certainly agree, at least with our line of reasoning, in picturing the kind of person we have as a suspect, an associate, somebody that dealt dope and somebody that's in [the] notebook and in debt up to his ass.

This part of the interview concluded:

SMITH: Um'hum.

TROOPER: Now, Mike, you've sit here for the last hour or so and we've ... we've talked about your background; you've been pretty open and honest at least what we know about you, okay.

SMITH: Um'hum.

TROOPER: Ah, in regards with your dealings with Ron ...

At this point, the troopers shut off the tape recorder for approximately twenty-one minutes to "get some coffee." While the tape was off, Smith confessed to the murders. The troopers then turned the recorder back on, and Smith repeated his confession.

MAJOR KENNETH D. BARKER, USAF

I received a letter dated 24 May 1977, from Major Barker which I'm including below. He alludes to mauled victims for whom I'd searched to include in my first book.

Dear Larry,

After researching records at the Alaskan Air Command's Rescue Coordination Center at Elmendorf AFB, we were able to find information on three of the bear maulings mentioned in your letter.

On 8 September 1975, the Alaska State Troopers at Palmer notified the RCC that a Mr. Forrest Roberts had been mauled by a black bear 15 miles northwest of Anchorage. The report was made by a hunting companion, Mr. McCracken. An Air Force HH-3E helicopter from the 5040th Helicopter Squadron at Elmendorf was sent to the scene, where Mr. Roberts was found to be dead. The 5040th is now part of Elmendorf's 71st Aerospace Rescue and Recovery Squadron. We do not know who the crew members were on that flight, but chances are they probably are no longer in Alaska.

On 18 September 1975, a bush radio operator notified the RCC that Maj. William Carlock (of the 172nd Infantry Brigade at Ft. Richardson) had been severely mauled while hunting in the Talkeetna Mountains 100 miles northeast of Anchorage. The Alaska State Troopers requested assistance, but severe weather in Anchorage prevented the launching of aircraft.

Mr. Don Deering, a Eureka Civil Air Patrol pilot, was scrambled along with Peter Davidson, a CAP pilot from Gulkana. Mr. Deering picked up the victim and took him to the Glennallen

Hospital. He was later taken to the Elmendorf Hospital by a relay of military and civilian ambulances. Mr. Dering, who was credited with saving Major Carlock's life, is still in Eureka as far as the RCC knows.

The bear mauling of Ron Cole was earlier that same summer. Attached is a clipping from our base newspaper, the ***Sourdough Sentinel***, that gives details about that rescue. All of the crew members on that rescue have left Alaska.

We could not find any information about Ray Hose or Roger McGregor, who you indicated were mauled in 1975. There are no records going back to 1949, when Knute Peterson was mauled.

I am sorry that we could not find out any more specifics, but if I can be of further help, please contact me again. Good luck with your work.

Sincerely,

Kenneth D. Barker, Major, USAF

Chief of Information

Mat-Su Valley Hospital

The Mat-Su miracle is one that folks need to hear about. A few years ago I saw a horrific image on the Internet. It was so ghastly I shuddered at its starkness. I didn't want to see it. But I did. There was what appeared to be a man in cammo coveralls in the snow. Where his head should have been was a discombobulated mass of red. A faceless, mangled man. I learned a few months later the man's name was Glenn Bohn.

Not the Glenn Bohn I know? Yes.

Not long after, Glenn invited my wife and me to his home for dinner. I wasn't ready for that. I didn't want to see some scar-faced man. But we drove to their home.

Glenn met us at the door. When it opened, I was shocked. There stood the Glenn I remembered. Could not tell he'd been mauled. He looked great.

Glenn told us about his journey and afterwards we visited, he showed us the bear skull, took some pictures and we left. I was amazed at the incredible work his doctor did to restore his face to the old Glenn. I told Glenn and Lorraine I'd like to include his medical aspect in this book. He agreed and told his story.

Our plan was to meet Dr. Dean at her office October 11, 2021. We would visit, see if she'd consent to providing her part in the miracle and go to lunch. Just off the phone with Glenn who confirmed our meeting.

Turns out Glenn and Lorraine also invited us to their house November 1, 2021, to help celebrate Dr. Dean's retirement.

In the corner of the living room stood a life-sized mount

of a beautiful, almost black grizzly bear. Although its forelegs pointed somewhat forward, 4-inch hay hook claws festooning its paws, it had a look of peacefulness upon its face. However the amazing 8-foot bear posed a serious threat when Glenn faced him.

This mountain grizzly messed with the wrong man. I don't know if it was the water or the air or maybe the milk Glenn grew up drinking from the dairy cows he milked, but whatever it was, this Colorado man endured multiple physical injuries over the years, including a motorcycle mirror imbedded in his skull, multiple fractures including both collar bones broken and much more. This grizzly should have never messed with Glenn Bohn.

Glenn and his son showed us the empty .454 Casul brass from the event and we noticed the missing 3x5-inch portion at the top of skull. I told Glenn of all those I've interviewed, I couldn't imagine being in a bear's mouth. He quickly responded with a smile, "I can."

I asked him if he'd care to go into detail since so many people want to be friends with Mr. Bear. He said, "I prayed. I called for my son. Shouted he's killing me."

Dr. Sue Dean sent me her version of Glenn's brawniness in November 2021...and in her words she said:

I met Glenn Bohn on April 15, 2016. Mr. Bohn and I would likely never have crossed paths in our usual coming and going. He was a hunting guide, and I am not a hunter. I am a surgeon, and he prefers to avoid doctors. Yet, on that fateful day, God saw fit to introduce us.

I received a phone call from the Mat-Su Regional Medical Center physician covering that afternoon asking me if I was readily available because a bear mauling victim was on his way to the hospital. I assured her that I was, and got my camera ready. I called the OR to let them know that I would most likely need a room. Not even 10 minutes later the ER physician called me back, and there was panic in her voice. I immediately went to the Emergency Department to see what was up.

There sat Mr. Bohn, fully conscious, and able to speak. His face and scalp were wrapped in blood soaked bandages, as were his hands. There was a flurry of activity around his bedside comprised of nurses, radiology technicians, and phlebotomists. I walked to his bedside, and introduced myself. "Mr. Bohn, I'm Dr. Dean from plastic surgery. I'm the one that's going to put your face back on."

Glenn Bohn is unlike any other trauma patient I have met. Far from fearful, he was taking charge of his situation. He requested that I sew his face back on (and it was ripped from his facial skeleton) under just local anesthetic in the emergency room. I assured him that I was not that skilled, and his repair would require general anesthesia and an operating room. This negotiation went back and forth until the acceptable terms of his care were agreed upon:

I would not give him blood products.

He would accept a dose of antibiotics pre-operatively, but not afterwards.

He would accept the use of general anesthesia, but no sedating medications including narcotics post-operatively.

He would agree to stay in the hospital after his repair to allow me to maintain close surveillance of his tissue for any evidence of necrosis or a rapidly progressing infection.

When I told the OR team about the terms of the "contract" with this exceptional patient, they were understandably stunned. We were all about to learn that Mr. Bohn is no ordinary man.

The bear had managed to get Mr. Bohn's head in its mouth, and Mr. Bohn had some recollection of being told by "old-times" that bears do not like to have their tongues manipulated. With that thought in mind, he reached into the bear's mouth to pull on the tongue. (Years later he says that he would not recommend this maneuver.) This tongue pull resulted in severe damage to both of Mr. Bohn's hands. The facial injury included complete disruption of his nose, an injury to his left eye that eventually resulted in loss of vision in the eye, and a complete denuding of the right side of his scalp and face from the skeletal support of the skull.

I had the good fortune to have the help of a full team that included Dr. Chuck Lee from anesthesia, Dr. Tucker Drury from orthopedics, Dr. Evan Wolf from ophthalmology, and Dr. Elliott Gagnon, my colleague in plastic surgery. There are times when there are no turf wars, no grousing about late hours, and everyone is on the same team. This was one of those times.

To everyone's amazement, Mr. Bohn did well. Without blood. Without additional antibiotic. Without narcotic pain medication. He was discharged from the hospital on his 5th post-operative day and promptly went about living his life. Living it not with bitterness over what he had endured and lost, but with true joy and with gratitude for what had been saved and what he was able to do.

Several months after his repair when he was in for a routine post-op visit I mentioned to him that several people involved in his initial arrival to the emergency department had been somewhat traumatized by the nature of his injuries. I asked if he might be willing to go to the department to tell people that he was doing well and to show them that he looked great. He readily agreed and said, "Let's go now!" So we did.

Arriving in the emergency department with the legendary

"Bearman" was akin to showing up with Elvis. People flocked to him, and there was a definite energy and lightness to his arrival that was palpable. He was gracious, thanked the staff for helping him on that fateful night, and shook any hands that were offered, proudly displaying his healed wrists, now slightly crooked.

He has since volunteered at a bear safety class to demonstrate what could occur if one got on the wrong side of a bear.

He's been a constant source of comedy in the office, arriving to each visit with a T-shirt that references bear attacks. (My personal favorite is the one with a man flipping 2 birds at a bear standing on hind legs.) He has gifted me with a bear skull, because what girl doesn't need a bear skull on her shelf? But mostly, he has gifted me with gratitude and a true sense of the divine.

There is something otherworldly about Mr. Bohn and his family. They travel throughout life with grace, with a true relationship with God, and with a solid faith that He is involved in our lives on a daily basis. If I was able to give Mr. Bohn the gift of my surgical skills, he has given me this gift. He has touched us all at the hospital, and we travel with his gratitude and his faith in our hearts. I consider it a true blessing to count Mr. Bohn and his family among my friends. They have given me far more than I could ever have given them, and certainly more than I deserve. I feel a true sense of divine intervention in our meeting.

Al Thompson

One of the most courageous and remarkable stories involving people mugged by bears is that of Al and Joyce Thompson. I'd heard about their event and contacted them in the winter of 1975 for ***Alaska Bear Tales***—I desperately wanted their story. Before I knew it, Al was at our house. When he came through our front door, I thought "this guy couldn't have been mauled by a bear." But when he removed his Alaska State Trooper beaver hat and I observed the scar tissue on his forehead, I had to disagree with my first impression. Al kindly handed me his story enclosed in a Manila envelope with ***Reader's Digest*** printed on it. This is the story Joyce wrote for the Digest but they rejected.

Al's physical appearance belied his mauling until he took off his Alaska State Trooper beaver cap...*oh, yeh...that scar tissue on his forehead is for real. He's been mauled.*

A few months later I received a long distance call from Henry Hurt of ***Reader's Digest***. Small talk continued for several minutes when he finally admitted he needed a good bear story. I told him I'd promised the contributors I'd help them make money, if there were any to be made, by putting them in contact with magazines. I told him I'd give him five names and contact information and he could take it from there.

Wasn't too long later when I received another call from Henry allowing he was at Loussac Library in Anchorage and couldn't find anything, or, at least, much about bear mauling victims. I suggested he call Al and Joyce and drive to Sterling to express his needs. Before he signed off he said he would and invited Pam and me to dinner upon his return. I thanked him and told him I was too busy finishing our home addition and ***Alaska Bear Tales***.

After I hung up, I told Pam I was pretty foolish, after all, how often does an editor with a major magazine call and invite you to dinner? I told her if he called back maybe we could invite him to our home since he lives out of a suitcase and eats out all the time.

And he did call again. Within a few days Henry called and we invited him to our home for a delightful visit. Pam prepared Cornish game hens (Later he sent a copy of a book he'd worked on about Lee Harvey Oswald).

Henry explained he'd visited with the Thompsons and gotten their story. It came out in July of 1979 and took a distant second place to the original Joyce had submitted. ***Reader's Digest*** could have saved time and money had they accepted Joyce's submission. I thought it was weird that a major magazine would spend the time and money to send an editor to get a story that they'd rejected, especially since it wasn't on par with the original.

After Al Thompson gave me the folder with his and Joyce's story, he sent me a note which follows:

1. Hazards I've experienced

Fell off 30 foot buildings, run over by farm tractors, 50 knot winds and 40 foot seas in 38 foot patrol boat on Cordova bar, eaten by bear and had poachers draw guns on me. Enough excitement for 1 day

2. Feel I've lost 1/3 of stamina, wounds give some problems but Dr. did remarkable job on me. My oil was a little low on the

dip stick and I was starting to knock but they gave a good tune up and I'm doing OK now.

3. Have no different outlook on outdoors. No nightmares after first few weeks. Feel driving Turnagain Arm is more dangerous than bears (stretch of highway just southeast of Anchorage).

4. Dr. that did most of work was Dr. Joe Sangster of Soldotna Hospital. He is a surgeon—not only a good Dr. but is also a friend—a fine man and a really good outdoorsman.

5. Joyce no doubt saved my life by her quick action—she had remarkable courage like when the year we lived in the edge of Mentasta Mountains and had many bear encounters. One night I was bluffing a bear off that was standing on its hind legs 10-15 feet away by shooting past its ear with my handgun as I didn't want to hit it. I turned around and there stood Joyce in the rain and darkness in her underwear with a rifle on the bear.

She has taken bear, moose, caribou, sheep with gun and deer with a bow.

We live in our cabin on the Kanai River and every day is a good one.

Lee Hagmeier

It was a marvelous experience having Lee Hagmeier visit my literature of the North class at Dimond in 1979. He showed up with his 4 key typewriter and regaled the students about his mauling and recovery. He explained a blind person had heightened senses that allowed him to "see" things sighted people miss, such as an alley way or an empty parking spot along the street. He explained a blind person came to understand such voids.

He also told us he married Christy, who is deaf. They have a communication system where he hears the phone ringing and stamps on the floor...she feels the vibrations and answers the phone.

Don Chaffin

The news media vilified Don for slapping a window through which a polar bear peered. Is that really what happened?

Polar Bear Crashes Radar Station, Mauls Worker

ROBIN MACKEY HILL December 1, 1993

ANCHORAGE, Alaska (AP)

Donald Chaffin was relaxing in front of the television at a remote Air Force radar station when a visitor peeked in the window.

A polar bear, standing 8 feet tall, was peering inside with its nose and paws pressed up against the glass. Chaffin tried to shoo it away, swatting at the pane with a rolled up newspaper or magazine.

It was a mistake.

The bear ducked, then crashed through the window about seven feet above the ground. As Chaffin and a co-worker fumbled with a jammed door, the immense animal attacked, mauling Chaffin's face, neck and chest before another man shot it to death.

"Everything that moves is food to a polar bear," station manager Tom Loddy said Wednesday.

Chaffin, 55, a civilian mechanic from Wasilla, was in serious condition Wednesday at an Anchorage hospital. His injuries from the Tuesday evening attack included lacerations and a collapsed lung.

The bear was shot by Alex Polakoff, one of Chaffin's five co-workers at the Alaska Long Range Radar System site at Olitok Point, about 30 miles northwest of Prudhoe Bay.

"There was no way to protect Don," said Leddy. "He was just brutally attacked. (The bear) was just doing what bears do. ... It was just fortunate Alex had a gun."

Leddy, who didn't see the attack, said workers told him Chaffin and another man were relaxing in the lounge when the bear appeared at the window.

When it broke inside and attacked, one worker tried to distract the bear by spraying it with a fire extinguisher while Polakoff got his gun, which he kept for protection while working outdoors.

U.S. Fish and Wildlife Service spokesman Bruce Batten said a bear had been spotted recently in the area, apparently attracted to the radar site by whale meat stored nearby by native hunters.

Leddy said Wednesday he had been concerned the meat would attract bears and had been trying Tuesday to get it removed

Truth be known.

I phoned Don Chaffin shortly after his episode with Mr. Polar Bear. He told me that his

case was being litigated. I thanked him, thinking to contact him later. Not long after that his attorney called me, requesting I research for the details and wondered about my "rates." I told him I had no idea about my rates and he asked me if I'd work for $100 an hour. I told him he could hire a high school kid for five bucks an hour and achieve the same results. No, he wanted me. So I began the research.

I spent 110 hours contacting polar experts and researching the relevant information and presenting it to Don's attorney. Part of my research included information from Don, which contrasts sharply with the media accounts.

The long and short of it was that the contractor working for the government built that building on pilings ten feet off the ground...then promptly filled in the space between the ground and the bottom of the building with gravel...effectively giving Mr. Bear an opportune moment to view his meals beyond the window—which appeared no more than vertical ice—then select his entre and breach the "ice" to obtain it.

The building was built on a polar bear migration route.

Because it had deficient locks, bears had previously entered the building.

The natives stored whale meat about 300 yards from the building which was some comfort for the hungry bears.

Men were required to go into the dark to check things like weather in a building some 200 yards away...unarmed, of course.

The camp was equipped with a firearms locker which necessitated gymnastic procedures and about two minutes to open. Two men had keys to the locker—one man who was asleep—and Don Chaffin. Don't think the bear knew the signal for time out...so we can fetch the locker key.

Don told me that he'd been working a crossword puzzle and rose to leave room. He folded the paper up and put it into his pocket or may not have. He saw the polar bear at the window and started by when it broke the glass with its paws. Don grabbed a magazine, rolled it up and swatted the animal in the face until if fell back to the ground. He ran around table and tripped on a stool, then fell. The bear came through the window and lunged across the table onto him as he rose to leave.

All in all, fortunately Don's salvation came from an "illegal" firearm which his workmate engaged to save Don's life.

Michio Hoshino

When I wrote about Michio in ***SAFE with Bears***, I had only part of the story. Seven men were at a cabin at Kurilskoya Lake on eastern Russia's southern Kamchatkna Peninsula. Two Russian brothers were guides for a Japanese television crew. Because the TV gear took up much of the cabin, two men slept outside in their individual tents some twelve feet apart. Over a period of several days as they awaited the arrival of the salmon, they were visited by a nuisance brown bear. They banged on a metal bucket with a shovel and pepper sprayed the bear with little effect. One of the men was Michio Hoshino.

He was a superstar photographer from Japan. People loved his images. In 1996 he was killed by a boar. It wasn't until I read Ted Gorsline's volume 8 of his 9-book series (***Man-eating Black Bears***) that I learned more about the event. Before he became a white hunter in Africa Ted was the animal handler for Mutual of Omaha's television show *Wild Kingdom*. I've taken the liberty to cherry pick comments from Ted's book.

"Hoshino tried using pepper spray as repellent before he went to sleep, not knowing that the vegetable oil base in pepper spray attracts bears. Hoshino unwittingly turned his tent into a bear bait. *

"Bear 'expert' Charley Russell once shared a tent with Michio, and because there was an aggressive bear around, slept clutching his bear spray, but apparently did not warn Michio that spraying the inside of a tent is suicidal. Perhaps Russell did not know?

"Bear 'expert' Dr. Stephen Herrero didn't mention the role

pepper spray played in Michio's death. He blamed the death on inadequate food storage."

"Hoshino was killed because he used pepper spray as a repellent when it's a short term deterrent. He slept in a place where other wildlife photographers had habituated a bear to people, the bear lost its fear of man and then it became aggressive and unafraid."

"In 750 hours of watching bears on the Kulik River Smith had never seen this type of behavior. In no case did the bear spray ever keep the bears away...

"In a 1998 United States Geological Survey report Smith said, 'If my study observations hold true elsewhere, then red pepper spray residues on the spray canisters, field gear, or on foliage near camps or other human high use areas may provide sites of interest to brown bears and consequently risk human safety.'

"Smith recommended that once fired canisters not be kept in or near the tents of sleeping persons. Michio Hoshino had sprayed the inside of his tent before he got eaten."

And Ted stated, "It's suicidal to use bear spray inside a tent, during an attack, because tents, as confined spaces that contain the billowing spray and you are far more likely to immobilize yourself than the bear."

(from Pages 106 to 107)

*Many years ago my friend Dr. Tom Smith told me about his experimentation with pepper spray...that he had sprayed the ground about a yard square and the brown bears on the Alaska Peninsula loved the inert spray. They rolled in it, ate the rubber bumpers from float plane floats that had been sprayed and knocked over an outhouse that had been soaked with it. Tom readily admitted that bears love the stuff and that one should always remove any residue after using the spray. (On another experiment near a heavily used bear trail Tom attached bear bells accompanied by fish line to bushes. When a bear approached the bells, Tom pulled the line to activate the noise. Of nearly forty bears which passed, none showed indications that it noticed the bell noise.)

Rollin Braden

In my quest for stories about man and bear encounters I interviewed Rollin in his Soldotna home for ***More Alaska Bear Tales***. He had been on a moose hunting trip with family members and a friend. When he heard noise in the brush, he assumed it was a bull moose and he stalked it. He was surprised to encounter two brown bears that charged him. After a nasty confrontation, he knew he needed medical attention and his party prepared to transport him in a 4-wheeler trailer six miles to the gravel road. He kindly responded to my request to update his life since 1984...which follows.

Hi Larry,

It took awhile but I got the letter that you sent to my commercial property in Soldotna. September 19th 1984 at 7:33pm I fought with 2 brown bears. Thirty-seven years later I'm still alive and doing well. I think I won.

I'm still hunting, fishing and trapping as much as finances will allow (10 months a year). My wife is mostly with me and she always shoots first. This moose season she got a huge 54" bull.

I have a 7-foot standing brown bear full mount in my house. He has a bow tie around its neck and arms outstretched with a wooden platter holding my beer and TV remote control. We call him the butler bear.

Great to hear from you and I like the name of your new book.

Scott Haugen

Scott and his wife Tiffany were in their first year of teaching on the North Slope of Alaska when Scott received an urgent call and armed himself to meet it. A villager at Point Lay had been snatched by a polar bear and villagers were looking for him that December 1990 morning. His story is in ***Some Bears Kill***. On October 5, 2021 Scott sent the following update, detailing his highly successful outdoor career and life.

It seems like yesterday I was tracking the man-eating polar bear in Point Lay, Alaska. But so much has happened since 1990.

Following the unfortunate incident, my wife, Tiffany and I, remained working as school teachers in the tiny Arctic village for three more years, followed by four years in Anaktuvuk Pass, on the northern slopes of the Brooks Range. Here, I also coached the boys and girls basketball teams, and our girls played for the state title in 1996.

After life in Alaska, Tiffany and I taught four more years at an international school in Sumatra, Indonesia. Going from the Arctic to 1/2-mile above the equator was a shock to my system, and that's where an unexpected writing career took root.

Nestled in my air conditioned office, I could look outside and see monkeys playing in our backyard jungle. Asian elephants, hornbills, and 18-foot long pythons also lived there and while I loved watching wildlife, I was not cut out for extreme heat and humidity.

While living in Sumatra I wrote a couple magazine articles on fishing and hunting, and editors asked for more. I immediately fell in love with writing and I gave them more, and before I knew it had a book deal with one of the world's most prestigious publishers of big game hunting titles. In 2000 Safari Press released a limited edition of my ***Hunting The Alaskan High Arctic*** book which became a best seller.

In 2001 I began a career as a full-time freelance outdoor writer. Before I knew it I was writing for over 40 hunting and fishing magazines around the world. This led to opportunities to guest host a few outdoor TV shows, and just like that, I went to work hosting big game hunting shows for the Outdoor Channel. I also hosted fishing shows. For a couple years I hosted two hunting shows which took me on more than 50 hunts a year around the world. Together, Tiffany and I juggled three months a year of public speaking and book signing events around the country, and during this time she was a full-time cookbook author and columnist for multiple magazines.

Over the next 14 years I'd host over 450 TV shows for various networks and companies, the last being shown on Netflix and Amazon Prime. Our final TV show, *The Hunt*, also aired in more than 50 countries, making it one of the widest-reaching hunting shows of all time.

I quit hosting and filming TV shows in 2014 but continued pursuing my true passion as a full-time outdoor writer and photographer, which I'd continued doing through all the years of filming. Over the years I've penned more than 3,500 magazine articles, had over 10,000 photos published, and my wife and I have written 24 books; mine on hunting and fishing, Tiffany's on cooking fish, game and other specialties.

In 2019 Tiffany and I returned to Alaska to teach school. We lived in Hyder, Alaska where we were the only two teachers in a K-12, two-classroom, school. We loved it. What a drastic change of lifestyle it was from the Arctic, where, three decades prior our married life began, pre-internet, where it sometimes took a month to get a letter from the Lower 48. Sadly, due to low student enrollment, the school in Hyder closed after one year so we moved back to Oregon where we now live near our two sons and extended family.

I still travel to Alaska multiple times a year, and while I love fishing and hunting throughout the state, it's photographing the animals that brings me the most joy, especially the bears. I often reflect on the incident of the man-eating polar bear, not only because of the horrific encounter, but because that's what launched my writing career; something I'll never, ever forget.

While filming various TV shows in Alaska in the fall of 2014 I found myself in Homer, Alaska. I went to the high school science room because I'd recently been made aware that the man-eating polar bear had not been destroyed–as I'd thought all those years–rather it was mounted, life-size. Seeing the man-eater face to face was far different than that initial encounter, 24 years prior in total darkness amid 42° below zero temperatures. It was a solemn moment, one where I thought deeply about the victim, his family, and the wonderful people of Point Lay, Alaska.

James Erickson

A normal deer hunt turned somewhat abnormal for James and his hunting buddy as they encountered a protective mother brown bear set on taking care of her cub. She meant business as she got James' head in her mouth with unkind intentions. The same day I received an email update from Scott Haugen I received the following update from James, a man who was chewed by a mama bear and whom I wrote about in ***Some Bears Kill***.

Recovery from the bear mauling went well despite having to change dressings daily and being on crutches for a few weeks to rehabilitate my left calf muscle.

One memory reminds me of your sketch that you had sent me of your experience on Dry Spruce Island, titled "My knees knock when I think of you." While a bear was approaching while your pants were down around your ankles while going to the bathroom. While I was a short distance from camp one morning using our outhouse I listened to what I thought was a bull moose making its way towards me. After finishing up and walking back to camp and going to wash, my brother Dale and Bob Brown witnessed a grizzly walk into camp. Luckily, it was easily scared off.

Another highlight was my marriage on July 21, 2018 to a wonderful woman.

In 2019, I had an episode at work in which my doctor Bob Urata suggested a brain MRI. I flew to International Falls, MN the following day after the MRI, as I had been planning a vacation to my home town in Northern MN. After receiving the results of the MRI, which indicated that I had a brain tumor, my brother Dale who initially invited me to join him and his wife Jean in Juneau in 1983 now reside in Fountain City, WI which is within an hour from the Mayo Clinic in Rochester MN. My brother had also been an RN at Bartlett Regional Hospital in Juneau, AK and on duty the day Ray Rusaw and I were medivaced in from Fresh Water Bay after the brown bear mauling. Upon telling my brother about my MRI results, he offered to drive up to International Falls and take me back to his place in Fountain City. We spent the next day touring the area and giving my doctor time to send my MRI results to the Mayo Clinic. The following morning my brother and his wife Jean, drove me to Rochester. After over 4 hours in the ER at the Mayo Clinic, I was scanned for CT and MRI and it showed that the tumor needed to be removed asap. As the tumor was blocking my spinal fluid which was causing hydrocephalus. I was admitted into the ICU that evening and the next morning had endoscopy surgery through the top of the head. My wife flew into Rochester that evening. The following day I was discharged before noon. The surgeons were able to remove 80% of the tumor while the other 20% was too close to blood vessel to be disturbed. The remaining 20% has since died off due to lack of blood supply. The tumor is called a colloid cyst, a nonmalignant tumor. I'm scheduled for future MRIs to monitor the area of the brain where the tumor was removed.

I had been a union carpenter for past 18 years and now I am retired. My wife and I frequent the outdoors and if in bear country, we try to carry bear spray. If we are at our cabin, which we purchased from my brother and his wife. The cabin located on a small island and it is extremely close to Admiralty Island, which is home to a brown bear every square mile. Every once in a while a bear visits the Island that our cabin is on so I feel most comfortable packing my S&W .44 revolver. We often walk across the island because one of our mooring anchors is located on the opposite side of the island.

Lastly, I often use the phrase "It's a good day to be alive".

Binky and Nuka

Binky shared a polar bear space with Nuka at the Alaska Zoo in Anchorage. They received some notoriety in the 1990's before they died. Binky throttled a photo seeking Australian nurse who got too close to his pen and later that summer he beat up a high school student whose alcohol induced actions fogged his brain.

Supposedly both bears died from liver failure, caused by a parasitic disease called *sarcoystosis*, Nuka on July 14, 1995, and Binky six days later. Supposedly both bears were buried on the zoo grounds. The local fish wrapper extolled the bears died of some rare "bug" from cat do-do. I heard about the falsity of that report...and that version.

But there is another.

After writing about the two folks Binky engaged at his pen, I learned from a reliable source that the cat feces story might be a little off the mark.

Supposedly, there's that nasty word again, the bears were buried elsewhere and they were not killed by the aforementioned means. They were poisoned.

Supposedly it was a right of passage for students at the nearby high school to sneak into the zoo at night and visit the inhabitants.

Supposedly after the high school senior was on his way to recovery from Binky's bites, the kid's pals formulated a plan.

Supposedly that plan included raw meat laced with arsenic.

Supposedly some of those seeking to avenge their friend's

injuries, chose to injure Binky.

Supposedly those persons sneaked into the zoo and tossed the poisoned meat to Binky. Seems Nuka also got some of it.

Two versions. Which is more accurate?

TJ Langley

I wrote the following abut TJ in ***SAFE with Bears***: In 2000 at a 40 year class reunion while discussing bear encounters a classmate informed me that her son was good friends with TJ Langley. I Googled TJ, made contact and received his story after a couple of revisions. Ten years later at another reunion I told my classmate that I'd acquired TJ's story and she said, "He's dead." Was I stunned! He died while solo hiking in Washington state's Glacier Peak Wilderness in October 2009.

Since that time I thought it might be a good idea to incorporate the following information from ***The Seattle Times***.

By Eric Pryne and Susan Gilmore

Originally published October 10, 2009 at 8:30 pm Updated October 10, 2009 at 10:46 pm

The body of missing Seattle hiker T.J. Langley was found Saturday afternoon in a remote section of the Glacier Peak Wilderness, the Chelan County Sheriff's office said.

Lt. Maria Agnew said two searchers on foot spotted his body near Luahna Peak, above Boulder Pass, at an elevation of about 8,600 feet. It appeared he had lost his footing and fallen about 300 feet, she said.

His body was recovered by helicopter and taken to a funeral home in Leavenworth, Agnew said.

Part of the route he followed crossed a glacier, she said, but it was unclear whether he was on ice or on a marked trail when he fell.

Langley, 42, failed to return Tuesday from what he told friends and family would be a two-day solo hike in the Okanogan-Wenatchee National Forest near Lake Wenatchee.

On Thursday morning, friends filed an overdue-hiker report, and the Chelan County Sheriff's Office initiated an extensive ground and air search.

Langley, an avid outdoorsman and experienced backcountry hiker, checked in at a forest trailhead last Sunday. His car was found parked at the Little Giant trailhead, a turnout on the Chiwawa River road about a half-mile past 19 Mile Campground.

Earlier Saturday, search dogs, using the scent they got from a piece of gear left behind by Langley, were among dozens of searchers looking for the veteran actor.

Searchers said they spoke to other hikers who said they saw Langley on the trail, but whether that was Tuesday or Wednesday wasn't clear.

He had told friends where he was going and when he'd return, so it was easy to map a search area, said his sister, Joy Langley.

She was flying from her home in the Washington, D.C., area to Seattle on Saturday.

T.J. Langley, who managed an apartment building on Capitol Hill, was also a veteran actor with a drama degree from the University of Washington.

He was a member of Seattle's Repertory Actors Theatre, a nonprofit group known for staging shows with primarily multiethnic and nontraditional casts.

The Simms Family

While researching my bear files September 2021, I ran across information that may have some value to the reader. Headlines indicated three people perished in the waters of a lake and fishermen shot suspected bears ("3 who drowned may have fled bear," May, 28, 1998, ***Anchorage Daily News***; "Fishermen may have shot Chena Lake bears over weekend," June 3, 1998, ***Associated Press***).

A year later Amanda's story of her bear hunt with her father appeared in NRA's ***American Hunter*** magazine. Her father Bert indicated that Amanda was a lifetime member of the NRA and her story was for an English assignment.

April 27, 2000, I contacted Amanda's mother who responded with the following letter:

Dear Mr. Kaniut,

Thank you for offering us the opportunity to discuss the "Bear Attack" on our daughter, son-in-law and his little brother. I don't' know if it would help save lives or not to tell the story as we know it, but it may well save the life of a bear or two. So here is what I know, and what I believe:

My daughter, Amanda, her husband, Joe, and his little 8-year-old brother, Evan, went fishing on Memorial Day 1998. Evan had never caught a fish before, and from a roll of film found in the tackle box we have photos of his first catch. They all three appeared very happy that day.

Amanda and Joe were both hunters and had each taken

the mandatory bear baiting clinic offered by DF&G. Amanda had taken a clinic on hunting Alaskan large game. She had bagged her first black bear May 21st, 1998.

Amanda and Joe would never have put Evan in danger or attempted to flee from a bear by running to icy water for escape. Evan did not swim, neither did Amanda, and it would never be her choice to go into cold water. The only reason she would go into that water would be to assist Evan or Joe.

Joe was an excellent swimmer but nobody can swim well or long in ice water, especially if trying to rescue someone else. When we knew they were missing, my husband and his retriever went to the lake. It was very early morning. Bert told me later that nothing was disturbed—not the tackle box, fishing poles or snack food.

My husband found Evan and stayed until Amanda and Joe were found. None of them had any marks on them and the state demanded autopsies. No marks, no internal injuries, no alcohol, no drugs. All three drowned.

To the best of my knowledge the twin bears implicated were innocent. My husband said the only tracks he saw were from our dog. Bears, especially aggressive, curious young ones do not pass up on an opportunity to snoop around "people stuff."

I was, and continue to be sickened by the myth that bears caused our tragedy and was horrified during the immediate aftermath when two men went "fishing" in the area and shot one of the twins, injuring it and causing a massive bear hunt. A wounded bear is a grave danger to humans. A poor shot/reckless hunter/unethical "sportsman"/inhumane person is also a grave danger to humans.

Not everyone involved in our family's terrible loss believes, as I do, that bears were not involved.

I believe that perhaps Evan got a yellow jacket or bee

threat and ran to the water. Or perhaps his first fish got away, we have a photo, but no one saw a fish stringer. Ice cold water and a sudden drop in depth, 2 non-swimmers. That there was a tragedy an irreplaceable loss I cannot deny, but the myth of bears I will adamantly argue.

My daughter and her husband were hunters. Bert continues to hunt and bear meat remains part of our diet. Bears are dangerous and deserving of respect, human safety relies on good information, preparation and training.

If you want to send a message that may save lives recommend hunter safety classes, bear clinics and keeping up shooting skills.

Campers and hikers that go unarmed an uninformed into the wilds of Alaska take responsibility for their own safety and we ought not blame bears for human failing.

CJ Thomas

Bear on Ice

A publisher asked me to compile a book about Alaska bear encounters and such. One of my students, Bill Reynolds, had lived in Homer, Alaska, and spun a vivid story about his bear on ice. He and a brother had been sledding and he witnessed his brother disappear just ahead of him. Was he surprised when he descended the snow-covered hill to find a brown bear den…out of which the bruin lunged. It chased Bill and his brother down the hill, into their cabin where his mother was preparing a meal for Christmas day. But the bear broke in and they retreated to the ice-igloo they'd built. And when papa returned home, they spent the night in the straw covered ground in the igloo.

BUT…the real story I heard July 4, 2024, 39 years later. They say that truth is stranger than fiction. I'm beginning to believe them.

En route to our daughter Jill's for dinner, I noticed a red, 1957 Chevy a couple of hundred yards behind us. I pulled over and let him pass then followed the awesome vehicle as it journeyed toward our daughter's home. When he pulled into a driveway, I pulled in behind him and he told me about his rig. He'd purchased it, restored from the ground up, from a Floridian seven weeks prior. He showed me the interior and the engine.

I asked him if he'd been born in Alaska. He replied that he had and went to Dimond High school where I taught from 1966 to 1992. He said he'd graduated in 1980 and his name was Scott Reynolds. Brother of Bill. They had spent some time in Homer, Alaska. I told him that I was there then and he asked my name. "Kaniut," I replied. And he said, "Larry. I read your book

Alaska Bear Tales all the time. Then he related that Bill's story about the glissading bear was not true, that he'd made it up.

APPENDIX 1: Bears I Have Met

c. 1950-52 Black bear on roof near Duvall, WA, eating apples from angular tree that sloped up the roof, some half dozen miles from Monroe

1956 Yaak River logging camp dump, bears appeared at night looking like black stumps; driving from Spokane to Yaak River around Moyie Springs, a cinnamon bounded across road around 7 a.m.; bear "growling" (Yaak logging camp area) while I fished (considered crawling into culvert and climbed tree armed with rocks)

c. 1958 or '59 Blue Mountains behind Cloverland and Clarkston while traveling a forest service road and deer hunting I saw a skinned black bear hanging from a meat pole at a hunting camp. It looked, weirdly enough, like a man's body.

1967 Chester Meeks, Paul Kendall, 2 college boys, me on Palmer Creek Rd. near Hope, AK, climbing hillside for closer look, Chet and I roll rocks down on mom who fled when a pillow-sized boulder nearly brained her; I have pix of them in distance taken through binoculars; August: Moose packing with Chet Meeks, Norm and Steve Boling, Bill and Gary Hinkle and Louie Jensen and me saw sow-2-cubs blacks and huge black grizz; c. October 16th: Sat. Ron Richter, Steve Boling, Louie Jensen, and I encounter grizz (track in trail, "want to be by here before dark on our return,") in dark near Gold Creek up Resurrection Creek—fired round into air, eye-high bear thrashed brush, breaking trees as we skedaddled.

1967 Summer Frank Morgan came to AK; Tazlina Glacier overlook, grizz tracks 9" wide in trail (Frank, Marcia Timmons, Louie Jensen, Pam and me).

1967 or 68 Gwennie's on Kenai, blacks at outhouse—sow and twins standing erect.

c. May 1968 Pam, Donna, Rodney and Melinda Meeks and I get blackie at Rainbow, AK

c. Nov. 1968 our family saw huge brownie tracks up Bird Creek (by dump), maybe 18" long in snow

1969 Pam, Gin and me see black near highway en route from Prince George to Prince Rupert

c. 1970s Hope Road, huge black near top of ridge on Turnagain Arm peak

August 1971 grizzly in sheep camp behind Gunsight Mt., AK, at cabin, retrieve Hodaka, on road next a.m. (Randy Terry, Tom Bentley and I—and Peterson?), probably 40-60 yards distant, crossed so quickly couldn't ascertain grizz or black, returned during the night--*thrub, thrub, thrub*/not porcupine, we went out, shone light to wood pile--I to retrieve wood build fire in front of doorway, green eyes looking back from wood pile, fired round into air, departed, returned next a.m. to retrieve bikes. Encountered same bear on way out. I told him to behave or I'd kill his butt. He was shot opening day. Had spent days watching folks wash their cars at Gunsight Lodge.

c. 1971 large black bear opposite Fresno Creek north of Summit Lake, standing in the fog

c. 1972 "dogging" moose for Kent Muehlhausen at Jonesville, huge brown track 14 7/8"

early 1970's up Fresno Creek w. Dan Hollingsworth and Duanne or "Roy Mullen and (?)" who wanted to go after a small black bear on opposite side of creek

c. 1973 Ralph, LaVonne and I floating Lake Creek on two separate logs from 4 miles upstream, variety bear tracks and partially eaten salmon polka dot the trail black that Ralph and I "scared"...it exhausted some digested materials as it fled.

c. 1973 Les Smothers, Ralph Ertz, Jr., Leslie Baldwin see lots tracks on Lake Creek, water fills black's track, sliding in mud on bend in river on our return (as it had jumped into tall grass alongside stream)

1973 Pam, Gin, Jill and I near Jasper (Canada) w. Smothers en route to Anchorage spot black emerge from woods on right nonchalantly approach shoulder of road about time biker ahead of us spot each other and they ignite—bear in retreat; biker in high speed pedal action

1973 Carrells (Bill, Dean, Norm and Cliff), Les Smothers, Tony

James and I see sow-2-cub blacks up Hawkins Glacier, we inadvertently adversely conditioned-fed them.

1973 Smothers' wounded black near Fuller Lakes, Kenai Pen., AK

1973 Smothers in Denali—prob. saw bears w. them

c. 1974 Bonanza Hills, Mulchatna caribou hunting with Ralph Ertz, Ralph, Jr., Dan Hollingsworth. Ralph and I spotted a large black on the breaks of a ridge above the river flying in to camp. A couple of days later when Ralph returned to bow hunt, the four of us saw a grizzly about a mile away on the far side of two caribou, and the bear appeared larger than the caribou. We were safe, however, as we had our bows!

c. 1975 moose hunt on Mystery Creek road, black tracks beneath Randy Terry's feet in dust as he slept in trunk of car; Smothers family and Kaniuts.

c. 1975 Lynn Roumagoux, Frank Morgan, Dan Hollingsworth and I on goat hunt near Hope's Walker Creek, possible Bigfoot vocalization...

1976-8 put Ben in birch tree on Russian River when I spotted brown bear cub across river, told him to climb if it came across—Les and/or Keith Gray may have been with

c. 1983 Chester, Roger, Ben and I returning from Seward deep sea fishing and see big black cross road, guardrail and scramble up ditch-cliff at railroad tunnel/culvert near summit before Moose Pass

c. 1985 Ben and I saw 13 bears in Denali while transporting Ben Holt and wife—cute little grizzly tosses flower clump and bounces it on head by bus (Ben Holt ? caterpillar company owner from Santa Fe, NM, and wife rented motor home from Ethan Fode's dad and we drove them)

c. 1988 Pam spots grizzled grizzly on outskirts of Whitehorse

1988 Larsen Bay, Kodiak Is. spotted couple from air

1989 Alaska ferry to Prince Rupert from Haines, Pam, Jill, Ben, Scott M and I see black on beach on Admiralty just after tour guide says Admiralty has NO blacks. On return up Alaska Highway Jill, Ben and I see small, probably adolescent, blonde grizz near Burwash Landing on Alcan, Ben and I throw rocks at it

c. 1990 Randy Terry and I sheep hunting, spotted huge black south Hershey Mine, Palmer Creek Road

c. fall 1992 Waha behind Lewiston with Dave Ellsworth, large black returning from apple orchard and in timber, Dave read regs while it left

probably 1992 at Clarence Espedal's farm w. Jamie Crawford, huge, very fresh, bear pile of processed apples

1993 Jill Rose encounters a "white legged-brown bodied horse" near Burwash Landing on return from Haines ferry pick up (August or September)

1994 Nov. 20 10-foot brown boar on Dry Spruce Island between Raspberry Is. & Kodiak grunted while I did the same

1995 July went to Karluk Lake with Evan Swenson and Buzz to photo bears—saw 35+ Browns on river, fishing, stripping willow bark and eating it—licking sap from tree

c. 1995 Colorado Creek, sow and 2 cub blacks near mouth canyon Ben K., Brad R. and I after John Duke and Bryce Clyne left us on hunt

1996 Moose hunt with Al Smay, Chris Adamson, Bob Smay, Larry Fisek, Brad Risch and me camping near grizz on moose gut pile. Night before Brad and I slept in Al's trailer under starlight, black had been sighted across stream

1996-97 Sonny Miller saw a huge black waddle down his driveway and onto our eastern property. He hollered and it split due south. He had thought of getting his rifle in case it tried to get cozy with Pam's horse Prince.

c. July 1997 Ben and I stopped at Dan France's and glassed two huge browns ¾ mile away—female blonde, black male, thought I'd wet pants, first thought=bigger gun!

1997 Jill, Nathan Mullen, Daniel (?) and Angela and I hiked up

DeArmoun toward Rabbit Lake, spotted black heading toward our tent and doughnuts as we climbed up slope

c. summer 1997 Pam and I saw black jump guard rail at Potter Valley subdivision entrance

September 1998 overnight at B&B in Seward, returning from town in dark, approaching car lights blotted out momentarily by "moose." Suddenly 2-3 feet in front of our headlights a gray "moose" whose back was below the hood of our car appeared/ vanished off our right bumper-fender

around 1999 at Exit Glacier we saw a black on the mountain north of the glacier about the same time Pam and I saw a black behind Helvey's in Seward, on the mountain north of Mt. Marathon

between 1996-1999 we spot and watch black high above Bird Flats on New Seward, (Pam, Jill, maybe Gin and Sarah)—may be the time we watched 4-5 little weasels zipping around with mother nearby in culvert-bridge area of Exit Glacier

c. May 2000 Pam, Jill and I return from Chair 5 dinner and watch 3 guys on Bird Flats hunt black, bikers bobbing by between them-us-bear; then Jill spotted sow and 2 black cubs a couple miles west on our return to town (just around the corner at west end of Bird Point)

August 25, 2000 Skilak Lake in Jerry Anderson's red/black Achilles raft with Brad Risch and Jeremy Anderson. 2-year old black on beach at 50 yards.

August 26, 2000 Surprise Creek Trail north of Bear Mt. and Skilak Lake, huge black at 800-1000 yards with Andersons and Brad Risch.

September 7, 2000 Denali Highway, c. mile 16 (from Paxson) turnout/overlook, man stalking grizzly. We entered the game to cut it off if need be, but it smelled him and spooked. Ben, Brad and I saw, though I just got a glimpse of its last two or three jumps before it disappeared.

Wednesday, October 11, 2000 Pam and I drove to Seward, Alaska, for the day. We saw 80 trumpeter swans, a dozen eagles, three sea lions. Pam kept saying that we'd see a bear before we got home. A half mile south of Rabbit Creek at 8 p.m. (in the dark) and a couple of miles from home, an average-sized black bear almost ran over us as it sped across the road in front of us.

Sunday, June 3, 2001 Returning home from Ginger and Brad's after their horses' morning feeding (they were via rail w. Sarah to Mt. McKinley Park) near the Stake Shop/Surveyor's Exchange we saw a yearling black bear run from the north side onto De Armoun pavement and begin walking the east side of Rocky Road. We stopped and watched it from about 30 yards, ambling south. It passed 2 seeded dandelions, and I commented to Pam that maybe it would eat them. It stopped just past them, turned and entered the woods on the east of the road.

August 6, 2001 Vickie Baer called to tell Pam there was a bear in her driveway/between their house and Stuits' so I rushed over with Brad Rish on my tail while Pam and Sarah stood in the street in front of our house.

I saw no bear in Stuits' driveway and told Brad to stand guard there and watch while I walked to the corner. It wasn't at the corner so I motioned for Pam to come down and Brad held Sarah while Pam spotted the bear in the shadows of the corner, then it walked into the driveway between Tom's pickup and the garage. It was about 30-inches tall at the back.

It walked toward Sasha, Tom's dog, popping its teeth and I heard a growl. I picked up a baseball sized rock and told Sasha, "Don't worry, girl, we won't let the bear get your food or hurt you." Brad stood nearby holding Sarah and Pam had left to walk home. The bear was about 20 feet from the dog when it turned and walked between the pickup and the garage, stopped to nip off a rose hip, stood on Tom's outside stairwell landing and advanced a couple of steps up before turning and walking toward the shed west of Tom's house. I watched it for a bit then left go get into the truck and drive to Baers (the direction in which the bear was heading) to warn them.

Monday, August 20, 2001

Brad Risch and I hiked the Fuller Lake Trail and spent last night atop a knoll 80 yards from the lake under the spruce trees on a level spot in my orange 2-man tent. After we arose and ate and started for the upper lake, we looked across the lower lake about a mile and spotted a black bear roughly ¾ mile distant on a slope west of Round Mountain. We watched it for a bit before moving on up-trail.

September 14, 2001 Drive through Denali Park with Gin, Brad, Sarah and Pam after staying night at Denali Princess, saw 6 grizzlies—a huge "black" one coming down onto flats at

Teklanika River, on the far side walking south; a sow and twins at Toklat River; then a couple of other solos with gold from the sun shining from their coats.

Around October 8th or so, 2001, before our first snowfall, Pam awakened me and thought there was a bear in our garbage. I shone my head lamp on it, saw only a black hole, shot Ben's air rifle into a garbage can to rattle and scare it. Never saw it move. Mayhave beendarkness. Moments later Pam aroused me and whispered, "Listen. I hear it breathing." I poked my head and headlamp out the bedroom window and heard and saw a black object breathing heavily. It had a long black tail, and I shouted, "Get outta here." It was a black lab between our window and fence, about 6-8 feet.

May 13, 2002—black crosses road in front of Brad and Ginger's... see In Search of Ursus Americanus, May 13, 12ish o'clock, 2002—see on the trail of *Ursus americanus* in completed folder herein.

May 27, 2002 We'd just returned from picking up Jill and 3 friends from Galena and stopping at Alaska Wild berry Products when Tom Stuits called about 4:30 p.m. "There's a black bear between our place and Sonny's."

I told Pam and Jill, grabbed my camera and headed outside where Pam said, "There it is" and pointed it out 10 feet west of Sonny's. It looked like it was going away, but it turned and was actually coming our way.

We watched it meander along the house and hot tub (saying that it would give Carol a thrill if she were in the tub—Pam called to let her know), turn east, walk across the yard to the swing set and lie down. I took a picture of it before it lay down, and we watched it. I walked out to the truck and moved to the hood to see it better.

Five minutes later Carol pulled into the driveway and I walked over, keeping my eye on the resting bear, told Carol and pointed to the bear. She went to get her camera. About then the bear started toward our house, gingerly dropped into the ditch and started up the road by Miller's mailbox.

I kneeled down to take a picture, did so, watched it walk into our yard toward the wood pile, stop at the white trailer as if sniffing a tire and I returned to the front yard, all the while watching it mosey along, through the wood pile path and out onto the side lawn where I took a picture of it. It walked toward the back yard, stopped and sniffed the horse rope fence and continued to the eagle swing.

I went through the house, out the back onto the picnic path, watched it, joined by Tom Stuits who was packing a big side arm. It walked across the east of our property, limping on its left hind foot, and under the horse rope at the southeast corner and across the neighbor's woodlot.

Just about then Risches came…too late to see the bruin.

Aug. 21, 2002

We left Gin, Brad and Sarah at Quartz Creek on Kenai Lake around 5:30 to drive Ben, Jeff and Heather to Seward and saw a few cars and tourists photoing an outhouse at Trail Lake. I stopped and went to investigate, but it was about a 6-foot black bear that Ben digitaled pix of Jeff in foreground and blackie in background, as bear approached garbage can and bit the corner of the outhouse a few times. He swatted at a plant 3 times, so fast it was difficult to observe the three swats!

The night before (20th) Brad and I towed a guy (Todd Petersen) and two 15-year-olds 10 miles to Trail Lake (lower unit on their boat went out), and we saw 2 blackies on the hillside a mile and 3 miles east of camp. (Petersen and boys quite excited when Brad refused the $20 Todd offered and Brad told them to go on line to order one of our books…they were in the presence of the "great one"!

Aug. 26, 2002 News from the homeland (email to Jill Rose).

Yest. I awakened to some excited chatter, talk, noise. It was around 9 and I was thinking church. I had run into Mrs. Terwilliger at Freddies on Lk. Otis, and when she asked about Benny, I suggested we might attend their church (her 50th wed. ann. this week)...but Ben and Jeff went to Heather's church. I jumped from bed to discover the noise was a bear in the yard. Your mother had been pulling weeds for the chickens while watching the horse. Carol called to say there was a bear coming our way. Mom rushed to put Prince away, not remembering if she told Carol bye or hung up or dropped the phone. Then she watched a med. black bear walk over the hump in the front yard and stand up by her hanging basket with a paw on it. She awakened J and B and the chase was on.

When I hit the floor and went into the living room, they were in the truck, driving out of the drive up Natrona. We observed the bear moseying around the back yard a bit, Jeff videoed, then it turned and walked past shed to barn, stopped near ladder, looked our way and bolted when the door opened--Ben had asked for a knife; and I threw a rock at it...I didn't want It to see the chickens.

Last night Hersh and Karen drove to Begich-Boggs Visitor Center, saw around 100 Belugas by hooligan area.

May 20, 2004

Don and Anita Meierhoff were visiting and discussing the process of putting her mother's writings on paper, sitting in our living room on Natrona. All of a sudden around 8 Don exclaimed, "There's a bear!" He sat near the piano and was looking east toward the well head. I jumped up and rushed to the window to see a bear walking—probably from the lawn glider—toward the kitchen-fireplace area. Jill, Dave Pavish, Crystal and a male friend rushed toward the living room and I told them the bear would probably walk right by the east kitchen window and not to make any quick movements.

The bear walked to the window, turned east toward the "I Love Rose" sign and walked up the east lawn past the woodpile, along the east property line and beyond the cedar rail fence.

We got a note from Meierhoffs today thanking for arranging a bear in the yard for them.

Summer 2004

Vickie Baer called excitedly telling us about a big bear that had just left their place. I asked her if she wanted me to come over and she said, "No, Vick's here." I decided to drive over to see what they could tell me about it. When I left the driveway I noticed the tail end of a bear turning into Jones's driveway at the end of Natrona. I drove down, turned around and watched it cross the road between the turn around spot and the corner, a small black with a green and a yellow ear tag (in each ear). I drove to Vickie's and told them I'd seen the bear. "Wasn't it big!" she exclaimed. No, it wasn't. Probably about 100 pounds.

About mid-May 2005

Vickie Baer called to let us know a bear was near Tom Stuits' swing set. I walked out and leaned on the white Suburban hood while looking in Tom's direction, much to Pam's dismay.

A few minutes passed and I heard a 10-yard diesel start up, rumble around the corner from the corner opposite Baer's and grunt by our house, pulling a trailer and a cat. About 30 seconds later I watched a black bear waddle around the same corner and head west down Natrona.

Sonny told Pam that he saw a bear in our garbage Saturday the 4th of June—probably while we were in the garden with Sarah working. Sonny said the bear stood up and looked toward the back yard, standing taller than your Suburban (probably as tall as—[author]).

June 11, 2005 8:15 a.m.

I was sitting at the kitchen table with my back to the bay window, about to put some scrambled eggs into my mouth when I noticed movement from the peripheral vision of my left eye. Thinking that can't be a squirr…I turned to see about a 150 pound black bear 7-9 feet away ambling at an angle from the southeast corner of the deck toward the kitchen window. I told Pam (between me and the sink and out of view of the bear), "Don't move." I didn't want her to move to the window and to startle it. I thought of the horse and chickens as I suggested she move to the window by me to see the bear. I tapped on the window, which Pam didn't appreciate because she wanted to watch the bear longer.

It ambled nervously toward the water faucet and around the corner of the house. I headed for the front porch and Pam went to the old living room where she watched it go around the corner, approach the 3-rail cedar fence, step one way, then the other, then step between the lower and middle rails. I watched it pass beyond-between the VW and the Blue (flag) Suburban. It was out of sight so I suggested she go up to the upstairs study. She couldn't see it and came back down. I tried to get her to go with me to the white Suburban to watch it at the garbage cans, but she didn't want to get too far away from the door.

About then it stood up and looked at us. We saw its head above the Toyota trailer with the Avon raft on it. Pam spoke gently to it telling it that it was cute and that it was nice of it to visit us. A couple of minutes later it walked onto the road, quartering towards Sonny's, looked over its shoulder with a semi-glare and vanished up the bank and into the woods between Tom's and Sonny's. Pam called and alerted Lori and Vickie.

Vickie called later and said that she never saw it but observed Lori looking from her deck.

July 2005 Kelsey Wilkins (Lynn and Kelly's daughter) wanted to see a bear and I told her I'd order one for her. One morning (before church I believe) I looked out the bay window and saw something black above the white planter on the left rear of the deck. A black bear walked from behind the planter and I told Kelly to tell Kelsey, who was in the guest bedroom/old living room. She looked out the window and watched it like it was an every day occurrence...Jill told her she'd lived here 30-some years and it was like the 2nd or 3rd bear she'd ever seen in our yard.

2006 We saw 7 black bears in yard. Memorial Day we had homemade chocolate-coconut ice cream, T-bone and NY steaks. Played croquet, badminton and horseshoes before retiring to deck where we observed a bear walk north to south across the area we'd just vacated. Gene Greenfield arrived about the time Risches, Bryan and Barry were leaving. Visiting on deck Gene said, “Is that a bear?” Sure enough 20-30 minutes removed from our game playing a black walked through our playground, under our split rail fence and moseyed through the neighbor’s yard behind us. It looked to be about a 200 pounder. Not huge, but big enough to do some damage if so inclined

June 17

Awakened at 5:10 this a.m. by barking dog. I peeked out guest bed window, saw him walking around paddock wagging tail and Prince next to him looking southeast as he often does. Then a black bear walked into view from the fire ring area, a behemoth 250-300 pounder (about 31 inches at shoulder), sauntering along, nose to ground, head down, straight toward Prince. The horse stood looking down as the bear looked up from about five feet, casually eyeing each other as if to say, “How’s it goin’, Dude?” Then the bear turned and walked toward the power line, put its front paws on the top cedar rail “gate” and knocked both down and sauntered into tall grass on power line. Think I’ll load .30-06 and have on the ready. That’s the third bear we know of in our yard in the last month (before Memorial Day Prince was grazing in back yard and ran to house where Pam said he was trembling to beat the band).

June 18

Went to car in front yard at 9:15 p.m., walked around it and noticed Pan in the street about 30 feet west of our property line--Pan is the nickname I gave Panhandler, the bear in our house yest. a.m. We exchanged stares from 35 yards as I watched it sniff a paper plate, then amble a few steps into the north ditch, fetch something, return to roadbed, sit on his rear and leisurely chew on it. I went into the house to tell wife and daughter and we returned to watch him until he moseyed around the corner to the north on Landers.

There was a young (15ish) girl in the street 10 yards east, and I asked her if she wanted a ride past him as I was heading to Huffman to get a paper. She said she'd take her chances so I followed Pan around the corner Landers north toward Shoshoni. He stood broadside in the street at Stuit's west driveway, head pointed east, and as I approached to within 20 yards, he ambled into the woods north of Tom's drive. I backed up and told girl I'd drive along between her and the bear's path if she wanted to walk to her friend's, the daughter of Ben the fireman (on Landers and Shoshoni).

She complied and when I reached Baer's drive, she said she'd run down path on west of road to Ben's. I backed into Baer's drive, drove around corner at Natrona and the bear was broadside at Stuit's south drive, bolted into Stuit's yard and angled toward Miller's. So, I'm not sure if he'll be back, but I think so.

Sitting in kitchen with Pam just before bedtime at 11:59 p.m. when we heard a loud rifle report which appeared to come from up the hill a few houses to the east. Jill was in bed and yelled to us in amazement as to what was happening to the neighborhood. I drove up 140th and Riverton with no results.

July 6

"Do you want to see a bear up close and personal?!" Pam stated excitedly as she awakened me at 7:45 this morning. I followed her hurriedly into the living room where she flopped onto the couch and pointed into the front yard. I saw the tail end of an average sized black—125-200 pounds—waddling across our driveway toward the street. It crossed the street, entered the ditch and exited into Sonny and Carol Miller's yard. *Hmmm.* Bear number 5 in 5 weeks.

We went into the kitchen and Pam said she'd been sitting on the bench when she noticed a dog on the chip trail past the bay window and realized it wasn't a dog. It walked past the east TV window and she ran to get me.

July 10 I was reading an email from sister Laura Lee when Pam rushed into the computer room and had me run to front door, just in time to see the south end of a big black bear disappearing north across/next to our neighbor's hot tub. We wondered if it was Pan, the panhandler that visited us June 17. It was good sized. I asked her if she wanted to drive around the block with me and Jill shouted from upstairs, "I do!" We hopped into the white suburban and drove with no results, though Pam thinks she saw it in the fireman's driveway (from where we parked east about ¾ block). That's 3 to 4 different bears since Memorial Day, (40 days or 1 bear a week). It must be the Year of the Bear!

July 15 Sarah was here part of the day, and her parents arrived around 11 p.m. to pick her up. They'd driven up Rabbit Creek and Elmore (the back way) and were excited to announce that they'd seen Pan, the big black bear. Brad said he was probably 40 inches high, over the top of their Saturn's hood. He ambled along about 35 yards in front of them and down Sanderlin's driveway. (awaiting email from Lee Aiken who supposedly saw and later measured 40-inch at shoulder—Roger Meeks told us his boss had spoken to neighbor about it).

July 21 (the world famous author interviews Pastor Pammy this morning). In the early morning dusk about 4:15 a.m. while sitting on a bench at the kitchen table with my cup of hot black currant tea, my precious daughter joined me.

Moments later I noticed a black dog just past our bay

window (less than 11 feet from me and less than 10 from Jill), then quickly realized the seventh bear of the season was here for us to enjoy. It left the bay window traveling around the corner on its way north, past the east window, angling toward Larry's woodpile. It disappeared on the path between stacks of wood, ambling along in a seemingly unconcerned manner. I ran out into the street to see it cross, but I didn't see it again. (it might actually be bear number 8 that we or the horse have seen/ sensed)

July 30 Paddy cake brownies. Ben, Jill and I left home around 7:12 p.m. to see if we could see the brown bears playing paddy cake with the fishermen at Bird Creek, 17 miles south of our house. On the way Ben apologized for not being there at 7 as he'd had trouble locating his ammo, stored separately from his pistol. I didn't think much of his pistol apology until he brandished 2 .45 caliber semi-autos and told us that we would each have one and he would have his 40 Glock. Then he began a 15 minute lesson for Jill on how to operate and quick draw her piece, including timing her…"one thousand one, one thousand two…you have to be faster than that or get eaten." I told him not to have a live round in mine as I figured I could outrun fishermen in hip waders!

We parked in the west Bird Creek lot and walked to the bridge. Partway across the bridge I looked upstream 300-400 yards, saw what appeared to be bears on an island with fisherman and asked, "Are those bears?" They were. It appeared to be a yearling and a new born but upon closer inspection—I had told Pam we'd stay on the "boardwalk"—it was a sow and yearling. We walked upstream on the south bank, keeping 30 fishermen between us and the bears, to about 100 yards and watched. At one point the sow came toward us and stopped about 50 yards away. We took a few pix and left an hour and twenty minutes later with rain trickling down.

It was funny watching the fishermen move ahead of the bears. Every time the bears moved, the fishermen moved!

June 2008

Flew over 4-5 blacks with Brad Risch in *Tundra Bunny* on return from Heather Whip's fish camp June 4.

Today (25th) Pam and I drove up Bear Valley and saw a big black on the left of the road on Honey or Black Bear Street walking a game trail on the opposite side of the draw about half mile away.

July 17, 2008 Read in the ***Anchorage Daily News*** on line about 17 dead bears so far this summer in Anchorage. *Waahhh.* So be it. I then Googled Alaska State and emailed Doug Larsen, Director of ADFG, (see email of today) and asked him if he anticipated an open archery season on bears and/or moose, to rid the Anchorage Bowl of the furry, 4-legged bear magnets called moose calves. Will see if he responds.

Shortly thereafter, around 10 a.m. Pam and I simultaneously answered separate phones to hear our neighbor Tom Stuits state that he'd seen a black bear walk into our yard near our VW. With phone in hand I ran to guest bed, looked out the window onto a big eared black bear sitting 64-inches to 6 feet from me, opened the window and shouted for him to vamoose—Tom probably wondered what he was hearing. The bear looked mildly disturbed and rose to walk the path toward the chicken area. I asked Pam to bring the pellet gun.

I pumped it up, loaded a BB and fired at the black spot beyond the elderberry bushes, which probably deflected the BB. Then I ran to get my pepper spray and started out the door with it and the pellet gun. Pam insisted that I take more powerful medicine so I grabbed my .44 Magnum pistol and walked out the front door where Tom was standing in the street with his pepper spray and .44 Magnum. I told him I'd go out back and around the house to flush the bear toward him.

I picked up a couple of baseball sized rocks and hurled them against the cedar fence between the chickens and the VW where the grass is three feet high. I figured the loud noises would ignite the bear. Then I banged twice on the old Suburban hood just past the VW, walked around it and saw the bear watching me from the rear of the truck 18-20-feet away. I raised the pepper spray and fired a one second blast which got the bear moving, albeit slowly.

I shouted to Tom, "It's coming your way."

Tom saw the bear and shouted, "Git."

We chased it into his yard where we momentarily lost sight of it, then spotted it on Sonny and Carol's lawn east of Tom's. Wanting to get a blast of cayenne into its face or mouth, I chased it around Sonny's house and garage. It stayed 50-feet ahead of me. As it ran into the alders on the power line, I grabbed a handful of gravel and tossed it at the bear.

The surprising thing was that the bear seemed disinterested in leaving in a hurry, just looked at me and ambled along slowly. When I approached it in front of Sonny's, it stood broadside and kind of glowered at me before moving off.

This was probably a 2-3 year-old bear, long legs, long fur and big ears. Somewhere between 100-150 pounds.

My one shot of spray probably went 15 feet, 3 feet shy of the bear. I think the noise startled him into motion. It was rainy with no wind and the propellant carried well. The can expired in 2006 so I was pleased that it still functioned. It was the first time I'd used it.

I called neighbors Marcus and Ingrid and Carol to alert them. Carol called back later to tell me it was probably the same bear that awakened her yesterday morning at 12:30 a.m. And probably the same animal that strewed a black garbage bag's contents in the street in front of Steve Couture's, our neighbor to the east. Went to Tom's and had Hunter take pix of the neighborhood bear watch guys.

July 23 Garbage day. I noticed something in the ditch across from our house, walked out to investigate, saw garbage and heard a *whoomp,* which sounded like it came from Sonny's. Walked into house to fetch the .44 pistola and pepper spray and walked to Sonny's where I found his black plastic garbage can on its side with a white garbage bag on the porch and wet black bear tracks between the porch steps and the bag. Went home and raked up garbage into cans and placed them into the trailer for better visibility and protection, planning to contact Lienhardt for an electric fence.

July 24 Pam and I returned from shopping (noon to 5 p.m.) and found one smashed garbage can in the trailer and an empty one with garbage strewn about on the ground. Armed self with pepper spray and pistola and went to Sonny's to find garbage strewn along the walkway beneath his steps, from the same can I'd refilled yesterday morning.

While on a long distance phone call (Elsie O in WA) Pam came in to tell me the bear was back. I ran outside to find Tom Stuits on our walkway armed with his .44 and pepper spray. I grabbed my spray and slipped into my boots and joined him, watching the bear in our trailer 20 yards away happily engaged in looking through scraps.

I wanted to get close enough to spray it in the face. About

then the bear shifted to the rear of the trailer and it tilted like a teeter totter and bounced off the ground, causing the bear to jump out. I ran over to spray him just as Tom shouted "Git!" and the bear ran through the alders toward George and Nancy's.

I paralleled it running down the road as it ran along the fence behind the high grass. We met at George's driveway but not close enough to spray it. The bear reversed and I did. It stood up twice and looked at me from about 20 feet, and I gave it 1 blast each time. It ran out onto the road as neighbor Madonna drove toward us and it crossed in front of her.

Tom chased it west of Sonny's to the back and I ran around to the east, hoping to get close enough for a facial shot. Not so.

We cleaned up Sonny's garbage in one sack and Tom took it home. I returned home and Madonna told us that they'd had a huge bear on their deck yesterday morning, attracted by neighbor's trailer garbage can with bears there regularly.

I cleaned up the scraps into one garbage can, took it to the barn loft and leaned the ladder against a tree. Hope the bear comes to bother our chickens or horse.

August 9 "Something's bothering the chickens," Pam stated. It was around 6:30 a.m. I jumped from bed, pulled on my pants and moccasins and grabbed the pepper spray by the back door and headed toward the chicken yard.

Rounding the Devil's club I spotted the juvenile delinquent black bear from above sitting inside the chicken run non-chalantly looking at me. I walked within 10-11 feet of him and gave him a pepper blast in the face. The spray blocked out his face but I assume it hit him squarely as he bolted south. I ran after stopping to spray toward him and shouting. I either imagined or heard him hit the wire mesh at the end. Hoping to eliminate his visits I ran into the house and frantically looked for ammo for the .30-06 or the .375 Ultra Mag with zero results.

I grabbed Ben's 12 gauge and tried loading slugs into it but was unable to. Grabbed .44 pistol.

I thought about going to Mark's on the corner but ran over to Tom's to see if he had ammo that would fit either of my rifles. He came sleepily to the door and acquired his .44 before I explained that I just wanted to borrow rifle ammo. He grabbed 125 grainers and we headed to our place, grabbed my .06 and loaded three into the mag, chambering one and putting it on safety before approaching the chicken run gate on the north end

The door, which I expected to be open, was still latched. *Hmmm. How did that bear get in?* I walked to the south end and saw no sizeable hole. *How did he get out?*

Tom and I chatted about the need to eliminate this bear and he went home.

Pam and I examined the chicken run later, and found the chicken wire roof near the door scrunched down with black bear hair on a couple of wires. Then I noticed a small opening with bent down wire at the south end where about three wires came together but not solidly and assumed the bear lunged at the small opening and his weight and momentum spread the wire before closing back. I assume he climbed the cedar fence or a tree to get out. I will check neighbor's tree as it seems the only way he could have come down through the roof.

Took a bunch of pictures of feathers, spray on the fence wood and chickens. Seems like all chickens are okay though the old gray Pepper is missing a bunch of feathers and moving slowly.

2009 After failed attempt to catch 2 red Dodge Ram pickups

racing up Natrona and while returning home, I drove up 141st thinking maybe the drivers had gone that way. About a quarter mile west of Goldenview I spotted a black bear on the left bank moving down from Arwezon's property. It crossed in front of me and I drove into Tomco's old place to apprise the owner.

The bear watched me as I walked about 25 feet from him to the house and a high school aged kid told me that he'd just cleaned up the garbage from a bear.

I returned to the white Suburban and watched the bear pussy-foot around, trying to get down a concrete wall while the kid tapped on the window from the second story then honked his pickup horn electronically—each time the bear jumped but stayed focused.

After about 15 minutes the bear grabbed a white garbage bag from the can and backed up the yard while the kid clapped his hands for his deck. The bear crossed the road to where I'd first seen it and tore open the bag to eat. I gave some thought to retrieving my rifle for a shot but decided to wait till the bear comes to our house!

July 24 (from the desk of Pamela Diane) I was pulling hard on a big weed trying to get its deep root free. Just as it came loose, I fell backwards and heard Ginger and Sarah yelling at me. We spent 1 ½ hours in the heat visiting and having root beer floats on the deck and then Sarah headed around the house for her bike as they were preparing to bike back home. Sarah yelled when she reached her bike because she saw a medium size black bear walking confidently in the road toward our empty garbage cans. Then the bear headed into the west side of the yard but soon turned and we saw him near the wood pile on the east side of the yard. Then he walked to the picnic area in the back but at the edge of it turned and came back to the main road—maybe because the horse was eating in the picnic area.

In the old, white Suburban I followed Ginger and Sarah as they headed home on bikes. I left them a little lower on the hillside and soon they passed by a large moose.

I was so proud of them for biking home.

They arrived home safely.

2010 On the way home from Camp Challenge Sunday July18 we saw a black sow run across the road with her three cubs by Service High. As of July 27 we've not seen a bear in the yard though know that we've had 3 occasions where one was in the yard—twice at garbage and once in road in front of house (neighbor's nephew Duane Johnson saw a huge black). Neighbors north and south have had them in their yards the last two weeks—Sonny had one in his garage and Tate's wife told me she had a large black in her driveway. They're all over town.

Ginger had one at their beehive about ten days ago and one in their yard Saturday morning—Sarah was in the barn and saw it by their raspberries. From 2 to 4 a.m. yesterday morning Sarah's horse was fidgety and they discovered that a black was thrashing away in their electric fence.

A neighbor told Ginger that a griz was in her yard a week ago.

Jill had a black in her driveway a week ago Saturday.

2011 June 10, day Ben brought Heather, Lincoln and Reuben to get Logan, Preston and Cannon—they were greeted by black bear (see next piece).

"Better than a Month of Sundays"

Friday June 10, 2011 was kinda-sorta-normal. Kinda-sorta. But ever so unusual.

Pam volunteered to watch grandsons Logan, Preston and Cannon at the farm while Ben took Lincoln to Providence Hospital to pick up Heather and 5-day-old son number 5 Reuben Wyatt. When Ben dropped off the boys, I was at the post office mailing kaniut.com book orders and on my way to Freddies on Abbott to get three bunches of daisies for Heather.

As I entered Freddies, I saw Ben and Heather in the Starbucks shop, waved at Lincoln, walked in to say hi and told them I wouldn't look at Reuben until Pam had a chance. I shopped and headed home to discover their Suburban in our driveway—Ben had taken Lincoln into the house while Heather waited with Reuben. I waved at her and went in. While playing with the boys in the living room, I heard a small eruption from the kitchen. Pam exclaimed, "There's a bear cub!" Jill exhorted me to "take your pistol and shoot it."

I ran into the kitchen and saw the bear at our wood pile. I headed out that way giving new meaning to the phrase "going to the wood shed."

The average-sized bear moseyed past the trailer while I went to the Suburban and asked Ben if he wanted me to kill the critter. He said no and we watched the bear walk south across our east lawn. I went to the back yard, grabbed Pam's horse Prince, turned him around, pointed to the bear and said, "It's a bear. Go get him." Prince advanced toward the bear which slid under the split rail cedar fence.

As I started toward the fence, I discovered our neighbor behind us Julie and shouted, "Julie, there's a bear in your yard!" Her dogs Piper and Buddy were barking and advancing toward the bear, Buddy within inches. Julie ran toward the dogs shouting, "Buddy!" And I figured Buddy was a swat away from doggie heaven. While awaiting a squeal from Buddy, I spotted a rock, picked it up and tossed it at the bear. The rock sailed past the bear but when it hit the ground near the bear, the animal moved away from the dogs, just in time to allow Julie to rush in and grab Buddy up in her arms.

That night Pam and I took Ginger, Brad and Sarah and Aunt Jill to the Golden Corral for dinner. When we reached home, Prince was rolling on the ground in his paddock and exhibiting symptoms of colic. The girls went into action calling vets and neighbor Tom, dispenser of vet drugs. No vet was available. Pam called Mary Bolin around 11:30 and Mary said she had some Banamine so yours truly headed in that direction.

Meanwhile Ginger and Jill swapped turns on one end of a towel with Sarah on the other end—lifting on Prince's belly to alleviate pain and/or redirect intestines. When I returned, Sarah took the syringe, placed a shoulder under Prince's jaw and an arm over his snout, inserted the syringe and emptied it before I could blink. With his upper lip thrust skyward, Prince was not enjoying the treatment of the Banamine. No matter. Sarah held him in that position for 2-3 minutes and he seemed to calm down and come around. I went to bed around 1 and they stayed with Prince until 2:30 AM.

I checked Prince at 3 and 6. He stood motionless in his stall, apparently asleep.

So there, my friends, was a day better than a month of Sundays.

July 15 black cub wanders past bay window and into woodpile. Sarah, Ginger and I went out armed with camera and bear spray, thimble-sized cub scooted up dead tree by wood trailer 15-feet and whimpered as Sarah took pix and I called ADFG.

c. August 18 Ginger noticed a black cub—probably the same one from July 15—on our deck sniffing our grill. It wandered off beneath the tree house then out to the power line.

August 21 Pam told us—Jill and I hunted Denali Hwy. with Al Smay—that a huge boar and sow black bear were in our picnic area, walking the length from west to east three times before departing into the power line.

Had about a 250 pound black sniffing our grill on the deck a couple of days in a row. Then it walked beneath the tree house and off toward the barn and disappeared into the power line bushes behind the barn.

Aug. 26 Ginger discovered junior bear on deck again by grill, he stood up and sniffed before padding over to check out the ceramic pic then departing for Sonny's. We called Sonny to apprise and he said the bear was there.

Sept. Ginger noticed a black cub on our deck by the grill about early Sept. Around mid-Sept. Pam was visiting on our deck with neighbors, and when the husband left, she and Vickie came in to have tea and warm up. Just about then they spotted a black cub walking our sawdust path by the bay window. It looked in the window at her and Pam then wandered off toward the power line.

Sept. 15 Dale Steele invited me to visit his bro's B&B in Moose Pass then hike up to Russian River falls. We decided to hike the river back to the car and anticipated the possibility of unlimbering our .454 Casul or .44 mag (mine) if not careful. Lots of dead salmon and seagull poop on trail. Reached power line that crosses the river and boardwalk bordered by railing—missing a hunk from bear bite—when 4 men pointed out a bear to us. We'd just walked past her. We took pix of brown sow at mid-stream 35 yards away when we noticed a yearling cub about 25 feet away approaching us, then crawling under the railing. We decided to depart before the cub—or its mother—chose to shake hands with us!

Oct. 26 a week ago I got an email/YouTube clip from Dave Goggins relating 3 brown bear cubs a quarter mile west of us in a neighbor's yard. And today neighbor Marcus (Kucera's old place) had the 3 brown bear cubs in yard all day. At least 9 so far in yard this summer.

2012 Friday 29 June, 3:45 P.M. Pam and I worked in garden pulling weeds with Preston when I went to the house to turn on the water for raspberry transplants. I turned on the water as Preston held the hose in one of the 5-gallon buckets. As I watched him having fun with the hose, I looked towards Rachel's house and spotted a dog. Whoops, not a dog. About a 60-80 pound black bear just emerged from the vegetation by the devil's club on the lawn.

I called to Pam twice and she walked out the garden gate and I pointed to the bear. She hustled Preston into the barn as I moved toward her, not wanting to spook the bear her way. It bolted onto its back trail as I hucked rocks against Rachel's fence, scaring it back toward the garden panel fence. I fired a few more making noise against the fence, got Pam and Preston into the house, grabbed the pepper spray and rocked the fence as I walked to the road. No bear.

Pam suggested I walk to Vickie's "who is outside working

in the yard." I startled her and she told me the neighbor dog went ballistic ten minutes prior. Prob the bear.

July 18 Laura Lee Smothers washed dishes at kitchen sink when small black bear (40 pounds?) walked up shavings path from picnic area. I grabbed camera but critter disappeared into wood pile and I didn't see it again.

July 10 Laura Lee, Les and I drove east on Huffman and watched a small black run across the road a block east of Elmore, south to north. We stopped and watched it in a driveway-parking lot and I jumped out to chase it from behind garage for Les to take pix. No cigar. It vanished.

July 21 Black bear in street in front, walked up Sonny's driveway.

July 25 I discovered two garbage bags ripped beside overturned garbage can. Looked like work of a bear.

2000 to 2012 bears in yard that we saw

2000 0

2001 0

2002 0

2003 1

2004 1

2005 3

2006 7

2007 0

2008 3

2009 1

2010 0

2011 9

2012 4

2013 Summer drive to Point Woronzoff, saw bikers jammed along bike trail and cop up ahead, then he hopped onto the hood of a police car and cruised ahead where we saw a black bear cross the road.

5/16/2016 Sixty to eighty pound black walked up trail from fire pit to deck, behind grill, saw Sarah's horse Boomer, turned and ambled back down trail and to Tate's garage and trailer and west lot.

June 6, 2018 2 large blacks crossed our back yard as I walked onto deck. I clapped hands and gave them the angry eye-to-eye and they barely hastened their stride. Then Pam observed one as it walked the pathway toward our house from the back yard.

July 29, 2018 We drove Karen Timblin to Indian Valley Bible Chalet and spotted a black on the hillside on our return (just west of Beluga Point turnout). We stopped and watched it for several minutes while Karen took pictures of it on her phone. The next day she called and asked if we'd heard about the bear that ate the Cobra. Last week her client's Shelby Cobra, parked overnight at Alyeska, was "vandalized" by a black bear that wanted Fig Newtons left in the car—ripped open the vinyl top for the goodies. Karen was pretty sure it was the bear we saw!

August 27, 2018 speaking of outlaws...we headed to Ben's to deliver his b-day present and at 140th noticed ahead at the bridge corner a grizzly walk toward the bridge, as if to cross it. Couldn't tell if she came from the 140th driveway or the creek. She saw us, stopped, looked toward De Armoun and rose on her hind legs to peer at an approaching vehicle, dropped to her all-fours and retreated toward the creek. We passed slowly, noticed a pile of fresh stool and headed up De Armoun when Pam noticed a cub in the first drive by the A-frame house. I pulled into the next drive on the left, turned around and parked on the shoulder--out of the way of traffic--with emergency lights on. Spotted 3 grizzly cubs of the second year playing in Mary Western's yard. Mama was between Mary's and the next yard west. She was darker while the cubs varied in color from dark blonde to brown. She meandered back and forth while one fiddled in Mary's raised beds and two wrestled; we watched them until the mother disappeared. I figured she was going to cross the creek again so decided to drive to the original "crossing" spot. As I approached the bridge, I noticed in our rear view mirror the three cubs run behind us across the road.

June 26, 2020 Pam saw a "small, brown colored bear" in yard today…just below east kitchen window. It wandered at a medium pace across front yard, road and up bank into Toby's yard.

June 29. 2020 We saw a black bear near the corner of Evergreen Ridge and Rabbit Creek. Pam said, "There's a bear"…so we watched it near a trailer in the driveway south of the house. About ten minutes later it disappeared into the bushes behind the trailer and we slowly drove north, seeing 2 adult brown and 2 younger brown bunnies standing on hind legs and looking north.

Before long here comes mister bear and when the bunnies scattered, he noticed them and went into the high alert stalking mode. Three fled behind the bushes and one lay on the gravel, stretched out and lazed.

June 29 Overnight we had a visitor at our garbage can. I cleaned up the leavings. Must not have had much to eat cuz there was little to pick up.

July 3 While I patched back garage gable our neighbor hollered over the fence to know if I'd seen the black bear behind his house. No cigar.

July 4 Daughter-in-law showed phone vid of griz sow and 2 newborn cubs in her neighbor's yard, about 3 miles from us.

August 4 Probably the same June 29 bear in our garbage visited us the next two Monday nights and the following Saturday night…something like 4 weeks in a row. I was standing on the front porch talking with Roger Holland (running against Cathy Giesel) who had dropped off a yard sign. I asked him what he thought of BIT Alaska; he said he'd never heard of it. I said I made it up. Since you oppose bears in town, I thought I'd see if you could meet with a group and discuss Bear In Town. He agreed and about then I said, "There's a bear" as a 2-3 year-old-black walked from Christina's west yard across the street toward our neighbor's fence to the west.

Today Jill called and asked if I'd heard of the bear mauling (I later looked it up and a man was mauled behind Kodiak).

2021 The middle of June a neighbor lady told me there'd been a sow brown bear and two adult sized cubs in her garbage at 1:30 AM. Within a week the neighbor two houses west had a brown sow and a cub in her garbage. Around July 2 a homeowner unleashed 5 shots at 4:30 AM, killing a sow and a cub and injuring another cub. That was about the same time we saw a black bear strolling along New Rabbit Creek Road near its junction with Old Rabbit Creek. I calculate there are 375 bears within the Anchorage bowl—from Birchwood to Potter Marsh. Yikes.

2024 Pat, the neighbor, told me he'd seen a brown bear on power line behind his house.

2025 We had a small blackie in yard today around 11:15 AM. Some time in June. It climbed Skrukrud's tree.

APPENDIX 2: Our Book Titles

I thought a little history of our books was appropriate and my wife, Pamela, wrote the following.

Alaska Bear Tales was followed by ***More Alaska Bear Tales*** in 1989. With this second book Larry's royalties went up and the publisher provided him with a tape transcriber and a 7-inch Mac Intosh, his first computer.

Between these two bear books, our friend, Steve Phelps, and Larry put together Instant Sourdough, a serious and humorous booklet. Steve did the line drawings while Larry provided the definitions. They had 2000 printed.

Publisher Kent Sturgis of Epicenter Press "came calling" next. ***Cheating Death*** soon was being handed out in LA at the behest of American Booksellers Association. At the Convention Center Larry was asked to do another bear book. He had thirteen stories and with this start, he agreed to write ***Some Bears Kill,*** published in 1997.

Along the way he helped Eddie Feigner (King and His Court) with his autobiography.

Stepanhie Evans met with us in California and offered to be our literary agent. She presented ***Danger Stalks the Land*** to St. Martin's in New York.

At this point publishers owed Larry a combined $20,000 so we began self-publishing.

We produced ***Bear Tales for the Ages***.

Our family next created ***Alaska Fun Bears***, a monster coloring-activity book designed for adults to interact with children as they learn about bears and Alaska.

In 2014 with Jack Gwaltney Larry co-authored ***Alaska Air Tales***, a collection of true stories from those who have flown in the Great Land. It features a photo fold out of post-World War II fighter planes parked in Anchorage.

Larry was inspired to write ***Brachan***, a Roman soldier's mission from Rome to Judea as he monitors John the Baptist... before seeking John's cousin Jesus.

A very positive Alaska romance titled ***Trapped*** was published in 2018.

Following closely on its heels was ***SAFE with Bears,*** forewarning people of the need for safety from bears in the outdoors.

In 2020 we published a novel about high school and the need for loving our youth, titled ***The B.G.***

Swallowed Alive, Volumes I and II, survival and related outdoor stories, is completed which will be followed by non-violent bear stories and titled ***What's Bruin?***

Then, of course, we will publish Larry's ***Charlie's Tails,*** 400 cartoons of outdoor events.

Snatched from Death is on the drawing board.

Alaska...Comin' 'Atcha is now available, an anthology of some of our stories.

www.ingramcontent.com/pod-product-compliance
Lightning Source LLC
Chambersburg PA
CBHW062118020426
42335CB00013B/1014